11699763

**The Adoption of Innovation
by Local Government**

The Adoption of Innovation by Local Government

Richard D. Bingham
University of Wisconsin-Milwaukee

with the assistance of
Thomas P. McNaught

Lexington Books

D.C. Heath and Company
Lexington, Massachusetts
Toronto   London

Library of Congress Cataloging in Publication Data

Bingham, Richard D
    The adoption of innovation by local government.

    Bibliography: p.
    Includes index.
    1. Local government—United States. 2. Diffusion of innovations—
United States. I. Title.
JS341.B54   352.073   75-41922
ISBN 0-669-00484-7

Copyright © 1976 by D.C. Heath and Company

All rights reserved. No part of this publication may be reproduced or transmitted in any form or by any means, electronic or mechanical, including photocopy, recording, or any information storage or retrieval system, without permission in writing from the publisher.
This project was supported by the National Science Foundation, Office of National R & D Assessment under Grant No. DA-44312. The conclusions and recommendations contained in this report are those of the authors alone and do not necessarily reflect the official position of the National Science Foundation.

Published simultaneously in Canada

Printed in the United States of America

International Standard Book Number: 0-669-00484-7

Library of Congress Catalog Card Number: 75-41922

**The Adoption of Innovation
by Local Government**

352.03
B513a

Contents

List of Figures		vii
List of Tables		ix
Acknowledgment		xi
Chapter 1	**Innovation in the Public Sector**	1
	Analytic Framework	4
	Design and Methodology	13
	Summary	32
Chapter 2	**Adoption of Innovation by Public Housing Authorities**	33
	Process Innovation	33
	Product Innovation	57
	Conclusions	77
Chapter 3	**Innovation Adoption in Public Schools**	81
	Process Innovation	81
	Product Innovation	104
	Conclusions	118
Chapter 4	**Innovation Adoption in Public Libraries**	121
	Process Innovation	121
	Product Innovation	138
	Conclusions	147
Chapter 5	**Adoption of Innovation in the Common Functions of City Government**	149
	Process Innovation	149

168569

Product Innovation   166
Conclusions   195

Chapter 6   **Toward a Policy Perspective**   199

Innovation Diffusion   199
Hypothesis Testing   205
A Model of Innovation Adoption   214
Political versus Bureaucratic Innovations   216
Policy Alternatives   226

Appendix   **Geographic Diffusion of Innovations**   231

Notes   243

Selected Bibliography   253

Index   265

About the Authors   273

List of Figures

Figure

1-1   A Model for the Adoption of Technological Innovation
      by Local Government   6

2-1   Percentage of *Journal of Housing* Articles Devoted to
      Computer-based Management Information Systems
      (1964-1973)   41

2-2   Revised Model for the Adoption of Process Innovations
      in Public Housing   45

2-3   Percentage of *Journal of Housing* Articles Devoted to the
      Use of Prefab and Modular Construction   63

3-1   Percentage of *Today's Education* Articles Devoted to
      Methods of Individualized Instruction (1964-1973)   86

3-2   Percentage of *The National Elementary Principal*
      Articles Devoted to Methods of Individualized
      Instruction (1964-1973)   87

3-3   Revised Model for the Use of Individualized Instruction
      in Public Elementary Schools   92

3-4   Percentage of *Today's Education* Articles Devoted to the
      Use of Videotape Recorders as an Aid to Teaching
      (1964-1973)   108

4-1   Percentage of Articles in the *American Library Associa-
      tion Bulletin* and in *American Libraries* Devoted to the
      Use of Computers in Library Management (1964-1973)   126

4-2   Revised Model for the Adoption of Process Innovations
      in Public Libraries   129

5-1   Percentage of *Police Chief* Articles Devoted to the Use of
      the Computer by Police Departments (1964-1973)   155

5-2   Revised Model for the Adoption of Computer Systems
      by Police Departments   158

5-3   Percentage of Articles in the American Public Works
      Association *Reporter* Devoted to Vehicle Fleet-
      Management Systems (1964-1973)   171

5-4   Revised Model for Contracting for Mainstem Services   176

6-1   Mean Housing Percentage Modular, by State   203

6-2   A Model for the Adoption of Technological
           Innovation by Local Government   215
6-3   A Model for the Adoption of Innovation by Local
           Government   218
A-1   Mean Housing Computer Score, by State   233
A-2   Mean Housing Percentage Modular, by State   234
A-3   Mean Housing Prefab Score, by State   235
A-4   Mean Percentage Teachers Using Individualized
           Instruction, by State   236
A-5   Mean VTRs per Secondary School, by State   237
A-6   Mean Library Computer-Use Score, by State   238
A-7   Mean Theft-Detection System Use, by State
           (Percentage of Libraries with Theft-Detection
           Systems)   239
A-8   Mean Police Computer-Use Score, by State   240
A-9   Percentage Using Mainstem Services, by State   241

List of Tables

Table

1-1	Technological Innovations Examined in this Study	2
1-2	Varimax Rotated-Factor Matrix of Selected Census Variables	26
1-3	Factor Matrix of Selected Attitudinal Variables	28
1-4	Varimax Rotated-Factor Matrix of Selected Attitudinal Variables Including Vote for Nixon	28
1-5	Zero Order Relationships Between Size-Related Variables in the Housing Process Model	31
2-1	Public Housing Authority Computer-Use Questions	35
2-2	Zero Order Relationships Between Housing Process Independent Variables and Housing Computer-Use Score	36
2-3	Local Government Reformism	37
2-4	Summary of Stepwise Regression Explaining Housing Computer-Use Score	47
2-5	Distribution of Housing Prefab Scores	58
2-6	Zero Order Relationships Between Housing Product Independent Variables and Housing Product Innovations	60
2-7	Relationship Between Expected and Observed Use of Modular and Factory-Built Housing	62
2-8	Interrelationships Between Technological Innovations in Public Housing	78
3-1	School Board Reformism	83
3-2	Zero Order Relationships Between School District Process Independent Variables and the Percent of Elementary Teachers using Individualized Instruction in Elementary Schools	84
3-3	Zero Order Relationship Between Measures of School Board Reformism and Individualized Instruction in Elementary Schools	85
3-4	Relationship Between Community Environment and Organizational Environment Controlling for Demand	90

3-5   Zero Order Relationships Between School District
        Product Independent Variables and Average
        Number of Videotape Recorders per Secondary
        School   107

4-1   Questions Concerning Library Computer Use   122

4-2   Zero Order Relationship Between the Public Library
        Process Independent Variables and Library
        Computer-Use Score   123

4-3   Relationship Between Demand and Organizational
        Characteristics Controlling for Community
        Environment   127

4-4   Relationship Between Demand and Community
        Environment Variables Controlling for Remaining
        Community Environment Variables   127

4-5   Relationship Between Community Environment and
        Organizational Characteristics Controlling for Demand   128

4-6   Zero Order Relationship Between Public Library Product
        Independent Variables and Library Adoption of a
        Theft-Detection System   139

5-1   Zero Order Relationship Between City Process
        Independent Variables and Police Computer-Use
        Score   150

5-2   Relationship Between Demand and Organizational
        Environment Controlling for Community Environment   156

5-3   Relationship Between Community Environment
        Variables and Computer-Use Score Controlling
        for Remaining Community Environment Variables   156

5-4   Summary of Stepwise Regression Explaining Police
        Computer Use   159

5-5   Zero Order Relationships Between City Product
        Independent Variables and Mainstem Use   168

5-6   Relationship Between Community Environment and
        Demand Controlling for Remaining Community
        Environment Variables   175

5-7   Summary of Stepwise Regression Explaining Mainstem
        Use   177

6-1   Zero Order Relationships Between all Innovations Studied   201

6-2   Zero Order Relationships Between State-Innovation
        Scores for all Innovations   204

6-3   Summary of Findings of Hypothesis Testing Over All
        Innovations   209

6-4   Public Visibility Rankings of Technological Innovations   222

Acknowledgment

We wish it were possible to acknowledge all the individuals and organizations whose assistance and cooperation in completing this study were so valuable. Unfortunately, space does not permit proper acknowledgement. A special debt of gratitude goes to the many local officials cooperating in the study and particularly those individuals participating in the field studies, the majority of whom were more than cooperative and willing to share their time and expertise.

Special thanks are also due to the professional associations and service vendors for their assistance and cooperation. A special remembrance is due Robert Martineau and Mainstem, Inc. for their extra help.

Of course the job never would have been finished without the contributions of the work study assistant Susan Brown, secretary Vaddie (Dorris) Hill, and Research Assistant Thomas J. Westerheide. For correcting our spelling and editing and typing the final manuscript, we are grateful to Susan Hoffmann and Amy McLees. Ann Mallinger and David Bertram of the Computer Services Division of Marquette University provided willing assistance during the data collection and analysis phase.

And finally, we express our appreciation to our professional colleagues, J. David Roessner, Irwin Feller, Donald Menzel, and Robert Yin, for their helpful comments on the original manuscript.

The Adoption of Innovation
by Local Government

1 Innovation in the Public Sector

Recent years have seen an ever increasing body of literature concerned with the adoption of innovations by formal and informal organizations within our society. Today there are literally hundreds of publications dealing with the diffusion of innovations, many developing their own terminology and leaving the reader in an obvious state of confusion. Fortunately, several authors have recognized the need to draw together this widely disparate body of literature and have done so with some success.[1] Nonetheless, the area of innovation in organizations is complex at best and hopelessly confusing at worst. Part of the confusion lies with the fact that the literature concerned with the diffusion or adoption of innovation comes from a variety of disciplines, with management and business, sociology, and psychology somewhat in the lead. Added confusion develops as we note the variety of different types of organizations under study— business corporations, federal bureaucracies, state bureaucracies, local government, schools, health organizations, social clubs, and dozens more. Due to problems of differing organizational goals, variations in the need for profit, diverse methodologies, and many other factors, it is difficult to transfer the findings concerning the diffusion of innovation in one type of organization directly to an organization with completely different structure and goals.

The research presented in the following chapters attempts to narrow the scope of the discussion of innovations in organizations to local governmental units while at the same time comparing a variety of innovations across four different types of local government agencies. Innovation is examined in (1) public housing authorities, (2) school districts, (3) public libraries, and (4) two common functions of city government. The study covers these governmental units in all American cities with 1960 populations of 50,000 or more. Within each of the governmental categories two types of technological innovation have been examined: those requiring adoption of physical change (*product innovations*) and those requiring a change in method (*process innovations*). In all cases, however, the innovations include the adoption of a new technology. Table 1-1 lists the innovations studied.

There is a commonly held belief today that state and local governments are highly resistive to innovation. Frederick O'R. Hayes and John E. Rasmussen, for example, believe that state and local governments have little surplus energy to devote to innovation.[2] Robert Crawford, in a recent summary of efforts to bring science and technology to local government, suggests that the fractured structure of local government seriously hampers any effort to increase technology

1

Table 1-1
Technological Innovations Examined in This Study

Type of Government	Process Innovation	Product Innovation
Public Housing Authorities	The application of computer systems to housing authority management	The use of prefabricated components in high-rise construction and the use of modular or factory-built components in low-rise construction
Public Schools Districts	The use of a system of individualized instruction in elementary schools	The adoption of videotape recorders by secondary schools
Public Libraries	The application of computer systems to public library management	The adoption of a theft-detection system
Municipal Government	The use of automatic data-processing equipment by police departments	Contracting with Mainstem, Inc., for vehicle maintenance management service

utilization in local government.[3] Thus a far-flung and fragmented market tends to limit local government's use of science and technology to products initially developed for other purposes.[4] And yet technologies are adopted by local government—often for reasons not entirely understood. This study attempts to answer two fundamental questions pertinent to the adoption of technological innovations by units of local government.

First, why do some local governmental units readily adopt technological innovations while others virtually ignore them? Second, what are the processes usually followed in adopting innovation? Since these questions involve two separate but related issues—namely, (1) *why* innovation is adopted versus (2) *how* innovation is adopted—the level of analysis differs regarding the two questions. The study has attempted to answer the first research question through rigorous quantitative analysis utilizing model-building and empirical investigation of theoretical propositions, while examination of the second research question is more exploratory with investigation confined to a number of selected field studies.

The first task was to clarify the meaning ascribed to the phrase "adoption of technological innovation." There are significant differences of opinion among innovation scholars concerning what constitutes an *innovation*. One major problem with the literature is simply with the definition of innovation and the concept of "newness." Some scholars do not require that a process or product be new to society to be innovative, only that it be new to the organization under study[5] while others require that the innovation be new to the particular situation.[6] While in the past this definition has been largely a matter of the scholar's personal preference, there is some evidence, somewhat ignored in the literature, that "newness" may be of critical importance in innovation research.[7] Terry N. Clark suggests that after the newness wears off, a program is no longer innovative and adoption becomes a function of factors other than those explaining innovation. Clark reached this conclusion while attempting to explain the difference between his findings concerning the relationship between a centralized community power structure and urban renewal success and the findings of a similar research project conducted by Amos H. Hawley a decade earlier.[8] Hawley investigated the relationship between highly centralized city power structures and urban renewal expenditures and found that cities with a high concentration of the power function showed a greater success in urban renewal endeavors than those with a diffuse power structure.

Clark, however, found a positive correlation between decentralized decision-making and urban renewal expenditures. He reconciled his findings with Hawley's by suggesting that *fragility*, loosely defined as newness, may play an important part in identifying innovation. Clark suggests that fragile issues are often difficult to adopt—that opposition by even a small group of dissonants may prevent action on the issue. He thus reconciled his differences with Hawley by suggesting that Hawley studied urban renewal adoption when it was innovative while he studied renewal at a later time when the issue was "less fragile."

Thus the operational definition of innovation is critically important. A definition suggested by Selwyn W. Becker and Thomas L. Whisler defining *innovation* as "the first or early use of a set of organizations with similar goals"[9] formed the basis for the definition of innovation adopted in this study. A time constraint was thus introduced into the research—an idea must have been adopted "first or early" to be considered innovative.

The study was further limited to technological innovations—that is, to innovations that constitute "new development or combinations of the material, as distinguished from the nonmaterial, culture."[10] Everett M. Rogers' definition of *technological* thus presents a framework broad enough in which to conduct this investigation.

It was further necessary to consider two specific types of technological innovations—the product and process innovations mentioned earlier. As long ago as 1953, Homer G. Barnett, in an anthropological and psychological analysis of the adoption of new ideas by individuals, recognized the distinction in innovations among thought, behavior, and things.[11] Later Kenneth E. Knight discussed innovation in four aspects of the organization.[12] They may pertain to (1) the product (or other output) of the organization, (2) a new process or new way of doing things, (3) changes in the organization structure, or (4) "people innovations" or innovations in social practice. The technological innovations examined here are variations of Knight's first two categories. We considered product innovations to be physical. That is, the product innovations under study all involved the adoption of a new physical product—a product produced by another organization. For example, one of the product innovations studied here is the adoption of factory-built housing and the use of prefabricated walls and flooring in the construction of public housing.

The process innovations do not necessarily involve the adoption of a new physical product. Process innovations require a change in method or the way things are done in the organization. Again as an example, one of the process innovations studied here is the use of the computer in housing authority management. While this process involves the use of a new product, computers, it also requires the use of a new process—a new way to obtain and evaluate management information.

In broad terms, then, the preceding paragraphs introduce and define the nature of the technological innovations studied and the study environment. The remainder of the chapter is devoted to a brief summary of a very complex topic— the theory and research findings of others interested in the diffusion of innovations in organizations, the development of the hypotheses, and a discussion of the research design and methodology.

Analytic Framework

The literature concerning organizational behavior in the public sector presents no coherent framework for the analysis of innovation adoption. In part, this is probably due to the extremely diverse nature of the innovation studies. It does seem, however, that a modification of David Easton's application of the systems approach to the study of political science provides a satisfactory framework for analysis of the adoption of technological innovation by local government.[13] This approach has seen widespread use in the area of public policy analysis[14] and appears to be a satisfactory framework in which to research innovations.

Figure 1-1 presents a model for innovation adoption by local government. The organizational literature suggests that organizational decisions to adopt innovations are based on a wide range of variables. These variables, however, seem to fall into four broad (although by no means mutually exclusive) categories. The categories are: (1) community environment, (2) demand, (3) organizational environment, and (4) organizational characteristics. The model suggests that the community environment independently affects innovation adoption, generates demand variables, and works through both organizational factors to effect innovation adoption. In a similar manner, the demand variables affect innovation directly and through the organizational factors. The organizational environment is expected to directly affect innovation adoption and to indirectly affect it through the organizational characteristics. The effect of the organizational characteristics on the adoption of innovation, then, is only direct.

Community Environment

Within the community environment there appear to be two classes of variables that might influence innovation adoption: demographic variables and attitudinal, or cultural, variables. The importance of demographic variables as determinants of community policy outputs (in this case decisions to innovate) has been repeatedly stressed by economists and political scientists over the past quarter of a century. Analysis of both an aggregative nature and disaggregative nature (e.g., investigation of specific federal grant programs rather than of the determinants of grant expenditures in general) support the contention that local demographic and socioeconomic variables are determinants of city policy output.

Much of the quantitative work explaining the use of federal grant programs, for example, points out the importance of community characteristics as determinants of program use. The studies of urban renewal by Hawley and Clark mentioned earlier are excellent examples of this work as are other studies of public housing and urban renewal by Michael Aiken and Robert Alford[15] and by Richard D. Bingham.[16]

City characteristics may also be indicative of the kinds of innovations communities adopt, and certain innovations may appeal to only special classes of cities.

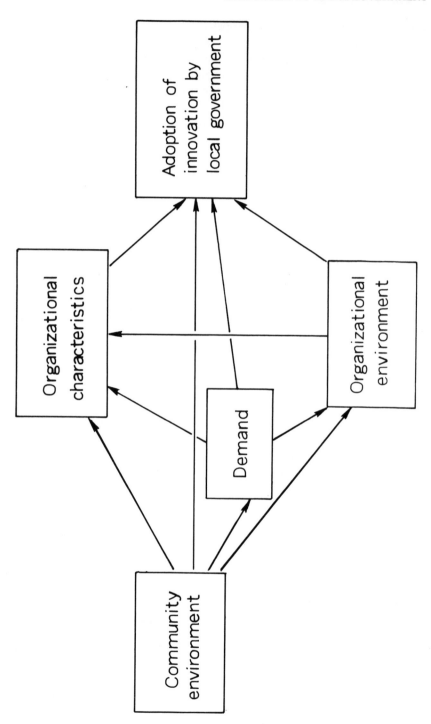

Figure 1-1. A Model for the Adoption of Technological Innovation by Local Government

Oliver P. Williams and Charles R. Adrian, for example, use the term "amenities" to "distinguish between policies designed to achieve the comforts and necessities of life as opposed to only the latter."[17] They note that city policies designed to provide amenities emphasize the home environment rather than the working environment and that certain types of cities are more prone to emphasize amenity value than others. In other words, one can expect that amenity-type innovations will be adopted by cities with high socioeconomic status while cities with low socioeconomic status will adopt innovations designed to correct some specific deficiency. For example, when considering the two school-related innovations in this study—the adoption of individually guided instruction methods and the use of videotape recorders—individually guided instruction was expected to be related to low socioeconomic status. This innovation was presumably adopted to improve the educational achievement of deprived populations. Videotape record-ers would not alleviate such "educational emergencies." In this case, the innova-tion of videotape recorders might be strongly related to measures indicating high socioeconomic status. Thus the direction of the relationships found between variables should be a good indicator of the type of innovation being considered.

There is still the necessity, however, to distinguish between *amenity* and *need*. For the purposes of this study, technological innovation based on need includes those innovations designed to upgrade substandard performance or to significantly reduce governmental operating expenses. *Amenity technological innovations* will be defined as those innovations designed to improve already adequate performance, to upgrade systems or management techniques, to pro-vide additional information or more comprehensive information to decision-makers, and/or to make other such improvements not directly related to up-grading substandard performance (or physical deficiency) or directly reducing operating costs.

Physical factors or characteristics are not the only components of the com-munity environment. There is also an attitudinal component to communities that need not be related to physical factors but that colors the kinds of things cities and/or public organizations do. In political science, for example, one often hears of the conservative nature of the Orange County suburbs of Los Angeles. Voting behavior is occasionally used to identify such community attitudes. Aiken and Alford used an electoral variable, i.e., the percent voting Democratic in the 1964 presidential election, as an attempt to isolate the presence of a population holding private-regarding values.[18]

Bingham used the 1964 Republican vote as a measure of community political conservatism. He also used the Wallace vote in 1968 as a surrogate for racism. Neither variable was found to be significant in explaining community differences in public housing or urban renewal. In several case studies, however, Bingham did note the importance of community attitude in determining pro-gram use. A radical conservatism in Beaumont, Texas, for example, was found to be the overriding reason that Beaumont did not participate in the federal urban renewal program.[19]

Research by Robert D. Wrinkle and Jerry L. Polinard also associates the Wallace vote with racism.[20] Using county-by-county data in Texas, Wrinkle and Polinard found a strong relationship between percent black and the Wallace vote. Their data did not support the populist explanation of the Wallace vote, and they suggest that the Wallace vote is closely related to a feeling of hostility toward blacks.

Daniel J. Elazar also suggests that political attitudes are part of the overall political culture in the United States. He identified three dominant political cultures in American life: individualistic, moralistic, and traditionalistic.[21] He traced the origins of these dominant cultures and their migration across the United States. He also noted the dominant culture in each state and broke up the areas within each state into regions based on the dominant culture.

The public policy literature thus suggests several hypotheses relating the community environment to the adoption of technological innovation:

1. City size is positively related to the adoption of technological innovation.
2. Community socioeconomic factors are related to the adoption of technological innovation.
3. The dominance of conservative political values in a community is negatively related to the adoption of technological innovation.

Demand

The second category of variables, demand, also includes variables that are representative of the community in which the organization is located. These variables, however, do not represent the community in general but pertain only to the specific organization under study. In the school model, for example, "demand" for innovation in educational programs might be stimulated by a high student dropout rate for the school system. The demand area or classification thus includes only those variables applicable to the specific innovation and/or governmental unit under study.

Organizational Environment

Organizations face another environment—one well beyond the communities in which they are physically located. For the firm, this environment consists of its industry, market, etc. For the public organization, it consists of its relationship with other governmental units, the private sector as it affects the organization, and other similar entities. In other words, the organizational environment is that environment within which the organization operates above and beyond the local community.

Various works in economics and political science suggest that the organizational environment of local governmental units consist of four basic areas: (1) intergovernmental relations, (2) professionalism, (3) private sector influence, and (4) slack resource availability. Much of the recent research concerning program use, or the adoption of innovations by public organizations, stresses the significance of one or more of these areas.

The intergovernmental influence, or influence of one level of government on another, was noted by Alan K. Campbell and Seymour Sacks in examining metropolitan fiscal behavior. In examining the relationship between state and local taxation, they noted that the assignment of revenue responsibility to local governments was stimulative of total state and local tax revenue.[22]

Intergovernmental grants, transfers, or technical assistance also have an impact on the recipient governmental unit. Many grants are in fact designed to induce other governmental units to take an action which the granting unit desires—although the desired results are not always achieved.[23]

Jack L. Walker recognized the importance of a national system of emulation and competition between states. He noted that states are grouped into regions based both on geographical contiguity and a specialized communications net. It is through this network, he believes, that national standards are established.[24] It is likely that a similar diffusion network also exists among cities.

Much of the recent literature concerning innovation in public agencies stresses the importance of professionalism in innovation adoption. Many aspects of professionalism have been studied in some depth. Rogers and Shoemaker, for example, list 203 separate studies relating education to innovation adoption.[25] Some 74 percent of these studies conclude that early adopters have more years of education than do late adopters.

Maw Lin Lee posits a negative aspect of professionalism that may account for early adoption of programs or innovations.[26] In examining the diffusion of open-heart surgical facilities in local hospitals, he suggests that innovation may not be a function of need. The "innovative" behavior of organizations such as hospitals may be a function of status within top-level administration. Executives adopt innovations in an attempt to show their progressiveness—to show their peers that they are leaders in the field.

Williams and Adrian associate form of government with community goals. They see four different roles for local government: (1) promoting economic growth, (2) providing or securing life's amenities, (3) maintaining (only) traditional services, and (4) arbitrating among conflicting interests. They associate the council-manager form of government with economic growth and/or amenities. Cities oriented toward economic growth or toward amenities provide the city manager with the opportunity to "do things" that will show concrete achievement. Maintaining traditional services is thus in conflict with the professionalism of the city manager.[27] Such conclusions are in complete accord with Lee's findings in hospital administration.

It is also possible that professional norms lead to conservative expenditure patterns. Bernard H. Booms studied expenditures for police, fire, interest on local debt, noncapital expenditures for highways, sanitation, and public health in Ohio and Michigan cities with populations between 25,000 and 100,000. He found a definite difference in expenditure levels based on the type of government. He concluded that the form of government has an independent effect on the level of per capita expenditures. Booms found that expenditures were generally lower in council-manager cities and suggests that the city-manager administration may lead to governmental efficiency.[28]

As with professionalism, the concept of slack resource availability has been of increasing concern to diffusion scholars. Becker and Whisler suggest that *slack*, defined as a feeling of well-being or perceived success, "is not a systematically predictable variable except to the extent that the level of aspiration of the organization is a function of previous experience."[29]

But experience and success are not the sole determinants of slack. Other resources come into play. In summarizing Victor A. Thompson's research,[30] J. David Roessner suggests that the existence of unprogrammed resources of many types promote innovation. Thus slack resources include variables such as personnel, finances, material, and motivation.[31]

Research by Heinz Eulau and Robert Eyestone calls into question much of the "slack resource" theory of organizational behavior. They developed typologies of cities defined by different stages of development based on expenditures for planning and amenities over a five-year period. Eulau and Eyestone then correlated the typologies with census data, expenditure data, and questionnaire results (attitudes of city councilmen). The policy orientation of councilmen was not related to city size, growth, or revenue capability; however, councilmen more favorable to development were found in the more developed cities. They concluded that resource capability (slack resources?) may be an important constraint on policy development in some cases; but the willingness of policy-makers to draw on those resources that are available seems to play a more important role in explaining city policy development.[32]

There is considerable evidence that private sector activity has a great deal to do with the adoption of technologies by public sector agencies—in spite of the institutional idiosyncrasies of the public sector. Irwin Feller, et al, for example, document the importance of vendor activity in the adoption of impact attentuators by state highway-transportation agencies. They suggest that when the possible benefits to the private firm are high enough, the vendors will attempt to cope with many obstacles to have their product adopted. Thus they believe that the willingness of manufacturers of impact attentuators to have their products tested under federal supervision can be explained by future profit considerations.[33]

Political considerations may also play an important part in the adoption of innovation by governmental units. In summarizing the literature on public technology, Feller, et al, identify a number of impediments to rapid diffusion of innovation in the public sector. Political considerations appear to be a major impediment. Elected officials, it is suggested, operate on a short-term time horizon limited by their term of office.[34]

Unquestionably the organizational environment plays a role in innovation adoption. The literature in the previous discussion suggest a number of hypotheses relating organizational environment to innovation adoption. This study tested the following hypotheses:

1. The adoption of innovation by local government is positively related to federal or state assistance.
2. Cities adopting innovations are located in close physical proximity to other innovation-adopting cities.
3. "Professionalism" in local government acts to speed up the innovative process.
4. The existence of slack resources in the organizational environment is positively related to the adoption of innovation.
5. Vendor activity is positively related to the adoption of innovation.
6. The adoption of innovation is positively related to a "reformed" structure of local government.

Organizational Characteristics

Much of the diffusion research suggests that organizational characteristics are important determinants of innovation adoption. Characteristics of the organization such as size, structure, and professionalism often affect innovation adoption. Edward C. Banfield and James Q. Wilson note that the mere structure of organizations tends to affect the kinds of policy decisions made. They found, for example, a number of differences in local policy which they attribute to reform characteristics in local government.[35]

Another factor common to the writings of organizational theorists is the concept of a performance gap. Zaltman, et al, suggest that a performance gap is present when the decision-makers perceive a difference between what the organization is doing and what they think it ought to be doing.[36]

Feller, et al, suggest that there are certain organizational variables that might increase the likelihood that a performance gap will be perceived. They suggest that factors such as diversity of tasks and number of occupational or functional specialists are likely to be correlates of organizational innovation. They believe that these organizational factors are likely to increase the probability that someone in the organization will perceive the performance gap which will lead to organizational innovation.[37]

Formalization and organizational complexity are two other attributes of organizations believed to explain significant differences in the adoption of technologies.[38] The assumption is that emphasis on following rules and procedures does not give lower levels in the bureaucracy room to innovate. Again, a high degree of centralization of organizational authority tends to stifle innovation. The higher in the organization decision-making takes place, the more centralized is the organizational structure. Such a strict emphasis on hierarchy of authority often causes lower-level members of the unit to adhere to specified channels of communication and to feed back only positive information concerning performance. Thus negative information that might help the organization to innovate is often suppressed. Both formalization and complexity are characteristics of organizations that are expected to suppress the detection of a performance gap.

Agency resources, particularly financial and personnel, are often believed to be conditions necessary for innovative adoption. Mohr notes that size is expected to be a predictor of innovation, although he refuses to accept a strict causal relationship.[39] There is evidence, however, that factors related to organizational size are related to innovativeness. Large organizations are more likely than smaller ones to be specialized and professional. These characteristics, as hypothesized earlier, are likely to be related to the perception of a performance gap.

In an outstanding summary of the diffusion literature, evidence presented by Rogers and Shoemaker suggests that the presence of certain types of individuals in organizations is an important determinant of diffusion. They conclude that individual innovators are more educated, more cosmopolitan, more likely to be opinion leaders, and more professionally oriented than their less innovative counterparts.[40]

Feller, et al, identify inflexible civil service or union agreements as impediments to innovation adoption. They suggest that many innovations are labor-saving or require readjustments in work schedules and thus are resisted by public employee organizations.[41]

A number of hypotheses were suggested relating organizational characteristics to innovation adoption:

1. The adoption of innovation is positively related to an appointed (versus elected) decision-making body.
2. Governmental units directed by elected officials have a high propensity to adopt innovation based on need (versus amenity) value.
3. A formal decision-making structure is negatively related to the adoption of innovation.
4. A centralized decision-making structure is negatively related to the adoption of innovation.
5. Organizational size is positively related to the adoption of innovation.

6. The level of organizational funding is positively related to the adoption of innovation.
7. The presence of a large number of professionally oriented individuals in an organization is positively related to the adoption of innovation.
8. The presence of a civil service structure and/or employee unions is negatively related to the adoption of innovation.

Design and Methodology

The first steps in the research process involved the selection of the governmental units to be investigated, the identification of the innovations to be studied, and the operationalization of the concepts of the community environment, demand, the organizational environment, and the characteristics of the organization.

The Governmental Units

The governmental units (public housing authorities, public school districts, city governments, and public libraries) were selected for the uniqueness of their organizational patterns. Local school districts, for example, vary greatly in organization. In thirty states, they are independent governmental units; in five they are agencies of the city, county, or state governments; and in the remaining fifteen, the organizational pattern varies.[42] In contrast, housing authorities exhibit a different organizational pattern. Housing authorities are generally semiautonomous public bodies with the governing body appointed by the mayor with council approval. Of the authorities studied here, 89 percent indicated that they maintained this independence from the city government while 11 percent operated as a department or section within the city bureaucracy. Public libraries also exhibited a diversity in organizational structure. Of the libraries studied, 58 percent were governed by the city or the local school district, 17 percent were county libraries, 19 percent were city-county, and 6 percent were regional.

The Innovations

The selection of the specific innovations was generally accomplished through a telephone survey of applicable professional association staff members and heads of the appropriate governmental units throughout the country. These officials were asked, "In your opinion, what do you consider to be the major innovations in (public housing, public education, etc.) over the past ten years?" Several staff employees of the National Association of Housing and Redevelopment Officials (NAHRO) were thus asked to name the major innovations in public housing over the past ten years. Then the executive directors of twenty-one housing authorities throughout the country were asked the same question in telephone interviews.[a] Two major innovative areas emerged. The first was a process innovation—the application of computer systems to authority management. The second was a product innovation or, more correctly, a number of product innovations, involving the use of prefabricated components in both low-rise and high-rise housing construction.

Utilization of computer-based systems of management currently ranks as one of the most innovative measures introduced in public housing authorities in the last ten years. Ranging from simple automated data-processing (ADP) equipment to sophisticated computer hardware, local housing authorities (LHAs) across the country are using automated systems of management for the ever-increasing number of public-housing units under their jurisdiction. Where initially the innovation was confined to facilitating accounting functions of the housing authority, which included tenant accounting, payroll, accounts payable, central stores control, equipment inventory control, and general ledger accounting, it has now advanced to the point where it is providing management reporting. Using the same data as that used in accounting, housing authorities have been able to program Department of Housing and Urban Development (HUD) management reports, tenant information and statistical reports, and applicant information.

In the past, a housing authority, for lack of an alternative, was forced to dedicate a substantial percentage of its supportive staff to the manual and detailed tasks of accounting, the preparation of required reports for HUD, and the provision to top-level management with information needed for management decisions. With the introduction of ADP, however, LHA management has been able to reduce clerical staff as well as accompanying time and dollar costs faced by the administration of the office. Using one or two clerks to keypunch tenant or administrative data on punchcards or terminals, authorities have been able to automate the record keeping and the reporting and analysis of data, thereby eliminating the high cost of processing time and manhours.

For example, the forms used for tenant application and tenant information include data such as name, income, family status, employer, service status, assistance and benefits entitled to, project location, and rent payments. Once

---

[a]Geographic distribution was believed important. In each case involving the governmental units, an attempt was made to ensure that both those units most likely to be innovative and those least likely to be innovative were consulted in the selection of the specific technologies. Thus the initial survey of housing authorities (and later, state education associations, public libraries, etc.) included authorities in the "least innovative" as well as the "most innovative" states as specified by Jack L. Walker, "The Diffusion of Innovations Among the American States," *American Political Science Review,* 62 (1969): 883.

this data is keypunched, it is readily available for a wide variety of management uses.

Inasmuch as there are a number of private firms offering computer management services to housing authorities (such as Management Data Systems, Inc.; Boeing Computer Services, Inc., and Erie Data Processing Housing Service Center), the availability of a computer in the area is not a necessity. These private firms enable public housing authorities to implement computerized management either by mailing the input to the data-processing center or transmitting it by a terminal located in the LHA. In the event that a LHA does have access to a computer, it is able to lease the software systems from the private firms, develop its own program with consulting firms such as Touche Ross and Co., or hire its own in-house programmer. In short, the adoption of automated management systems is not restricted to any particular type of LHA or hardware availability.

The NAHRO staff members and LHA directors were also in consistent agreement on the innovative nature of recent advances in the building and construction industries and the application of these advances to public-housing construction. In general, two areas emerged. The first was the development of industrialized, or factory-built, homes (generally in low-rise construction), and the second was the development and use of prefabricated components in high-rise construction.

"Industrialized housing" is a term that has been used interchangeably with "manufactured housing," "modular" or "instant housing," and "prefabricated housing." For the purpose of this study, *manufactured housing* shall be defined as standardized off-site construction of total housing units (walls, floor, utility cores, and all exterior and interior finishing) built essentially by unskilled labor and shipped in sections or modules to the housing site.[43] For the sake of clarity, *modular housing* (the completely preassembled, three-dimensional unit) shall be distinguished from *prefabricated housing* (components such as utility cores, precast floors, and walls shipped separately and assembled on-site).

The modular-housing industry is perhaps best known for its production of mobile-home units. Factory-built, the unit emerges as a home on wheels complete with kitchen, bathroom, bedrooms and living room. It has been estimated that nearly 450,000 mobile homes are produced each year, accounting for 20 percent of total housing production.[44] Although mobile homes themselves could not provide relief for urban housing shortages,[b] the possibilities that such mass production of living units offered to public housing certainly did not go unnoticed. If residential units could be manufactured on a scale equal to that of mobile-home production and could at the same time meet the strict zoning and construction codes set by communities, a large percentage of the urban housing need could be met. In 1968, Stirling Homex Corporation of Avon,

---

[b]Virtually no mobile home meets conventional building codes.

New York, using factory-assembled modular units, erected 275 dwelling units in Rochester, New York, in just thirty-six hours.[45] This publicity-seeking display by no means went unnoticed in Washington. A year later the HUD initiated a program called "Operation Breakthrough" in an attempt to cut housing costs through volume production and to aggregate housing markets.[46] Public housing, of course, was viewed as a likely aggregated market. The Secretary of HUD, George Romney, summed up the operational goal as "seeking to shift from conventional to industrial production and from local to national housing markets."[47] HUD's Operation Breakthrough provided the impetus, through funding and a market, for further development of the concept. Of 200 applicants with complete housing proposals, twenty-two participants were selected in Februrary, 1970. Projects included precast concrete modules, wood modules with steel structural framing, and modules wrapped on a mandrel with reinforced plastics.[48] Modular construction, however, was not limited to the contracted companies of Operation Breakthrough. A survey taken in 1972 by the industry magazine, *House & Home,* determined that 222 companies were modular producers.[49]

Although such modular units can and have been used in high-rise housing, they are more widely used for multifamily, one-, two-, and three-story structures, or single-family sectionals. The box-like units, complete with plumbing, wiring, utilities, and all interior and exterior finishing, are literally dropped into place on waiting foundations, connected with other modules, and made ready for occupancy within a week. With the increasing demand for housing units, coupled with the high costs of labor and inhibiting weather factors, modular construction offers the low-rise category of housing the advantages of reduced skill, acceleration of erection time, and centralization of control and responsibility for construction.[50]

The development of prefabrication techniques in high-rise construction is a considerably more advanced innovation than modular housing; however, the European construction industry has far surpassed the United States in utilizing such techniques.[51]

High-rise construction is regulated by strict building codes that require the use of concrete, steel, elevators, and nonflammable materials for a structure over three stories high. Consequently, all prefabricated construction has concerned itself with such materials. Moving away from the brick-by-brick method of erection, high-rise housing construction now utilizes factory-built, hollow-core and solid load-bearing wall panels, thin floor and ceiling slabs, subsystems such as a bathroom-and-kitchen core, hollow-core floors, floor panels assembled with lateral and electrical work inside, and precast exterior brick and concrete panels. Shipped by truck from the factory, these panels are assembled on-site into a complete high-rise housing structure. Although public housing authorities have been moving away from high-rise structures for families (concentrating more on the scattered-site concept of low-rise housing), multistoried projects still remain the favored mode of accommodating the elderly. Construction of high-rise projects, therefore, remains a concern of housing authorities. The advantages of prefabricated components of precast panels, utility cores, and structural components allows for centralized control, unskilled and therefore less costly labor, and speed in erection. Modular and prefabricated housing appear as the most innovative breakthroughs for the construction industry and consequently for public housing.

Educational innovations were selected in much the same manner as were the innovations in housing. Several staff members of the National Education Association and education professionals in the Office of Education of the Department of Health, Education, and Welfare were initially consulted. In addition, professionals in ten state education associations were queried by telephone for their opinions concerning recent innovations. A number of technological innovations were suggested including cable television, computer-assisted instruction, videotape recorders, PPBS, performance contracting, and various types of individualized instruction. Again, two innovations were selected for detailed study—one product and one process innovation. The product innovation was the adoption of videotape recorders in the instructional program of district secondary schools, while the process innovation concerned the use of some system of individually directed teaching in elementary schools. Specifically, three instructional programs were considered—Individually Guided Education (IGE), Individually Prescribed Instruction (IPI), and Program for Learning in Accordance with Needs (PLAN).

As an alternative to what Alvin Toffler's *Future Shock* describes as the industrial concept of education where the student (raw material) is processed by the teacher (worker) in a centrally located school (factory),[52] educators across the country are developing and implementing the innovative concept of individualized instruction. While it may be argued that such an approach is not new and that progressive teachers and schools have for decades tried different methods of humanizing education, it nevertheless remains that not until the late 1960s were formal programs of individualized instruction offered to all interested school administrators regardless of district size, wealth, or location.

Individualized instruction, as opposed to traditional methods of teaching, is characterized by the rejection of the classroom approach and by the recognition that each student is a unique personality whose ability and desire to learn is different from that of other students. Inasmuch as all students are not able to achieve their greatest potential under the teacher-lecture approach, individualized instruction attempts to offer a diverse environment that ranges from the traditional large classroom to small tutorial groups. Because of the impossible task of determining which schools had introduced such methods as the nongraded approach, the open classroom, differentiated staffing, multi-aged pupil populations, and prescribed instruction, only those utilizing one of three formal programs of individualized instruction (IGE, IPI, and PLAN) were classified as individualized schools.

Individually Guided Education (IGE) is perhaps the most widely implemented program of the three, with over 1,000 schools in thirty-three states utilizing the program. Developed by the Wisconsin Research and Development Center for Cognitive Learning during the period 1965-1971, IGE implementation became accelerated in 1966 when the Institute for Development of Educational Activities, Inc. (IDEA), the educational affiliate of the Charles F. Kettering Foundation, committed itself to developing new ways to accelerate improvement in education.

In an IGE multi-unit elementary school, the nongraded instructional unit replaces the traditional self-contained classroom. Each unit consists of one unit leader, three to five professional teachers, one or two school aides, and 75 to 100 pupils. This differentiated staffing permits teachers to vary the medium of instruction to fit students' individual learning styles. Under the IGE approach, the unit has a multi-aged pupil population, a nongraded approach to curriculum, and specific learning programs designed for individual pupils. Essentially there are four steps in the IGE cycle: (1) assess the student's level of achievement, learning style, and motivation level by use of criterion-reinforced tests; (2) set short-term specific instructional objectives for each child; (3) implement the learning program; and (4) reassess students for attainment of initial objectives and for setting the next set of instructional objectives.

Although the open classroom is architecturally desirable, any school's physical plant is adaptable to the IGE method. As for the actual implementation of the program, IDEA and Wisconsin's R&D Center offer the instructional materials necessary for training in-service professional staff as well as programmed learning materials for students. In short, IGE has been made available to all and does not cater to only progressive or specialized laboratory-type schools.

Individually Prescribed Instruction (IPI) is considerably different from the IGE approach in that it is more behaviorally oriented with a heavy concentration on diagnostic testing devices and daily prescriptions of learning for each pupil. The IPI program, older than the other two individualized instructional methods, was initially developed at the Learning Research and Development Center at the University of Pittsburgh. Research for Better Schools, Inc., (RBS) a federally funded, nonprofit education laboratory, assumed responsibility for field testing and disseminating the program; and by 1974, over 600 elementary schools across the nation were utilizing one of the RBS individualized programs.

The third approach to individualized instruction, Program for Learning in Accordance With Needs (PLAN), is a computer-managed individualized learning program developed in 1967 as a collaborative effort on the part of Westinghouse Learning Corporation and the American Institute for Research. Because of the integral role played by the computer in this instructional approach, far fewer schools have adopted it than the other two methods. PLAN provides for a Program of Studies (POS) for each student. The POS is a list of the objectives that the students are scheduled to follow; students are encouraged to work out their own POS with the teacher, using the computer printout data for guidance. After completion of their learning direction sheets, the students undergo an evaluation exercise which is input into the computer. The computer is programmed to score tests, keep records of each student's progress, project a program of studies based on the pupil's evaluation exercises, and printout on the school's terminal a specific program for each individual. PLAN currently offers programs designed for individualized instruction in math, language arts, reading, science, and social studies.

It should be stated clearly that in no way do the previous short summaries of IGE, IPI, and PLAN do justice to these innovations in educational instruction. However, so as not to lose perspective on the intent of the summations, they are provided to explain the difference between traditional and individualized approaches to education, as well as the diversity within the innovative approach itself.

While the blackboard and chalk still reign as the most important instructional aid for educators, videotape recorders have gained a number of strong proponents among professional educators. Videotape and videocassette recorders remain a relatively new innovation for audiovisual departments in secondary schools where for quite a few years the application of hardware technology in education has been limited to record players, film, slide and overhead projectors, audiotape recorders, and, in the 1960s, instructional television. It was not until manufacturers of the television networks' videotape recorders were able to develop a less costly system that their use became feasible for school administrators.

The videotape recorder (VTR) system employs a camera similar to that used by commercial television, except that it is portable and far less complicated to operate. The videotape itself is a magnetic tape that records both sound and picture and that allows immediate recording and instant replay. Developing the tapes is unnecessary as the sound and picture are recorded in the same way as a regular tape recorder, allowing for simple erasure and reuse. The videotape can be played back on either a receiver or a monitor. A receiver is a standard TV set sold for home use that can be adapted to videotape playback. A monitor, on the other hand, is designed specifically for use with the VTR system and is capable of displaying a picture directly from a video camera. In that the VTR requires only natural lighting for taping, only a camera and videotape recording machine are required.

An even more recent innovation-within-the-innovation is the introduction of videocassettes. Unlike the reel-to-reel half-inch videotape used in portable and inexpensive equipment, the videocassette offers three-quarter-inch magnetic tape used exclusively on videocassette recorders, eliminating tape threading, facilitating operation, and allowing for library collections of videotape recordings. The advantages of the latter type of VTR system rest primarily with the availability of quantity production, distribution, and storage.

Despite initial standardization problems among manufacturers, the VTR system is currently becoming more feasible for secondary school audiovisual centers and could be well on its way to becoming a standard medium of education.

The selection of the two library innovations—a theft-detection system and computer use in library management—was accomplished in a manner similar to that used in selecting housing and school innovations. Interviews were held with several officials of the American Library Association (ALA). Based on information obtained from the ALA, twelve librarians in cities throughout the country were contacted for opinions on the most important technological innovations in recent years. Thus theft-detection systems and computer use were selected for analysis.

The automation of library operations is inextricably tied to the use of the computer. While there were a few early attempts to apply punchcard machines to routine library work (1940s and 1950s), it was not until the 1960s that the potential applications of computer technology to library operations were recognized. So important were these developments that the ALA formed an Information Science and Automation Division in the mid-1960s. Until recently, applications of the computer to library operations were largely confined to technical processing and circulation. Now, however, the computer is becoming a real tool in library management.

Paul L. St. Pierre sees wide application of the computer to the library system and its various subsystems. Thus computer assistance is possible in serials, cataloging, acquisitions, circulation, and reference, as well as in administration and planning.[53]

There are at least four major functions of automated catalog systems: listing, control, search, and combined systems. Listing systems list or print output such as catalog cards, book catalogs, and labels. Control systems provide support for catalog operations with products such as shelflist inventories. Search systems assist in locating books by using data such as author, title, subject, and call number. And finally, the more sophisticated combined system attempts to put as many operations under computer control as possible.

The basic systems in the acquisitions area include fund accounting and order control. Fund accounting relates to automation of management and control of fund allotments and expenditures. Order control is automated through machine-readable input of order information with a variety of outputs, including computer-printed orders. The third function again combines the other two.[54]

Since serials have traditionally been the most difficult type of material to control in a library, automation of serials functions has become extremely important. The first serials system is listing. Typical serials lists might include, for example, lists of titles by location or titles by subject. A second function, check-in control, provides mechanisms for controlling receipt, recording, and routing of incoming serials.[55]

Circulation is the main area of library operations where manufacturers have developed equipment specifically for library use. Thus many types of badge/card readers or microfilm systems tie in circulation to computer operations. Such systems keep control of inventories, print circulation lists, lists of overdues, overdue notices, etc.[56]

Administrative functions have, of course, many computer applications—largely in the areas of fund and property management. Other important areas of potential application include the automation of reference and bibliographic functions.

Because of rising theft in libraries across the country, manufacturers of library theft-detection systems have found a receptive market for their innovative product in a number of public libraries. Theft-detection systems identify library books and other materials that are being removed from the library without authorization. All systems use some type of sensitive material hidden in the book to be protected. When the book or protected material has not been properly checked out by a library attendant, it triggers an alarm.

There are two types of theft-detection systems: the bypass system and the full-circulation system. With the bypass system the patron hands the library materials to the attendant who sees that they are properly checked out and passes the material around the detection point. With the full-circulating system, library materials are desensitized prior to the patron passing through the detection point. This may be accomplished in two ways: by deactivating the sensitive piece or by shielding it perhaps by an appropriate card usually placed in the book pocket.[57] A library has the option of either sensitizing only certain sections of its collections, i.e., reference and rare books, or the entire collection. A library may have to restructure the floor plan, and in some cases the architecture, for the effective installation of a theft-detection system. As for the cost of installation, the ALA survey quotes the price of equipment as ranging from $4,500 to $8,300, with installation fees of $1,000 and under. Sensitizing pieces are quoted as costing 2 to 18 cents each. For a library, therefore, installation of a full-circulating system with sensitizing pieces for 100,000 volumes would run in the vicinity of $20,000. A noncirculating system, similar to the familiar airport security gates, would cost a little less. Currently, there are seven manufacturers offering library theft-detection systems on the public market.

The selection of the product and process innovations adopted by city governments was undertaken in a somewhat different manner from that used in housing, schools, and libraries. As with the other governmental areas, the leading professional associations were initially surveyed. An official of the American Public Works Association (APWA) was interviewed as the first step in selecting an innovation in the public works area. One innovation mentioned was in the area of city vehicle fleet management. The APWA official further noted that only one commercial firm, Mainstem, Inc., of Princeton, New Jersey, provided a complete vehicle-management service. A single vendor service provided a unique opportunity to study vendor influence in the adoption of innovation, so that contracting for a Mainstem vehicle and equipment-maintenance management service was selected as the product innovation. (Admittedly, the "product" is a service, but it fit the basic definition.)

In the area of public works, fleet and vehicle maintenance remain a special concern for management, if only for the reason that hundreds of millions of dollars are spent annually for the acquisition, operation, and maintenance of city vehicles. Because of the rising costs of fleet maintenance and the necessity to maximize efficiency in the area of vehicular management, since 1968, APWA has been working toward the development of a public works equipment data bank.

Mainstem, its name derived from Management Information Systems, is a private firm that offers a computerized data-reporting service for local governments, as well as commercial firms. Officially endorsed by the APWA, Mainstem services have been contracted by over sixty local governments for their fleet-maintenance service. Local governments contracting with Mainstem are provided with:

1. all data input forms;
2. implementation of the system and complete installation within thirty days;
3. training of personnel at all levels in the use of the system, both input and output;
4. data conversion, editing, keypunching, and verification;
5. data processing and report preparation and distribution to appropriate levels of management; and
6. report analysis and fleet advisory service to and in directing management toward corrective action.

Mainstem operates essentially on the historical data system. Utilizing computer forms to register a designated code for the vehicle and the labor spent on maintaining it, the mechanic assigned, the gas used, the mileage accumulated, the parts replaced, the time spent on each job, and the location of garage where maintained, PW departments subsequently receive a computer printout from which intelligent and cost-saving decisions can be made. Mainstem, after training garage personnel in how to code and complete the forms, is then able to provide the managers of fleet maintenance with the historical data needed to reform and restructure garage procedures. For example, included in the output provided by the New Jersey firm are reports summarizing direct labor repeat work by component, direct versus indirect labor, average hours and dollars per repair, number of units repaired, maintenance and operating cost per vehicle, location of vehicles repaired and/or fueled, and a breakdown of work performed on each vehicle such as commercial work, labor hours and dollars, tires and tubes, gasoline charges, and total charges. Additional reports include the complete detailed history of each vehicle by component from acquisition to disposal, notification of each vehicle falling outside the norms developed specifically for its function, and a monthly billing to leasing activities or customers, computer by activity and by vehicle.[58] Although the aforementioned do not include all the reporting services provided by Mainstem, one can begin to understand the enthusiastic endorsement given by APWA to the private firm. With such data at the service of management, decisions concerning depreciation, trade-in, and retirement of vehicles are no longer guess-work. Poor labor performance, as well as the quality of commercial products used, become ascertainable, and cost-effective management of fleet and vehicle maintenance becomes a simple matter of utilizing and acting on the data received.

It might be noted here that the APWA has been working to develop an equipment service program and data bank with Mainstem. Utilizing Mainstem's governmental client files, the APWA has been seeking to develop a uniform system of coding and forms that could be applicable to all fleet-maintenance departments. Further progress towards this goal was made in 1973 when the APWA and Public Technology, Inc., combined their formerly separate efforts into a united project of developing the "Equipment Management Information System" (EMIS). Both desired a software system that could be adaptable to most types of computers, thereby allowing all cities to implement it. Should their efforts prove successful, the cost for contracting with Mainstem would become unnecessary for those local governments having their own computers. Nevertheless, Mainstem remains the pioneer in the development of an equipment-maintenance system, as do the local governments who initially implemented the innovative management practice.

The selected process innovation in local government was the use of automatic data-processing equipment by police departments. The significance of ADP in police work was initially pointed out by officials of the International Association of Chiefs of Police (IACP). Fortunately, the International City Management Association (ICMA) had recently surveyed American cities on the use of ADP by police departments and made their data available for this analysis.

An early write-up of the survey results succinctly describes computer applications in police work. Kent W. Colton reports that the substantial expansion of computer use by police departments is due to three factors: (1) the need to process large amounts of information with speed and accuracy, (2) the need to increase efficiency of operations, and (3) the availability of large amounts of federal money to support local police operations.[59]

Police computer use has grown rapidly during the past ten years. Between 1964 when St. Louis became the first city in the United States to install a real-time computer system, and 1971, when the ICMA took its survey, almost 50 percent of the larger (25,000+) cities had adopted a computer or punchcard equipment for police work. Colton groups police computer systems by four functions: (1) administration, (2) operations, (3) management, and (4) planning and research.

Administrative applications include, for example, payroll, personnel records, inventories, fleet-management records, and budget analysis. These applications are very similar to the administrative uses of the computer in other areas of city government.

In support of operations, computers also have a number of applications. Inquiry systems allow the police to make real-time inquiries as to the identification of people or property. Traffic systems provide automated records of accidents, traffic citations, and parking tickets. Computer systems are also used in dispatching and for greater control of vehicles. Crime patterns, criminal associates, modus operandi, and other supporting information can be computerized and made available in criminal investigations.

In some instances computers provide increased information for police management. Colton reports, for example, that programs have been developed that can help predict workloads and alter police deployment to meet changing crime patterns.

In the area of planning and research, statistical data on crime and patterns of criminal activity are two examples of data being gathered to facilitate research on criminal careers and to evaluate alternative methods of crime control.[60]

Computer application in police work thus covers a wide range of activities. The growth of computer use and the professional interest in its applications make it an ideal technological innovation to study.

Quantitative Analysis

After the innovations were selected, the next step—and the first step in the analysis of innovation adoption—was the development of the community environment factors, factors of both a physical and attitudinal nature. On the basis of past research,[61] twenty variables were selected that were believed to be adequate descriptors of the physical characteristics of American cities. Twenty variables, however, are much too cumbersome to fit successfully into the model for the adoption of innovation. The mathematical technique of factor analysis was therefore used to group the variables. Factor analysis provided a viable method for identifying the underlying dimensions of the twenty variables that might accurately describe a city in quantitative terms.[62] The use of cluster, or factor, analysis to identify the underlying dimensions of American cities has substantial precedence.[63]

Orthogonal rotations were performed on the data using principal-component factor analysis. The number of factors produced was limited by Kaiser's criterion (eigenvalues greater than unity). Orthogonal rotation was selected for a number of reasons: simplicity, conceptual clarity, and amenability to further analysis. In orthogonal rotation, the factors are, by definition, uncorrelated as the axis are 90 degrees from each other. Thus an orthogonal restriction ensures that the factors are statistically independent of one another.[64]

Four factors were produced under this criteria. Eighteen of the twenty selected variables had substantial loadings on one or more of the factors. While Rummel is not specific on what constitutes a substantial loading, there is precedence for giving little attention to loadings below .40. Bruce M. Russett, for example, believes that "it is reasonable largely to ignore correlations below .40 since the factor in question accounts for less than a sixth of the variance."[65] Thus the two variables apparently load on factors that did not satisfy Kaiser's criterion. These two variables, percent of the population living in group quarters and percent population increase or decrease, 1950-1960, were considered independently in the analysis of innovation adoption.

The two variables were temporarily eliminated from the analysis, and a second factor analysis using the remaining eighteen variables was computed. Again, Kaiser's criterion was applied and orthogonal rotation performed. The result of this computation is found in Table 1-2. The four factors explained 73.3 percent of the total variance with Factor 1 explaining 31.1 percent; Factor 2, 21.9 percent; Factor 3, 12.0 percent; and Factor 4, 8.3 percent. All eighteen variables reached a minimum loading of .40 on at least one factor.

Factor 1 is an obvious measure of socioeconomic status (*SES*) and was so named. Seven variables had significant loadings on this factor. Median income, percent with income over $10,000, median school years completed, percent with a college education, and persons employed in white-collar occupations all had high positive loadings on this factor. Two variables, percent of the population residing in the same house for the past five years (residential stability) and percent of the labor force unemployed, both had substantial negative loadings. The factor is thus a clear measure of SES.

As with Factor 1, seven variables had significant loadings on Factor 2. Median income, percent with income over $10,000, percent sound housing, and the ethnic index—all had positive loadings of .40 or greater on the factor. The remaining three variables, percent with income under $3,000, percent non-white, and percent renter occupied, had significant negative loading on the factor. Factor 2 thus seems to capture a central city/suburb dichotomy. The factor was thus named *suburb*.

Again, seven variables loaded substantially on Factor 3. The ethnic index, percent renter occupied, population per square mile (density), median age, and residential stability—all had high postive loadings. As with Factor 1, two variables had high negative loadings—the dependency index and the percent of housing units in one-unit structures (single-family housing). This factor seems to be descriptive of areas like Boston's North End, that is, descriptive of high-density, multifamily, renter-occupied, European ethnic communities. The factor was thus termed *ethnic/ghetto*.[c]

---

[c]*Ghetto* is simply defined as "a quarter of a city in which members of a minority group live . . .," *Webster's New Collegiate Dictionary* (Springfield, Mass.: Merriam, 1973), p. 484.

Table 1-2
Varimax Rotated-Factor Matrix of Selected Census Variables

	SES	Suburb	Ethnic/Ghetto	Size
Percentage Same House	-.45973	.16590	.42751	-.12010
Median School Completion	.77803	.32721	-.26888	.01458
Percentage College Graduates	.88378	.01256	-.03097	-.00845
Percentage Unemployed	-.51376	-.20988	.01946	.03745
Percentage White collar	.83579	.23918	-.03345	.00887
Percentage Income +10,000	.69086	.55964	.16169	.02473
Median Family Income	.47565	.82346	.10692	.00337
Percentage Income -3,000	-.22698	-.87812	-.11985	.00601
Percentage Nonwhite	-.03230	-.64761	-.04064	.19046
Percentage Sound Housing	.38844	.76612	.03424	.00243
Ethnic Index	-.14166	.47885	.67454	-.06120
Percentage Renter Occupied	-.02257	-.57723	.76507	.08291
Dependents	-.17391	-.09527	-.61473	-.08388
Percentage One-family House	.09946	.11122	-.89765	-.02064
Population per Square Mile	-.15044	.07333	.63650	.12170
Median Age	-.03828	.11389	.65723	-.08728
Land Area	.05356	-.12735	-.08131	.67538
Total Population	-.06392	-.00135	.21877	.95444
Percentage Total Variance	31.1	21.9	12.0	8.3 73.3

Factor 4 was termed *size*. Only two variables loaded significantly on this factor—total population and land area—and both in a positive direction.

Factor scores for each of the 310 cities were then computed for each of the four factors.[66]

The aforementioned factors, however, captured only the physical dimensions of the city's environment. Missing still were dimensions attempting to capture the attitudinal characteristics of the population. Three variables were believed to be important determinants of the attitudinal environment. Two measures of voting behavior were selected as surrogates for local political attitudes. The vote for George Wallace for President in 1968 was used as a surrogate for an anti-integrationist, or racist, attitude. The vote for Barry Goldwater for President in 1964 was also used as a surrogate for conservative attitudes—but a more basic political conservatism concerning the use of federal programs. Voting statistics on a city-by-city basis were not available; therefore, the 1964 and 1968 voting percentages are figures for the county in which the city is located.[67]

The third variable considered in the attitudinal environment is an operationalization of Elazar's concepts of political cultures.[68] Each of the 310 cities was assigned a classification based on the location of the city in relation to Elazar's map of dominant political cultures. The cultures were then operationalized as follows:

MT	*M*	*MI*	*IM*	*I*	*IT*	*TI*	*T*	*TM*
0	1	2	3	4	5	6	7	8

These attitudinal variables were then subject to factor analysis under the same criterion as were the physical variables. The results of this computation are shown in Table 1-3. One factor was produced explaining 70.5 percent of the total variance. All three variables loaded significantly on this factor with all three variables loading in the negative direction. The factor appears to catch the underlying dimension of a conservative/liberal political dichotomy. Since all of the loadings were in a negative direction, a positive value on the factor score for a given city will be indicative of a "liberal" community political attitude. Conversely, a high negative score for a city will indicate a "conservative" political attitude. For these reasons the factor was named *liberalism*.

To ensure that the factor did indeed capture conservative political values, a second factor computation was made—this time with an additional variable. The vote for Nixon in 1968 was added to the other three variables with the results shown in Table 1-4. The three conservative variables still loaded on one factor, although a second factor was produced. With positive loadings of the Nixon and Goldwater votes, this new factor apparently represents traditional Republicanism rather than conservative values. Since our theoretical concern was with

Table 1-3

Factor Matrix of Selected Attitudinal Variables

	Liberalism
Wallace	−.93633
Goldwater	−.67479
Elazar	−.64192

Table 1-4

Varimax Rotated-Factor Matrix of Selected Attitudinal Variables Including Vote for Nixon

	Conservatism	*Traditional Republicanism*	
Nixon	−.11189	.84706	
Wallace	.92707	−.34282	
Goldwater	.83749	.42187	
Elazar	.59272	−.15117	
Percentage Total Variance	53.9%	30.8%	84.7%

conservatism and not Republicanism, the factor scores for each city were computed from Table 1-3 matrix.

Thus all the studies of innovation have the four demographic factors, two demographic variables, and one attitudinal factor included in the computations under "community environment."

While the community environmental factors previously discussed are standard for all the models tested in the substantive chapters to follow, variables selected to represent demand, the organizational environment, and the characteristics of the organization were not. While the demand variables obviously pertain only to the specific governmental unit under study, every attempt was made to select similar variables to operationalize the concepts of the organizational environment and the organizational characteristics. Obviously, this was not always possible. Data availability, to some extent, dictated the selection of variables to represent these categories.

In the analysis of each individual innovation, all the independent variables in the model were individually correlated with the appropriate dependent variable. In some cases, Pearson's correlation was not the most appropriate tool for analysis. In cases in which the data required a lower level of analysis, the appropriate statistical techniques were used. However, the product moment correlation coefficient was by far the most common tool.

Since the model of innovation adoption suggested indirect, as well as direct, influences by some variables, the study also incorporated causal modeling techniques into the data analysis wherever possible.[69] With the large number of variables in each model, strict adherence to causal modeling was obviously impossible. Nevertheless, partials were computed in a causal sequence in order to best test the models. Initially, partials were computed between the variables indicative of the organizational characteristics and the dependent variable representing innovation while controlling for the organizational environment, demand, and the organizational characteristics. Next, partials were computed between the variables of the organizational environment and the dependent variable controlling for the organizational characteristics, demand, and the community environment. This procedure was followed until all of the possible linkages depicted in Figure 1-1 were tested.

There is a definite time lag built into the innovation models. The dependent variables measure the level of innovation adoption as of 1974. The community environment, however, is represented largely by factors computed from the 1960 census. The variables in the categories between the community environment and the dependent variable—demand, organizational environment, and the organizational characteristics—were measured at various times between 1960 and 1974. Often, data availability determined the exact date. When the *NAHRO Housing Directory*, for example, was the source of data, the date was 1968 simply because this is the only directory of housing that NAHRO has published.

Throughout the study, then, there is a time progression from 1960 to 1974. The community environment is measured at t_1 (1960), innovation levels at t_3 (1974), and the other three model components at t_2. The variable t_2 is simply defined as some time between t_1 and t_3.

Only partials statistically significant at the .01 level were ultimately used in the explanation of the innovation process. While in causal modeling there seems to be reasonable acceptance of the idea that when $r < .10, b = 0$,[70] this analysis included only those variables statistically significant at the .01 level in model building. This decision was prompted by several considerations. First was the need for parsimony. Model building with the large number of variables included in this analysis would have been virtually impossible. The second reason for the use of significance level as a criterion for inclusion/exclusion was standardization. Since the degrees of freedom of the relationships within the models vary widely depending on the quantity of missing data, the selection of some arbitrary inclusion value such as $r = .10$ would not be very meaningful. In instances with few cases of missing data, a partial coefficient of .10 might be substantial, but where there were large quantities of missing data, a coefficient of .10 might be substantively meaningless.[71]

In the following chapters, all partials computed in the analysis are not reported. Due to space limitations and an attempt to reduce the complexity of the chapters, partials not significant at the .01 level are not reported or discussed.

In those cases where there were more than one significant linkage between

independent variables and the dependent variable, stepwise multiple regression
was used to attempt, in a general way, to evaluate the importance of each
independent variable to innovation adoption.

Qualitative Analysis

In this research the investigation into innovation adoption largely emphasized quantitative analysis. However, a number of case studies were also built
into the design to posit tentative explanations for the unexplained variance in
the quantitative models and to add "richness" to the quantitative explanations.
To this end, a small number of cities were examined through field investigations.

Regression equations were used to select the specific cities and organizations to be examined in depth. It was important that deviant organizations be
selected, that is, organizations in cities where the quantitative explanations of
innovation were unsatisfactory. First simple correlation coefficients were computed between each of the independent variables and the applicable dependent
variable, or innovation. Similarly, partial correlation coefficients were computed
between each of the independent variables and the applicable dependent
variables while controlling for all other independent variables in the model. Then
all independent variables found to have relationships with the dependent variable
that were statistically significant at the .05 level (either zero order or partials)
were included in stepwise multiple regression equations to explain the variation
in the independent variables. However, only six stepwise regressions were performed. There were so few significant relationships between independent variables and either the housing or library product variables that virtually none of the
variation in the use of these innovations could be explained by the quantitative
variables. The regressions were also limited in another way. In each model there
were four or five variables representing size that were highly intercorrelated. In
the housing process model, for example, the size factor, the number of housing
units in management, city total general revenue, and the size of the LHA were all
highly intercorrelated (see Table 1-5). All variables in one way or another were
indicative of size so only one of the four variables, the size factor, was used in the
regression. This was true in all the innovation models.

The constant and B-values for each stepwise model were then used to predict an expected level of innovation adoption for each innovation in each city.
Again, since the purpose of this prediction was only to select a few cities for
case study, cities with missing data for any of the variables in each equation were
given a missing-data value for the predicted level of innovation. This procedure
ensured that cities selected for case study were selected in the most conservative
manner possible.

The expected level of innovation, or the predicted dependent variable, was
then subtracted from the value of the actual dependent variable creating a residual

Table 1-5
Zero Order Relationships Between Size-Related Variables in the Housing
Process Model

	Size	Units in Mgt.	City Revenue	Size of LHA
Size	1.000			
Units in Mgt.	.905	1.000		
City Revenue	.864	.976	1.000	
Size of LHA	.881	.993	.989	1.000

variable. The mean and standard deviation of the distribution of the residuals were then computed. Organizations with residual values one and one-half standard deviations above the mean were considered high deviants in that their actual level of innovation was much higher (1 1/2 SD) than predicted. In a similar manner, low deviants were selected from organizations having a residual value lower than one and one-half standard deviations below the mean.

Deviant cities are not identified by name in this study. In each case, approximately five to ten organizations were high deviants and a like number were low. Several cities had two deviant organizations, while two cities had three. Due to the possibility that certain cities in themselves might foster deviant organizations, both cities with the three abnormally high or low residuals were visited.

The first step in the field research was designed to identify the actors in the decisional unit. This was accomplished through the use of the positional and reputational approaches. For the purposes of this study, the decisional unit was broadly interpreted and did not necessarily correspond to the governmental unit adopting the innovation. Private consultants, for example, were often identified during the initial interviews as playing an important role. The same was true of state officials and others. Initially, the researcher obtained a copy of the organization chart of the unit under investigation and selected a number of positions likely to be knowledgeable of the unit's decisional processes. These people were then interviewed, and the reputational approach was utilized to identify members of the decisional unit. Through interviews with the positional and reputational leaders, the research thus traced the adoption from the initial identification of need (or performance gap) through the adoption of the innovation.

Organizational characteristics of the adopting unit were also examined. Further, data were obtained on formal rules and procedures followed in innovation adoption, professionalism, and centralized or decentralized decision-making.

In the case of low deviants, decisions *not* to innovate can be as important as decisions to innovate. Again, field research was used to identify the actors in the decision-making process, the adoption process, and the organizational characteristics of the adopting unit. It is in this area that the "nondecisions" of the community power studies were shown to be important.[72]

The investigators were cautious about biasing the results of the case studies through knowledge of the quantitative findings. Thus research tasks were divided. The researcher doing most of the case work completed the case studies (and the write-ups) prior to being advised of the quantitative results. Thus the field researcher was not "looking for" support for the quantitative results.

Summary

This chapter detailed where this study is going and why and also how we are going to get there. Much of the chapter is abbreviated, however. It would have taken hundreds of pages to spell out the exact variable names and data sources. Such material is available from the study codebook.[73]

The following four chapters contain the substantive findings of the research effort. All the chapters follow the same basic organization. Each is divided into three basic sections: process innovation, product innovation, and concluding remarks. Within the process and product sections, the results are presented in the same order in all the substantive chapters.

The quantitative analysis is followed by a series of descriptive studies (two to six) that present the results of the field work. The qualitative analysis is then followed by a short summary merging the findings of the two types of analysis.

Once both process and product innovations have been examined in this manner, the conclusions attempt to draw the findings together. Thus at the end of each chapter, an attempt is made to suggest some generalizations about innovation based on the particular unit of local government studied.

2

Adoption of Innovation by Public Housing Authorities

This chapter documents the findings of the investigation of innovation in the public-housing area. The chapter is divided into three sections. Initially, the adoption of the housing process innovation is examined. Within this section both quantitative and qualitative data are presented. The quantitative model is presented first followed by a series of case studies. Finally, some conclusions about housing process innovation based on the findings of both methods of analysis are drawn.

The analysis of the housing product innovations are presented in a similar manner; that is, the quantitative findings are followed by the qualitative which in turn are followed by a short summary.

The final section of the chapter draws together the findings of both the process and product sections and discusses, in general terms, innovation adoption by public housing authorities.

Process Innovation

The first step in analyzing the housing process innovation was to take the general model for the adoption of technological innovations presented in Chapter 1 (Figure 1-1) and translate it into a specific model for the adoption of computer applications in housing authority management. The model suggests that the community environment generates demand for computer use in housing management by determining the size of the management problem, that is, the number of public-housing units to be managed. In addition, it was expected that the community environment would directly affect segments of the organizational environment (e.g., city reformism) and the characteristics of the organization (e.g., authority size), as well as the level of computer use.

The number of housing units (demand) was also expected to directly influence computer use, as well as segments of the organizational environment and organizational characteristics. The organizational environment was expected to directly affect innovation adoption and certain organizational characteristics. Finally, the organizational characteristics were also expected to directly influence housing authority computer use.

While Table 2-2 lists the independent variables used in the quantitative explanation of computer use, the design is equally applicable to the more qualitative data generated by the case studies. Thus the model provides the basic framework for both quantitative and qualitative analyses.

Quantitative Analysis

The first step in the quantitative analysis was to operationalize the dependent variable—public-housing computer use. Data on authority computer use were collected through the use of a mailed questionnaire. A response rate of 97 percent was achieved with 300 of the 310 cities with 1960 populations of 50,000 or more responding to either the first or second questionnaire mailing. The response rate includes the few large cities without public housing.

Fifteen questions concerning computer use were asked and are shown in Table 2-1. The dependent variable, the computer-use score, is merely the sum of the *yes* responses to the fifteen specific computer applications. Of the public housing authorities responding to the questionnaire, computer-use scores ranging from 0 to 12 were noted. The computed mean was 1.7 with a standard deviation of 2.6 and median and mode values of zero. Of the responding authorities, 144 had a computer-use score of 0—indicating that they do not use the computer at all. The fact that some 57.6 percent of the cities had a computer-use score of 0 indicates that computer use in housing authority management has achieved only limited acceptance.

The variables shown in Table 2-2 are the independent variables selected to represent the community environment, demand, the organizational environment, and the organizational characteristics. The variables representing the community environment were discussed in detail in Chapter 1 and are therefore not discussed here; nor are they discussed in relation to subsequent models.

The demand characteristic was the number of housing units to be managed—the hypothesis being that a large number of units makes authority management extremely complicated, and thus such organizations are most likely to rely heavily on a computer to simplify data management. The data were obtained from the questionnaire responses.

Five individual variables were included in the model representing the possible influence of the organizational environment in innovation adoption. First a dichotomous variable, participation in the Management Improvement Program (MIP), represents intergovernmental influence as a determinant of computer adoption.

In an effort to minimize costs and improve efficiency in management in the 2,500 LHAs across the country, HUD initiated the Public Housing Management Improvement Program (PHMIP) on January 22, 1972, in thirteen test sites. Under the dual direction of HUD's assistant secretaries for housing management and for policy development and research, PHMIP contracts were awarded, after nationwide competition, to Dade County, Florida; Atlanta, Georgia; Greensboro,

Table 2-1
Public Housing Authority Computer-Use Questions

For which of the following do you use the computer?

1. Are accounting and budgeting of department revenues computer managed?

2. In tenant rent collection, is billing automated?

3. Are delinquent-payment reports automatically assessed and systematically output to project managers?

4. Do cashiers use a data-input terminal at the central collection office?

5. Are tenant application forms computer processed and recorded?

6. Are tenant profiles computed for the basis of tenant selection?

7. In maintenance, are service requests data processed?

8. Is the computer programmed to assess high-cost *units* based on past maintenance records?

9. In a similar fashion, is the computer programmed to pinpoint high-cost, problem *tenants* based on past maintenance records?

10. Are inventory and purchasing computer managed?

11. Are job-cost reports data processed?

12. In the area of personnel, is the computer utilized to schedule work?

13. Is the computer used to monitor personnel location at all times by means of computer-linked time-clocks?

14. With regards to community services, is the computer used in compiling tenant profiles based on need, such as transportation for the elderly and handicapped, job placement and counseling?

15. Are statistics compiled by the computer for federal authorities?

North Carolina; Milwaukee, Wisconsin; the District of Columbia; San Juan, Puerto Rico; Detroit, Michigan; Honolulu, Hawaii; Richmond, Virginia; Wilmington, Delaware; New Haven, Connecticut; Hartford, Connecticut; and Worcester, Massachussetts. The three-year program provided $25 million for the participating LHAs to evaluate and implement new approaches to public-housing management. These developed approaches would in turn be analyzed by HUD for nationwide use by other public-housing agencies. Areas falling under the cost-effective management approach included fiscal and budget control, maintenance standards, security approaches, management information systems, and management training.

Table 2-2
Zero Order Relationships Between Housing Process Independent
Variables and Housing Computer-Use Score

Variable	r
Community Environment	
Liberalism	.055
SES	.062
Suburb	−.032
Ethnic/Ghetto	.105*
Size	.286**
Population Increase	−.110*
Group Quarters	.050
Demand	
No. Units in Management	.221**
Organizational Environment	
MIP Participant	.408**
City Total General Revenue	.168**
City Per Capita Revenue	.248**
City ADP Score	.320**
City Reformism	−.133**
Organizational Characteristics	
No. of Employees	.180**
Age	.133*
Authority Organization	−.029
NAHRO Participation	.203**

*Significant at the .05 level.
**Significant at the .01 level.

Financial resources were also hypothesized to influence computer use.
Representing financial resources in the city are two variables: 1969-1970 city
government per capita general revenue and 1968 city government total revenue.
Representing equipment resources available is the variable city ADP score. It
was expected that a city with substantial financial resources (either per capita or
total) would devote some resources to ADP use (ADP score) and that this computer availability would stimulate housing authority use of the computer in management. Financial indicators were taken from census data.[1] The ADP score is
the sum of a substantial number of specific ADP applications in municipal
government. The data were obtained from the International City Management
Association.[2]

Also representing the organizational environment is a reformism score for
city government. Reform measures include council-manager form of government,

at-large representation, and nonpartisan elections.[3] Values were assigned as shown in Table 2-3. The reformism score varies from 0 to 3 and is the sum of the values assigned to the three reform measures.

Finally, four variables were selected as measures of the characteristics of the individual housing authorities that might bear on innovation adoption. The first two were the size (number of employees) of the LHA and the age of the LHA.[4] Housing authority status or independence was also expected to be a significant determinant of innovation. Thus a dichotomous variable concerning authority independence from city government was developed from the questionnaire.

As an admittedly rough measure of authority participation in the major professional association, a NAHRO participation dichotomous variable was developed. Authorities were divided into two categories—having a major NAHRO official or not having one—depending on whether any one or more authority employees was an NAHRO national officer, member of the board of governors, national committee member, regional officer, or chapter officer.[5] It was believed that an LHA with an employee (usually the executive director) closely tied to NAHRO would be more likely to adopt NAHRO-supported innovations than an authority without such ties.

Findings. Of the seven community environment variables, only size showed a substantial zero order relationship with the dependent variable with $r = .29$. A

Table 2-3
Local Government Reformism

Type Government	
Mayor-Council	0.0
Commission	0.5
Council-Manager	1.0
Representation	
Ward	0.0
Both	0.5[a]
At-large	1.0
Type Election	
Partisan	0.0
Both	0.5[b]
Nonpartisan	1.0

[a]A value of 0.5 was given to a city with both ward and at-large representation if neither category represented the type of representation of more than two-thirds of the council.

[b]A value of 0.5 was given to a city with both partisan and nonpartisan elections if neither category represented the type election of more than two-thirds of the council.

slight positive relationship between ethnic/ghetto and computer use was noted ($r = .11$), as was a slight negative relationship between population increase and the computer-use score ($r = -.11$). It thus appeared that larger, slow-growth cities and those with ethnic/ghetto characteristics were most likely to use the computer and to have high computer-use scores.

The demand variable also showed a significant relationship with the dependent variable with $r = .22$ between number of units in management and computer-use score. On the basis of previous research, however, it was expected that the community environment characteristics would lead to a demand for public housing which in turn produced a high number of units in management.[6] The expectation is substantiated with significant relationships between ethnic/ghetto and number of units in management ($r = .27$) and between size and number of units ($r = .91$).

The simple relationships found thus far point up the need for the slightly more sophisticated analysis to be presented later. The interrelationships between two of the characteristics of the community environment, ethnic/ghetto and size, the number of units in management, and the computer-use score illustrate the difficulty in ascribing "cause" to the various independent variables. Does size "cause" number of units which in turn "causes" high computer use, or is there an independent relationship between size and computer use? Later analysis utilizing partial correlation coefficients will answer this and other questions.

Virtually all the variables selected as indicators of the influence of the organizational environment were significantly related to computer use at the zero order level. The relationship between MIP participation and the computer-use score was $r = .41$. While only twelve of the 310 cities in this study had housing authorities participating in this HUD sponsored program, it seems that this participation was an important link in computer management development. It thus appears that intergovernmental influences play a significant part in innovation adoption and development.

Another aspect of intergovernmental consideration was the presence or absence of reformism in the structure of the city. It was expected that a reformed government would insist on innovative or progressive behavior from its bureaucratic agencies. While most housing authorities are semiautonomous agencies, professional "spillover" was nonetheless expected. The findings, however, did not support the expectations. In fact, a slight but significant negative relationship was found between reformism and housing authority computer use ($r = -.13$). When the form of government component of reformism was correlated with computer use, an even more substantial negative coefficient of -.23 was obtained. It thus appears that housing authorities in unreformed cities are most likely to embrace computer management.

The other three variables within the organizational environment were designed to measure the impact of external resource availability on the adoption of innovation. City per capita general revenue attempted to assess the availability of excess, or slack, funds that might be used to upgrade housing authority computer capability. Such slack would obviously be made available in equipment or technical assistance and *not* through cash contributions. It is possible, though, that authority expenses might be less in a wealthy city than in a poorer one.[a] The relationship between this measure of financial slack and computer use was as expected with $r = .25$.

City total general revenue, another measure of financial slack, was also significantly related to authority computer use with $r = .17$. Thus total wealth, even in poorer cities, might contribute to authority innovation. There is some difficulty with this revenue measure, however. Table 1-5 showed the intercorrelations between the size-related variables in the housing process model. The high correlation between this variable and the other size-related variables makes it impossible to conclude that revenue and not size or number of units in management is truly related to computer use. In fact, the interrelationships between the size-related variables were so high that it was impossible to partial out the independent relationship between total revenue and computer use while controlling for the other size variables. Thus, while it is necessary to keep total revenue in mind when considering slack resources, no further analysis including this variable is possible.

The city ADP score was included in the model as a measure of availability of equipment slack. It was expected that a city with a highly developed computer software system, as measured by the ADP score, would be likely to extend computer assistance (both hardware and software) to the local housing authority. This appeared to be the case with a significant zero order coefficient of $r = .32$ between ADP score and the housing computer-use score.

Only two of the four organizational characteristics exhibited substantial zero order relationships with the housing computer-use score. Again a positive relationship was noted between another size variable, number of full-time authority employees and the computer-use score with $r = .18$. As expected, large organizations are more likely to adopt the computer as a management technique than small organizations, but again this does not tell us much.

NAHRO participation showed the strongest zero order relationship with computer use of any of the organizational characteristics with $r = .20$. Of the 310 cities, in 1971, eighty-two had a local housing authority official serving as a NAHRO national officer, member of board of governors, national committee member, regional council officer, or chapter officer. This measure of professionalism thus appeared to make some difference in innovation adoption. Perhaps close ties with the major professional association stimulates progressive behavior or innovation adoption.

In a second attempt to investigate the role of the professional association in

---

[a]Some cities, for example, refund the payment in lieu of taxes (most authorities pay to the city) to the housing authority. Here we might also expect the city to furnish the authority with a systems analyst "on loan" to upgrade computer operations.

accelerating innovation adoption, all issues of the NAHRO publication, the *Journal of Housing*, from 1964 through 1974 were screened for articles discussing computer applications in authority management. In discussing the development of new or "hot" fields of science, Jack L. Walker noted that the few early research reports are followed by an increase in books and articles on the subject during the "hot" period of development. This period of rapid publication is then followed by a steady decline as the field settles down and scholarly consensus is achieved. Walker also finds that the same process appears in many studies of the diffusion of innovations.[7] It was thus expected that professional associations might behave in the same manner—that is, it was expected that the *Journal of Housing* would contain articles on computer management information systems on a widely scattered basis during the mid-1960s, followed by a period of relatively intense concentration, and then a cooling off as the innovation became a standard practice. Figure 2-1 indicates that this appears to be the case. The *Journal of Housing* contained one article on the use of the computer as a management tool in 1965, one in 1968, and seven in 1971. The seven comprised 12 percent of the fifty-nine articles in the *Journal* in 1971.

It appears that innovation emphasis by professional associations follows the pattern suggested by Walker—at least as far as this innovation is concerned. A few scattered articles appeared during the mid and late 1960s, followed by a period of intense interest or emphasis in 1971 which in turn was followed by a cooling-off period. While no evidence was collected concerning the dates of adoption of each of the computer functions, it is evident that the articles largely reported computer applications already in use. Four articles, for example, documented computer use by the Philadelphia Housing Authority.

Returning again to the quantitative analysis, a slight relationship between the age of the housing authority and computer use was noted. Older (and probably larger) housing authorities are slightly more likely to use the computer as a management tool than are newer or younger authorities.

The fact that organizational structure made little difference in computer application was rather surprising. According to questionnaire response, 213 authorities (89 percent of those answering the question) indicated that they were independent of the city government while twenty-six (11 percent) operated as a department or section within the city bureaucracy. It was expected that these twenty-six would be much more likely to have access to city resources and would thus have higher computer-use scores. This was not the case; organization made virtually no difference in computer use.

Simple correlations do not give all the answers, however. The independent contribution of each of the independent variables is not yet determined nor has any evidence of the intervening nature of the organizational characteristics or the organizational environment been examined. To do this, a series of partial correlation coefficients between variables were computed. The large number of independent variables in the model made causal modeling virtually impossible.

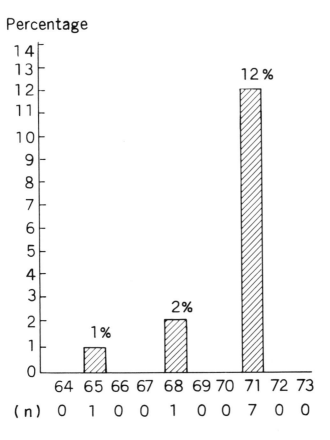

Figure 2-1. Percentage of *Journal of Housing* Articles Devoted to Computer-based Management Information Systems (1964-1973)

Due to the recursive nature of the model, however, inference concerning innovation adoption based on the partial relationships can be made.

Thus the first task was the compute the relationship between each of the organizational characteristics and innovation adoption while controlling for variables in the community environment, demand, and the organizational environment. Of the four selected organizational characteristics, only number of employees showed a significant independent relationship with the computer-use score with a rather substantial negative r of -.50.

It was interesting to note the reversal of the relationships with the introduction of controls. Recall that the zero order correlation coefficient between number of employees and computer use was .18. Once controls were introduced, controlling for size, number of units in management, and the other independent variables, the relationship became negative. This fits logically into a model of innovation for efficiency.

Organizational size (in 1968) is logically negatively related to authority computer-use score (1974). Other things being equal, authorities with lower personnel levels are more likely to devote resources toward computer assistance than are authorities with higher personnel levels. Computer management information systems may then be partially the product of an internal demand system. Instead of raising personnel levels, it appears that authority decision-makers try to provide employees with a greater range of decision-making information and thus are prone to develop a more sophisticated software package than are decision-makers in organizations where personnel resources are not quite so scarce.

The second step in model development was to compute the relationship between the organizational environment and computer-use score controlling for community environment, demand, and organizational characteristics. As number of employees was the only organizational characteristic showing an independent relationship with computer use, the other three organizational characteristics were dropped from this and all subsequent computations. There is, after all, no longer any reason to include them.

Virtually all the variables in the organizational environment were substantially and independently related to housing authority computer use. Only reformism ($r = -.14$) was not. The remaining three partials showed that significant and positive independent relationships exist between aspects of the organizational environment and computer use by public housing authorities. Even with the introduction of controls, a significant relationship was found to exist between MIP participation and the authority computer-use score ($r = .37$). This finding again underscores the importance of intergovernmental influence in innovation adoption, at least as far as this innovation is concerned. Both of the city resource variables were also independently related to the computer-use score. Thus a high city per capita revenue, $r = .20$, and a sophisticated city computer system, $r = .45$, both appear to influence the level of computer application in housing authority management.

In this investigation it is important not only to find the correlates with innovation adoption, but also to identify the environmental characteristics related to those factors that directly influence adoption. In this vein then, a partial correlation coefficient was computed between city per capita revenue and number of authority employees while controlling for community environment and demand. Virtually no relationship was found with $r = .01$. Nor was a significant relationship found between reformism and number of employees (-.06). Partials were not computed between MIP or ADP scores and number of employees as there was no theoretical basis for the relationship. In our model there does not appear to be a connecting link between the organizational environment and the only innovation-related organizational characteristic, number of employees. As reformism showed little relationship with innovation adoption or with number of employees, it was dropped from the model.

A partial was then computed between the demand variable, number of units under management, and number of employees while controlling for the community environment and the three remaining variables in the organizational environment. As expected, a significant coefficient of $r = .99$ was obtained. Obviously, large housing authorities have the most employees.

A partial correlation coefficient was also computed between the demand variable and MIP participation. A coefficient of $r = -.13$ (not significant) resulted from this computation. Thus demand, as defined here, has little relationship with the pertinent characteristics in the organizational environment. A relationship here had been expected. It was believed that a large number of units in management might stimulate MIP participation, but this was *not* the case. No independent relationship was noted.

A partial was also computed between number of units in management and the computer-use score controlling for the community environment, organizational environment, and organizational characteristics. A significant coefficient of $r = .38$ was noted. This relationship again supports the concept of an efficiency-based model of innovation adoption. The size of the management problem was independently related to the level of computer use—even when controlling for size characteristics. Thus demand (or need) seems to be a major determinant of innovation adoption in the housing process model.

The effect of the community environment on the number of authority employees was also computed, but only two of the relationships were significant. A large housing authority staff was positively related to rapid population growth and negatively related to size. It thus appears that fast-growing cities (usually economically healthy) tend to develop larger housing bureaucracies than their slower-growth counterparts, other things being equal ($r = .32$). The substantial negative coefficient of -.63 between number of employees and size is meaningless. The fact that the zero order relationship between size and number of units in management was $r = .90$, and the coefficient between number of units and number of employees was $r = .99$ undoubtedly created this partial.

The independent relationship between community environment and the organizational environment was also examined. Surprisingly, none of the community environment variables were independently related to MIP participation. Thus it was found that MIP participation was an important determinant of the housing computer-use score although the community or demand characteristics that make a housing authority likely to participate in the MIP could not be identified.

A number of community environment variables were related to city per capita revenue. Liberalism and ethnic/ghetto were both positively related to per capita revenue ($r = .25$ and $.52$ respectively) while size was negatively related ($r = -.27$). Thus politically liberal communities and those with the characteristics of a European ethnic population tend to devote higher levels of funds to the public good (on a per capita basis). Large cities, on the other hand, do not.

City ADP score also seems sensitive to the community environment. Size,

$r = .23$, SES, $r = .26$, and suburb, $r = -.28$ were all independently related to the city ADP score. Larger central cities with a high socioeconomic status were thus most likely to have a highly developed data-processing system.

It was noted earlier that the demand, or need, variable was independently related to the housing computer-use score. It was thus necessary to see if the demand variable was the product of the characteristics of the city. To this end, partials were computed between each of the community environment variables and the number of units in management while controlling for the remaining community environment variables. A number of the characteristics of the community environment appear to stimulate a large (in terms of number of units) housing authority. The most substantial result is also the most obvious. The coefficient of $r = .94$ between size and number of units merely indicates that large cities have a lot of public housing—a fact most of us already knew. It also appears that highly ethnic cities ($r = .56$) and those with lower socioeconomic characteristics ($r = -.24$) were also more likely to have more public housing than their counterparts without these characteristics. Thus, unquestionably, city characteristics are the major determinants of the level of public housing within a city.

The final partial computation was one of the most important of this investigation—that is, the relationship between the city environment and innovation adoption controlling for demand, organizational environment, and organizational characteristic. The results of these computations are quite surprising. There was no independent relationship between characteristics of the community environment and the housing process innovation! Community environment influenced computer management in public housing only through other variables in the model. In spite of a rather substantial number of public policy studies tying innovative behavior directly to city characteristics, these results showed no such direct relationship. Perhaps it is the nature of the innovation. Perhaps there is a distinction between policy innovation and technological innovation. A more thorough examination of the model might suggest some answers.

Figure 2-2 presents a revised model for the adoption of process innovation in public housing. The lines linking the variables indicate the partial relationships significant at the .01 level as discussed earlier. Translating the specific variables or operational definitions back into the characteristics they represent, it is possible to describe the system of process innovation adoption, at least for this process innovation in public housing, with reasonable accuracy.

Within the organization, the drive for efficiency appears to be a major factor in the adoption of the selected process innovation. This fact is suggested by the nature of the negative partial relationship between number of employees and the computer-use score. If one were to compare two housing authorities, each in a high-growth city and each with the same number of units in management, the authority with the fewest employees in 1968 would be most likely to have a highly developed computer-based management information system in 1974.

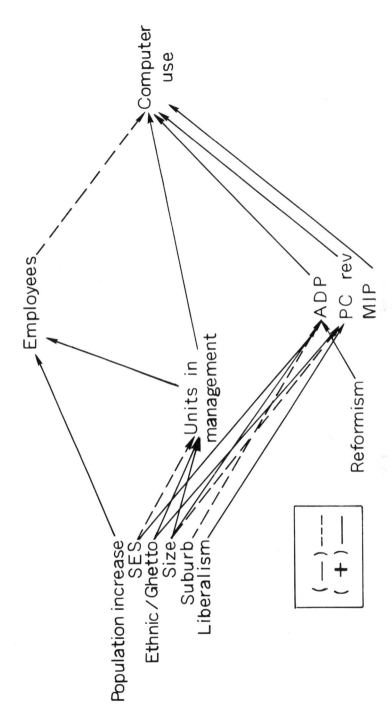

Figure 2-2. Revised Model for the Adoption of Process Innovations in Public Housing

While the organizational environment does not directly affect the structural nature of the organization, at least, as it is measured here, the environment substanitally affects innovation adoption. The existence of a high resource level within the city government is also an important determinant of housing authority innovation. Although most housing authorities are semiautonomous agencies, it appears that strong informal ties link city governmental resources with housing authority innovation. This suggests that the influence of the city in providing both equipment and personnel for authority use is a major determinant of process innovation in housing authorities. But what generates these resources? The model indicates that slack in the organizational environment is the product of the characteristics—both attitudinal and demographic—of the community in which the organization is located. Size appears to be the major determinant of resource availability, but many of the city characteristics also contribute to a high resource level. The relationship between political attitude and slack is particularly noteworthy. Apparently, attitudes concerning the distribution of resources for the public weal contribute to slack availability.

While city reformism showed no substantial direct link with innovation adoption or with the pertinent organizational characteristic of the authorities, it was suspected that reformism might have an indirect link in the innovation process. This appears to be the case. A partial was computed between reformism and city ADP score controlling for the community environment and demand. This computation produced a coefficient of $r = .18$, significant at the .01 level. It thus appears that professionalism in city government independently contributes to a higher level of computer capability in the city which in turn leads to a higher level of computer use by the housing authority.

Intergovernmental influence, or the activities of the federal government, substantially contributed to the adoption of this process technological innovation. Although MIP participation was limited to only twelve of the authorities studied, the influence of the availability of such a program was startling. The availability of this program was extremely important to the development of sophisiticated computer-based management information systems.

Demand also independently influences process innovation adoption. Size of the authority (in terms of number of units to be managed) presented authority officials with the management problem or goal. As the authority grew, the problems of management increased and became more sophisticated, control became more difficult, and information and communications channels more complex. Computer-based information was thus adopted to provide up-to-date data for management decisions.

In general, what can be said about this process innovation in public housing? First the model suggests that innovation adoption in public housing is a predictable process. Decisions to innovate appear to be based on very rational considerations—efficiency, need, and resource availability. Second the organizational environment appears to be the most influential determinant of innovation adoption—at least in this model. To further test this contention, a stepwise multiple regression was computed between the computer-use score and the five variables showing an independent relationship with it. Table 2-4 shows the results of this computation.

The five variables explain approximately 35 percent of the variation in the computer-use score. MIP participation was the first variable added with $r = .41$. Thus intergovernmental influence, a characteristic of the organizational environment, appears to be the most significant determinant of innovation adoption. When a second stepwise regression was computed, this time removing the MIP variable from the computation, another characteristic of the organizational environment, city ADP score, was the first variable added with $r = .32$. It thus appears that the proper organizational environment is most critical for innovation adoption.

Qualitative Analysis

The use of computer-based management information systems was examined in detail in four cities. Two cities had computer-use scores much higher than predicted, one had a score lower than predicted, and the fourth city had a computer score that was less than 1 1/2 standard deviations from the mean. The fourth city, Free City,[b] was used for field testing and to pretest the questionnaire. Thus Free City was not a deviant case but had developed a computer capability much to the extent predicted.

Free City. Free City was a participant in HUD's Public Housing Management Improvement Program. Participation in the program did not necessarily mean that a given housing authority would develop sophisticated computer management information and control capabilities; nevertheless, the additional funds

Table 2-4
Summary of Stepwise Regression Explaining Housing Computer-Use Score

Variable	R	R^2
MIP Participation	.408	.167
Number of Units	.453	.205
Number of Employees	.532	.283
City ADP Score	.591	.349
City per Capita Revenue	.591	.349

---

[b] "Free City" is a fictitious name, as are all the cities named in the case studies throughout this book.

provided under the program for management improvement did induce a significant number of the thirteen participants to utilize these additional resources in
this way. Certainly this was the case with Free City, a city whose housing authority developed a complete management data system with the awarded MIP funds.
Although the LHA switched its revenue budgeting to the city computer two
years prior to participation in MIP, it was not until a private consulting firm
helped prepare its proposed program for the federal government that an advanced
management data system housing program became a reality in Free City.

More than ten years ago, in 1964, the Free City Housing Authority switched
from decentralized rent collection by project managers to centralized collection
and control. It was a move that, at the time, caused considerable resentment
among project administrators who viewed it as an action motivated by a fiscal
department need to justify the cost of new equipment. As one administrator
recounted:

> There was really no justification at the time to switch tenant accounting
> to central control. Project managers were capable of handling rent col-
> lection and could tell you faster than the NCR who were delinquent in
> payments just by looking at their index cards. The switch also deprived
> the project managers of their personal contact with the tenants. The
> fiscal department needed to justify the cost of the ADP equipment. If
> it was used only for department accounting, it couldn't be justified. I'd
> agree that today it would not only be impractical but also dangerous for
> project managers to handle rent collection, but in 1964, I think the move
> was unjustified.

Despite such opposition, the fiscal department was successful in centralizing
tenant accounting and budgeting, using its newly purchased equipment for record
keeping and processing. Within six years, however, the workload exceeded the
capacity of the accounting department's "computer." From 1964 to 1970,
2,000 additional housing units were added to the authority's management burden;
thus record keeping of tenant accounts became overloaded. Reports were delayed, and consequently, it was difficult for project managers to locate tenants
who were delinquent in their rent payments. Although the adoption of ADP
equipment in 1964 had allowed the LHA to cut staff size, by 1970, they faced a
workload that either demanded additional staff and more record-keeping equipment or a completely new approach. In 1970, the fiscal department opted for
the latter solution.

As the old ADP equipment was no longer capable of handling tenant accounting, a computer provided the logical solution. Computer utilization in fiscal management was nothing new to the key LHA fiscal decision-makers.

The supervisor of administration, now deputy commissioner of administration and control, had three years' prior experience as a CPA with one of the

largest manufacturing firms in the nation. Describing himself as a "conservative accountant," he recalled how he had spent three months on a training program at the corporation's data-processing center and had been introduced to the application of computers in accounting. Inasmuch as he believed that public housing should be run on a business-like basis, it was not surprising that the supervisor of administration looked back to his experience in corporate accounting for a solution to the housing authority's needs.

The background of the supervisor of the budget and finance section, the other key decision-maker, was remarkably similar to that of his supervisor. Though not a CPA, his experience in the accounting department of a General Motors division introduced him to the advanced stages of fiscal control. With the same exposure as his supervisor to corporate use of the computer in fiscal control, there emerged in 1970 a consensus of opinion as how to best handle the Free City LHA's accounting overload.

In 1970, the administration and control department of the housing authority approached the city's central electronic data services department to negotiate a contract for LHA budgeting and tenant accounting. According to the director of fiscal control, the decision to tie in with the city computer was based on three factors. First and most important was the need to cut processing time; second was the availability of a trial balance; and finally, a cost savings was involved in using less expensive forms.

The decision in 1970 to convert the accounting and budgeting functions along with the tenant accounting and reporting functions to the city computer can be explained as a step motivated by need and operationalized by the past work experience of the key decision-makers. The work required for over 5,000 low-income public-housing units had exceeded the capabilities of manual fiscal operations. The need, coupled with the background of the individuals responsible for finding a solution, led to the computerization of fiscal management in the Free City Housing Authority. One may well ask, however, what steps were taken to bring Free City's application of computer management beyond basic fiscal operations, raising that authority's computer-use score of 4 in 1970 to 12 in 1975. The explanation is found in Free City's participation in HUD's PHMIP.

In 1961, Free City created the department of city development (DCD) by merging the housing authority, the city planning commission, and the redevelopment authority into one agency. The DCD was later expanded to include the community organization, relocation, and economic development division. By 1971, the organizational structure of the department of city development appeared to be deterring the effective management of its diversified responsibilities. Thus the city contracted with the private consulting firm of Touche Ross and Co. to conduct a reorganization study of the DCD with recommendations to be made for the improvement of DCD management procedures.

In 1971, the completed study was submitted to the city. After outlining the current problems within the DCD, the report concluded with detailed recommendations concerning methods for improving management within the various authorities and divisions. Included in the study was the recommendation that the department attempt to make a more creative use of federal programs and funding sources. Concerning the housing authority in particular, the report suggested the addition of a management information section.

Whatever the cost incurred by the city for the consulting firm's study, it soon became clear that it was more than justified. When the department of housing and urban development called for proposals from the nation's 2,500 LHAs to be placed in competition for HUD's MIP, Free City needed to do little more than submit a revamped version of the Touche Ross report and recommendations.

Fully heeding the consulting firm's advice for "a more creative use of available Federal funds," the LHA, with the assistance of Touche Ross, submitted a proposal for MIP funds. On June 22, 1972, Free City was selected as one of thirteen cities that would share $25 million over a period of three years for the development of management improvement programs. With their contracted access to the city computer, coupled with over $2 million they were to receive in federal money, Free City immediately began adopting advanced management applications of the computer contracting with Touche Ross for the software system.

Despite the fact that the fiscal office had considered further applications of the computer after 1970, the Director of Fiscal Control noted that only with MIP funding could advanced programming have been achieved. Prior to the federal award, plans for development applications were distant visions. However, once the funding was available and a system designed, the Free City LHA committed itself to a management information system and provided funding for a full-time system programmer. When in November, 1974, HUD ordered a halt to Free City's MIP program because of a dispute over a contract condition, LHA officials indicated that they would not abandon the computerization of management tasks, regardless of future HUD action.

Lakeview. Lakeview provides an example of a moderate-size city that has achieved a high level of computer management sophistication without participating in the management improvement program. The Lakeview Housing Authority had a computer-use score of 8—somewhat unique for a small housing authority. This score placed the Lakeview LHA more than 1 1/2 standard deviations above the predicted score for the city. The Lakeview Housing Authority was one of the first authorities, if not the first, to apply automated data processing toward LHA management that ultimately led to a state-wide automated tenant accounting system serving thirteen housing authorities.

Since the agency's creation in 1938, it has been managed by twin brothers who served as executive director and comptroller, respectively. It was a situation that, the director noted, "caused a few raised eyebrows" and in which only rigid record keeping eased the apprehension of the suspicious. It is this unique relationship, however, that enables one to better understand the earliest applications of ADP in housing management in Lakeview.

In addition to management of the city's low-income public housing, this particular authority also assumed responsibility for a state-aid program in 1949, and a federally sponsored veterans' program following World War II. In that all three required different accounting procedures, as prescribed by their respective overseeing departments, the LHA management was faced with multi-bookkeeping responsibilities, ranging from detailed cost-maintenance reports to tenant accounting. By 1961, the comptroller decided that automated applications were the only logical solution to management of bookkeeping without having to resort to a continuing increase of personnel.

Describing himself as a "virgin thinker," the now-retired comptroller recounted how he had seen the waste in using the same data over and over again manually for different jobs. Although he had no prior experience with data-processing equipment, he noted that it required only "brain power" for one to realize that ADP equipment could rapidly compile the same data for different management tasks. Reading whatever technical manuals he could obtain, he began educating himself in the use of ADP and began to understand the possibilities such automated operations could provide for his brother as executive director.

In 1961, the comptroller found an eight-year-old depreciated IBM Unit Record Processor for sale by IBM for approximately $10,000. With the support of his brother, the executive director, a proposal was put before the housing authority board of directors for the purchase of this equipment. The chairman of the board, coincidentally, was at that time purchasing similar equipment for his own manufacturing corporation and fully supported the proposal.

With board authorization, the brothers proceeded to develop an automated data-processing system. As the director would vocalize his needs for assorted types of information, his brother would proceed to develop a method of data processing by which it could be provided, oftentimes creating a unique system such as a 1-9 scaling of problem tenants.

If one judges level of professionalism only by the years of formal education or training in a specialized area, neither of the two brothers could be considered professional managers. The executive director received his degree in architecture from Carnegie Institute in Pittsburgh, certainly not what one would call training for administration and management. The comptroller never attended college and proudly remarks that, "neither did John Chancellor of NBC News. One thing college doesn't teach is brain power—how to use one's intellect." Yet despite this lack of formal training, these two men were pioneers in computer assistance to LHA management.

By 1964, the data system was so well developed that the comptroller was invited to attend a seminar in Washington, D.C., to explain his system. HUD made sixty copies of his operating instructions for distribution and offered him a job in Washington—a recollection he finds amusing in that Washington was initially opposed to his automation.

The Lakeview Housing Authority was soon contacted by the HUD regional office. HUD was interested in developing a system of tenant accounting that could be made applicable for other housing authorities. HUD held a number of seminars in Lakeview that included such participants as the National Capital Housing Authority, the housing authority of Philadelphia, and that of Baltimore. In 1965, the comptroller patented his tenant accounting system but found that the equipment he had was not capable of handling any greater number of units than that managed by the city itself. Although the package itself was adaptable to any city's tenant accounting and had in fact been contracted for by another housing authority, more sophisticated hardware was called for. The comptroller therefore organized a private company, the Data Processing Housing Service Center, and contracted with a local computer service to program and implement his system. In the past ten years, thirteen housing authorities across the state have contracted for tenant accounting with the Center for management of their tenant accounting. Although Lakeview has itself contracted for tenant accounting with the Data Center, it retains its own operation of other management data systems on its old IBM equipment.

The facts underlying the development and application of automated data processing to the management of low-income public housing for Lakeview certainly have no precedent. If indeed it was the first application of such management methods in the area of low-income public housing and if one is to accept the comptroller's statement that, "this housing authority was ten years ahead of the rest," then Lakeview offers a unique insight into the early development of this innovation. It lacks the trappings of decision based on precedent and experience of others; of government resources provided for the proven and desired innovation; of wide encouragement on the part of those seeking test sites; and it basically comes down to an idea developed, implemented, and refined by one individual— the comptroller.

River City. The River City Housing Authority also developed a computer capability well beyond the predicted. As might have been expected, the decision to utilize the computer in accounting and management was first based on the recommendations of the office of the fiscal director.

It was a decision, according to the current fiscal director, based on the need for efficient accounting for 2800 low-income public-housing units, a job that had outgrown the capabilities of manual operations.

Prior to contracting with Boeing Computer Services, Inc., for tenant accounting in July, 1972, the LHA attempted to keep management operations in-house. Using federal modernization money provided by HUD in 1969, the River City Housing Authority purchased a keypunch machine and sorter for about $26,000.

Whereas rent collection and accounting had formerly been carried out at the project level, there had been a gradual centralization over the years until all functions were directed by the central administrative office. It had been hoped that the ADP equipment might provide a solution for the tenant accounting problems, but this did not prove to be the case. The office of fiscal control, with the added tasks of keeping the general ledger, keeping track of maintenance costs, and directing the modernization of projects (the $5 million HUD grant), was simply understaffed and could not handle the tenant accounting and budgeting with the desired speed and efficiency.

In 1972, the River City LHA was approached by a representative of the Boeing Computer Services, Inc., a firm that was marketing a program developed by Management Data Systems of Madison, Wisconsin. Boeing Computer Services, Inc., and Management Data Systems teamed to market a family of computer programs that would provide tenant and management accounting and reporting for local housing authorities anywhere in the country. The programs were designed by Management Data Systems in cooperation with HUD. The system comprises a computer-based management system fulfilling basic tenant and general ledger accounting needs prescribed by HUD, plus information for more than twenty required periodic reports. It also provides a data base from which to draw information for better management control and tenant services. Boeing Computer Services (BCS) offers the system to local authorities through its nationwide teleprocessing network from data centers in Seattle, Wichita, Huntsville, and Philadelphia. Management Data Systems (MDS) offers the system from its Madison, Wisconsin, data center through the BCS network. River City contracted with the Boeing Corporation in July, 1972, for its services and the LHA's ADP equipment has been stored in the basement ever since.

As the fiscal director points out, there were two major factors behind the decision to contract with BCS. First the federal reporting requirements of HUD demand a considerable amount of time and work, particularly when a LHA must account for 2,800 units. And second, the director found that if an LHA employs more than one person solely to handle tenant accounting and billing, then the cost of computer management can be justified. The manpower saved by contracting out alone justified the expense. Because of the manpower saved, the River City LHA has since been able to catch up with the backlog of record keeping that had, in the director's opinion, added to the authority's management problems.

Prior to his employment at the River City LHA, the Fiscal Director had been the comptroller of a neighboring housing authority which also utilized an outside firm for computer management, tenant record keeping, and accounting. Although he played no part in the ultimate decision to contract for computer services in either authority, the fiscal director pointed out that the decision to turn to computer management in a housing authority was generally the comptroller's. And this decision usually rested on the comptroller's attitude and background. This particular comptroller was not a CPA, although he had trained at a business college and later taught there. His background was in accounting for small firms until he joined the first housing authority. Although he had some experience with computer use at the business college, his favorable attitude might be seen as emanating from utilitarianism, a need to get the job done.

Easton. Easton exemplifies an MIP participant without a highly computerized management system. In fact, the Easton Housing Authority did not use the computer at all. Just as the comptroller in both the Lakeview and River City LHAs had been instrumental in the development of computer-based management and accounting systems, so too was the comptroller in Easton found to be the key element in decisions *not* to adopt the computer.

Although all three were similar in their commitment to cost-effective management, the comptroller of Easton was of a conservative nature when it came to the application of automated bookkeeping. He strongly resented the popular attitude that computerization was the end-all solution for cost-effective management, and though he emphatically acknowledged the wide applicability of computers, he proceeded to develop and create his own manual accounting system that he believed was far more effective than any other system he had seen.

Hired by Easton in 1972, the comptroller was faced with what he called an "accounting mess." After twenty-four years' experience in the accounting department of a manufacturing corporation, he recognized the need for a good cost-accounting system. With the experience of his previous employment and formal training at the Bentley School of Accounting, the newly hired comptroller began reorganizing the bookkeeping of the housing authority into his own manual system.

One month prior to the comptroller's entrance, the housing authority was selected by HUD as a participant in PHMIP. The three-year contract provided $1.2 million to Easton, which had earlier contracted with a consulting firm to prepare its proposal for HUD. Concentrating more on safety and security measures than on actual management analysis, the first year of the program was a considerable loss. As the executive director noted, "we were warned by the U.S. Department of Housing and Urban Development because we were so slow."

In March, 1973, in an effort to give the MIP program some direction, the comptroller and two members of the consulting firm were directed to investigate the program and progress of the Wilmington (Delaware) Housing Authority, another MIP participant. Although their visit was for the purpose of examining the entire program, the topic of computer management was a recurring theme. Wilmington, which received a computer-use score of 12, had contracted with Boeing Computer Services, to implement computer management as part of its MIP. The Easton comptroller, who was currently implementing his own manual cost-effective accounting system, recounted how unimpressed he was with the Wilmington exhibition:

There appeared to be a flair for the flamboyant, but no one knew what it cost them, before or after. They couldn't even say what it cost them to prepare a payroll check. The Boeing representative couldn't answer my questions as to the exact cost of specific operations, and it was the unanimous opinion (comptroller and consulting firm representatives) that the answers just weren't there and such a system could not be justified.

Whether the comptroller set out for Wilmington with a preconceived negative attitude toward computerization is rather difficult to determine. More than once he emphasized that he would not be against computerization if it were economically justified. After twenty-four years of employment at the manufacturing firm, he claimed to have seen both the benefits and drawbacks of automated data processing. The key to the comptroller's attitude appears to rest with "economic justification." Under his own accounting system, "The costs of labor, materials, time, and location can be accounted for." Although he acknowledged the same ability of computerized management, the cost of such management for his housing authority could not, in his opinion, be justified.

The executive director of the Easton LHA (since January, 1971) was certainly open to the idea of computerized management information. A member of NAHRO, the director maintained contact with other LHA directors and had been invited to look at Greensboro's computerization under the MIP. He recounted how a couple of times he asked the comptroller's opinion on such utilization and received the same answer—it could all be done manually with the addition of one person to the staff. The comptroller said that, in actuality, it would require two more staff members, one in accounting and one in cost analysis. If indeed that was all that was required, no steps were taken to implement such programs on the manual level with the addition of staff.

When approached directly the following year by a Boeing representative, the comptroller indicated that his own lack of interest in the matter precluded the conversation from going very far and that those questions he did have could not be answered satisfactorily by the firm representative. The utilization of a computer, the comptroller noted, depends on what specific thing one is looking for. In his case, those "specific things," namely, payrolls, payables, rent collection, and cost-system maintenance, could all be done equally well at the manual level; something he believes he has already proven.

Summary

The case studies in general appear to support the quantitative model of innovation in public housing as well as provide additional insight into important variables not considered in the model. The attitude of the comptroller, or chief fiscal officer, takes on an apparent importance. In Free City, Lakeview, and River City, the comptroller was largely responsible for the initial move to the computer or ADP. In Easton it was the comptroller who effectively blocked the director's interest in computer systems. The case studies thus suggest that the comptroller is the key figure in computer-use decisions. At least the comptroller is a key figure in authority decisions which show deviation from expected patterns of behavior.

A second variable noted in the case studies and not apparent in the quantitative analysis was the emergence of the consulting firm as an important key to innovation. In Free City, for example, Touche Ross prepared the application for PHMIP while in River City, management information was provided by contract with the Boeing Computer Services. While Easton had a low computer-use score, the case study showed that the Easton PHMIP proposal was also the work of a consulting firm.

Demand and efficiency were important considerations. Lakeview, although a relatively small housing authority, had unusual reporting requirements generated by three different housing programs. River City consciously adopted ADP equipment and later contracted with Boeing with the expressed intention of keeping down manpower levels. Even Easton officials recognized that additional manpower would be needed to provide "Boeing-type" information if done by expanding the LHA's manual system.

In summary, certain facts emerge from the study of computer-based management information in public housing. First the data, both quantitative and qualitative, suggest that adoption is based on very rational considerations—considerations influenced by demand, efficiency, and resource availability. Community characteristics are obviously the first step in the process. The quantitative model shows clearly that community characteristics largely determine the management problem (number of units in management). They also determine some of the attributes of the organizational environment that lead to LHA computer use—attributes such as city per capita revenue or city emphasis on ADP use.

The number of units in management was obviously related to the number of authority employees. Case study findings, however, confirm the negative relationship between number of employees and computer use. Both sets of data suggest that computers and sophisticated management information systems are adopted in an effort to keep down manpower levels. That is, as authorities grow in size (number of units to be managed), authority decision-makers turn to the computer for assistance rather than to increased personnel levels.

The case studies also indicate that within the organization, the comptroller is perhaps the key decision-maker in computer use. While it is obvious that all authorities with comptrollers advocating computer assistance in providing management information have not adopted the computer, comptroller approval is probably necessary. Case study data suggest that an unfavorable attitude on the part of the comptroller will probably block computer adoption.

The organizational environment was probably the most important direct determinant of computer use. A high city ADP score (partially based on reformism) and a high city per capita revenue apparently provide the slack resources necessary for system development. MIP participation was, of course, the most important single variable. The intergovernmental influence took shape in two ways. First the PHMIP proposal competition allowed federal officials to influence the provision of computer management information by providing them with discretion in selecting program participants. PHMIP also provided the selected LHAs with adequate funding for the development of computer-based systems.

The influence of the consultant in obtaining federal assistance is strongly suggested by the case studies. Two cities, Free City and Easton, were MIP participants. In both cases the applications to HUD for participation in the program were largely the product of outside consultants. While this investigation was only indirectly concerned with PHMIP, it would be interesting to see how many of the approved applications were written by consulting firms.

Finally, the Lakeview and River City cases suggest that, at least in the case of high deviant cities, the contracting with private firms for management information and accounting software systems has a lot to do with the provision of data in sophisticated form. It appears that through market aggregation, the private firm is able to provide high-level computer-based management information to the housing authority—undoubtedly through standardization and efficient hardware utilization.

Product Innovation

The hypothesized model for the adoption of product innovations by public housing authorities is very similar to the process innovation model. Only a few of the specific variables in the quantitative model have been changed. There are two product dependent variables in the housing model, and each will be considered independently. The first is the use of prefabricated components in high-rise housing construction, and the second is the use of modular or factory-built housing in low-rise projects.

Quantitative Analysis

The first step in the quantitative analysis was to operationally define the dependent variables. A prefab-use score was developed from the housing authority questionnaire. Authorities were asked if any of the following components were utilized in constructing high-rise housing projects from 1964 through 1973: kitchen/bathroom utility cores, precast concrete exteriors, precast interior panel walls, and precast panel floors. The prefab-use score was simply the sum of the *yes* responses regarding each prefab component. Of the 170 housing authorities constructing at least one high-rise complex between 1964 and 1974, almost half (48.2 percent) used at least one of the prefabricated innovations selected. The prefab scores ranged from 0 to 4 with the distribution shown in Table 2-5. Thus only six of the housing authorities (3.5 percent) indicated use of all four of the prefab innovations.

The second dependent variable—percent modular housing—was computed to measure the percent of low-rise housing constructed between 1964 and 1974 utilizing modular or factory-built units. The data were again obtained from the mailed questionnaires.

Of the 167 housing authorities constructing low-rise units between 1964 and 1974, most had no experience with modular or factory-built housing. In fact, only 13.8 percent of the authorities building units used modular or factory-built housing—and with varying degrees of commitment ranging from 1 to 100 percent of low-rise housing units built.

Another independent variable, high-rise construction method, was added to the four organizational characteristics of the process model. This variable was obviously only used in the prefab model as high-rise construction method has nothing to do with modular use in low-rise projects. This variable was designed to measure contractor influence or dependence on contractor initiative. A score of one was assigned to authorities using only conventional contracting, 2 to authorities utilizing both conventional and turnkey, and 3 to authorities relying only on turnkey contracting.

Contracting technique was quite evenly split with 37.7 percent of the 175 authorities constructing high-rise projects relying exclusively on conventional methods. Another 37.1 percent reported experience with both methods while 25.1 percent relied exclusively upon turnkey.[c]

Within the organizational environment, all resource measures were eliminated. Housing authorities finance the construction of housing projects through the

Table 2-5
Distribution of Housing Prefab Scores

Score	n	Percent
0	88	51.8
1	43	25.3
2	18	10.6
3	15	8.8
4	6	3.5

[c]"Turnkey" housing called for the design and construction of rental housing by private contractors who sold the finished product to the local housing authority. The program was called "turnkey" because the developer "turned the key" over to the authority on purchase.

issuance of long-term, tax-free debt. The bonds are then paid off by annual contributions from the federal government. Since fiscal resources have little to do
with housing construction, the slack measures associated with the housing process
model were not included in the analysis. MIP participation was also eliminated
from the model as it, like resources, has little bearing on construction. Another
variable was added, however, representing intergovernmental influence—Operation
Breakthrough participant. It was expected that authorities participating in this
program would be most likely to adopt, or at least experiment with, new construction methods. City reformism remained as the other variable of the organizational environment.

Demand was represented by the number of high-rise projects built between
1964 and 1974 (prefab) and by the number of low-rise units built (modular)
during the same period.

The community environment remained unchanged from the process model.
The first step in the quantitative analysis was to examine the simple relationships
between each of the independent variables and the two dependent variables.
These relationships are shown in Table 2-6. Surprisingly there was virtually no
significant correlation between any of the independent variables and the two
product dependent variables.

Only high-rise construction method showed a significant relationship with
the prefab score with $r = .21$. It thus appears that contractor or vendor influence
is the only variable related to the use of prefab components—at least at the zero
order level.

Concerning the use of modular or factory-built housing, only reformism
showed a slight relationship with modular use ($r = -.15$), and this was significant
only at the .05 level. There is one other variable concerning modular use, however, that was not included in the model. This was method of construction. The
housing questionnaire asked a question concerning the contracting method for
the modular or factory-built housing units constructed since 1964. As only
twenty-three housing authorities used modular or factory-built housing at all, the
n was so small as to preclude inclusion in the model. Nevertheless, the results of
this question are extremely interesting. An extremely high 91.3 percent of the
modular-built housing projects were built through the use of the turnkey method.
Only two of the twenty-three projects were conventional. It thus appears that
contractor influence is an extremely important variable in predicting the use of
modular or factory-built housing by public-housing authorities.

While the results of the zero order correlations are somewhat dissapointing,
it is possible that partials might bring out other previously hidden relationships.
Thus the innovation model was tested using the same methodology as was used
in the process model.

Examining first the prefab score, the organizational characteristics were correlated with the innovation score controlling for the community environment,
demand, and the organizational environment. Only construction method was

Table 2-6
Zero Order Relationships Between Housing Product Independent Variables and Housing Product Innovations

Variable	Prefab Score r	Modular Use r
Community Environment		
Liberalism	.031	.087
SES	−.035	−.085
Suburb	.069	.077
Ethnic/Ghetto	−.068	−.015
Size	.041	−.026
Population Increase	.086	−.016
Group Quarter	−.052	−.054
Demand		
No. Low-rise Units Built		−.022
No. High-rise Projects Built	.044	
Organizational Environment		
Breakthrough Participant	−.011	.084
City Reformism	−.013	−.147*
Organizational Characteristic		
High-rise Construction Method	.210**	
No. of Employees	−.025	−.036
Age	−.055	.064
Authority Organization	−.091	.057
NAHRO Participation	−.012	.107

*Significant at the .05 level.
**Significant at the .01 level.

significant at the .01 level, although the relationship between number of employees and the prefab score was $r = .17$. While this relationship is not significant at the .01 level, it was interesting to note that the relationship is negative—much the same as in the housing process model.

Next, the organizational environment was correlated with the prefab score while controlling for the community environment, demand, and the construction method. Neither relationship was significant. Apparently the use of prefab components in high-rise public-housing projects is not independently related to reformism or participation in Operation Breakthrough.

It was possible, however, that the variables in the organizational environment might influence the construction method. As in the housing process model, however, there was no relationship between the organizational environment and the significant organizational characteristic. Since the organizational environment variables were not independently related to either the dependent variable or the relevant organizational characteristic, both variables were dropped from further analysis.

The relationship between the demand variable and high-rise construction method controlling for the community environment was computed. A coefficient of $r = .09$, not significant at the .01 level, resulted. Thus demand, measured in terms of the number of projects built, did not lead to the use of turnkey construction as expected. In terms of high-rise units, heavy construction activity does not lead to turnkey contracting.

Nor was there a significant independent relationship between number of projects constructed and the prefab score. Thus demand in terms of a high level of construction activity is unrelated to the use of prefab components in high-rise construction by public housing authorities.

Nor do community characteristics independently determine the method of construction contracting.

Finally, partials were computed between community environment and prefab score controlling for high-rise construction method. None of the relationships were significant.

Thus the model testing was not very successful. It appears that the community environment, demand, and the organizational environment do not contribute, directly or indirectly, to the use of prefabricated components in high-rise construction in public housing. Does this apply only to high-rise construction? To examine this possibility, the innovation model was tested using the percentage of low-rise units built using modular or factory-built components.

As with the prefab score, it was not expected that model testing concerning the use of modular or factory-built housing would yield much of significance. Nevertheless, the appropriate partials were computed. Partials were first computed between the organizational characteristics and percent modular housing, controlling for community environment, demand, and the organizational environment. No relationships of significance were noted. Since the organizational characteristics, as measured, show little relationship with the dependent variable, they were removed from further analysis.

Partials were then computed between the organizational environment and percent modular use, controlling for community characteristics and demand. Neither relationship was significant at the .01 level. As with the prefab/breakthrough relationship, the relationship between modular use and Operation Breakthrough participation was examined in tabular form (not shown). Again the lack of relationship was confirmed. Thus the variables selected as representative of the organizational environment were also removed from further analysis.

The next step in the analysis of the model was the computation of the relationship between the demand variable and percentage modular controlling for the community environment. Again the relationship was not significant. It appears that the use of modular components in low-rise public housing is much like the use of prefab components in high-rise construction—neither is related to demand as measured by a high volume of construction.

As noted in Table 2-6, there was also no zero order relationship between the community environment and the percentage modular use. The computations concerning modular use are thus even more disappointing (if that is possible) than the findings related to prefab use in high-rise construction. Only the relationship shown in Table 2-7 appears relevant to the model for the adoption of product innovations. Again, as with prefab, the method of contracting appears to be the only determinant of modular or factory-built housing use that could be found quantitatively.

Of the 82,053 low-rise housing units built by the responding authorities, 7 percent, or 5,428 units were modular or factory built. Of the modular units, 91.3 percent were turnkey built, and only 8.7 percent were conventional. HUD data show that as of December 31, 1972, 17 percent of the public-housing units under management and 69 percent of the units under construction were turnkey units.[8] Is there a significant difference in the use of modular or factory-built housing based on contracting method? Table 2-7 indicates that the answer is *yes*. There were two reasons for computing X^2. In part *a*, it is noted that if modular construction were proportionally distributed between conventional and turnkey units in management, 4,505 (83 percent) would be conventionally built and 933 (17 percent) would be turnkey. In fact, only 472 were conventional with 4,956 being turnkey. The X^2 is significant at the .001 level indicating that the null hypothesis is rejected and that the difference between the observed and expected could not have occurred by chance.

Part *b* of Table 2-7 shows the same relationships for units under construction. Recognizing that turnkey is a relatively new program, the "under management" statistics might conservatively bias the results. Thus X^2 was computed with an expected conventional of 1,683 units (31 percent) and 3,745 (69 percent) turnkey. Again the difference between the observed and the expected

Table 2-7
Relationship Between Expected and Observed Use of Modular and Factory-Built Housing

	Observed	Expected
a. *Modular under management*		
Conventional	472	4,505
Turnkey	4,956	993
(X^2 = 19,426.53)		
b. *Modular under construction*		
Conventional	472	1,683
Turnkey	4,956	3,745
(X^2 = 1,262.96)		

could not have occurred by chance. X^2 was significant at the .001 level. Thus the method of contracting is the only significant determinant of modular use.

As with the examination of the process innovation, the emphasis placed on the innovation by NAHRO was examined. Figure 2-3 indicates that the use of prefab components and modular units has received substantial emphasis from NAHRO via the *Journal of Housing*. There was considerable interest in the mid-1960s followed by a cooling off in the late 1960s and then renewed interest in 1970 when 13 percent of the articles were devoted to the selected construction innovations. Again the *Journal* follows the pattern suggested by Walker except that the emphasis on these products is more stable over time. There is an obvious peak in 1970, but the period of NAHRO interest is much more sustained than it was with the process innovation.

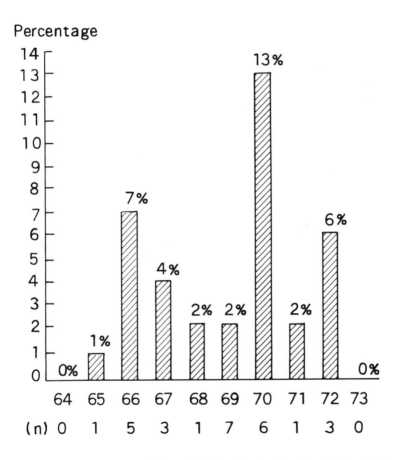

Figure 2-3. Percentage of *Journal of Housing* Articles Devoted to the Use of Prefab and Modular Construction

Surprisingly, housing authorities appeared to pay very little attention to NAHRO. The lack of innovation in conventional construction points up the inability of the major professional association to influence innovation adoption—at least in this case.

Qualitative Analysis

The case studies presented in this section cover a wide variety of innovation adoptions and nonadoptions. Three cities were high modular users while two other cities examined through the case study methods used no modular construction at all. In addition, prefab use was examained in two cities—one high deviant and one low deviant. The first city reported, Free City, was again used as a practice case and to pretest the questionnaire. In this case, however, Free City was a low deviant in terms of both modular and prefab construction.

Free City. For Free City the possibility of using modular units in the construction of the 497 low-rise housing units built during the last ten years was never considered. The reason, noted the deputy commissioner of operations for Free City's department of city development, was plain and simple: "The city building code prohibits the introduction of modular units." Despite the proximity of a well-known prefabricated home manufacturer, Free City has relied solely on stick-built construction. Although a number of communities (seventy-two) in the state, including twelve in Free City's county, have amended their building codes to allow off-site inspection by a third party, Free City has until recently resisted every effort to introduce prefabricated housing. In the spring of 1973, unions were even successful in preventing the erection and display of a prefabricated home in the convention center during the annual home show. As might be expected, it was the unions, not the city, that exerted the clout necessary to prevent building-code changes and therefore prevent the introduction of modular housing.

In the fall of 1974, however, proposed amendments to the code were brought before the city council. Free City's building inspector cited a number of reasons that accompanied his proposed amendments to the council. He noted that

> the structures themselves (prefab buildings) may be adequate and in some cases superior to structures built on the site. They have another asset in that a factory built building can be erected on site within two days, without any deterioration from the elements or damage by vandalism. Another asset is the fact that interest money is saved when a person can purchase a home with the anticipation of moving into it very shortly after the purchase, whereas many homes now being built on the site in the conventional way may take months to complete.

They would allow for "third-party inspection" such as that provided by Underwriters Laboratories, upon whose recommendation the city would base its approval. The prefab firms would be required to submit plans for city approval, and the city would retain the right to unscheduled on-site inspection.

The union reaction to these proposals was quite negative. A representative of the electrical workers stated:

> We are opposed to the whole concept of third party inspection. We believe the inspector should owe allegiance to no one but the city. We don't feel the code should be changed just for the benefit of the manufacturers. They should find ways of complying with existing codes. We have home rule, and rights shouldn't be given away to a third party.

A representative of the Plumbers' Union and a member of the building-code committee directed the inspector's attention to the fact that the local prefab firm used unlicensed plumbers and pointed out that 90 percent of all industrialized housing production used unlicensed plumbers. The inspector's reply was in no way conciliatory:

> It's not a matter of who does the work, but if it meets the code. Does the self-interest of unions override the benefits to the general community? The only real issue is: Is the code being met? There is no reason to question who does the job . . . God help us if the harness makers can obstruct the introduction of the automobile. If competition is keen, the industry and the unions here can erect their own plants and beat the others on shipping costs alone.

The proposals of the building inspector were submitted to the building code committee, an advisory body of the city council. The "third-party off-site inspection" proposal was amended and substituted with a provision for Free City building inspectors to travel to assembly sites where they would be responsible for assuring code compliance. After these proposals had been voted out of committee, they went before the council for approval. The aldermen, bowing to union pressure, sent the recommendations to the zoning and development committee for further study rather than acting on them. When asked if the code amendments situation was becoming a merry-go-round, the building inspector replied, "It certainly is. It will be several weeks before we know what the next move is to be."

Lakeview. One might suspect that a housing authority using modular or factory-built construction methods in over 60 percent of its low-rise construction in the last six years would indicate a certain preference for the innovative building practice. Such was not the case of one midwestern city in which industrialized housing accounted for 321 of the 500 low-rise units built.

In that Lakeview was holding 500 reservations with HUD for low-rise housing units, Washington's conventional/turnkey contracting preference was of a critical nature. When asked if a housing authority was required to utilize the turnkey method, the director noted that if Washington gave priority to turnkey, all applications for conventional developments would find themselves at the bottom of the pile. The director subsequently chose to use turnkey in low-rise construction. As required by HUD regulations, an invitation to interested contractors was placed in one or more newspapers of general circulation in the locality, at least once a week for two consecutive weeks. In addition to the local advertisement, the director placed the same notice in the *Dodge Reports,* a nationally circulated publication for contractors and developers.

This notice elicited ten proposals for thirteen sites, of which three were selected. None were to offer modular construction, although one was to utilize panelized construction. The area coordinator for HUD brought in an inspection team which approved all three sites and proposals. What were the criteria for the LHA selection? According to the director, it came down to site selection, meeting of cost requirements, prohibiting costs in excess of $3,150 per room, and the fact that the design met the minimum standards desired by the director. Because of the complete development responsibilities placed on the contractor by the turnkey method, local builders and developers found themselves in another league. As one local contractor noted,

> Local firms are frightened off by turnkey. They can't afford to invest a
> million dollars or more on purchasing and developing a site, constructing
> a large number of units and not being able to collect a cent until the first
> tenants move in. They're afraid of HUD and its regulations and are not
> familiar with the turnkey program.

It soon became clear that turnkey was a program that benefited large firms with the resources necessary to compete on a national level—characteristics all possessed by modular-producing firms. But in Lakeview, another factor was introduced that created an environment even more enticing to modular firms.

Despite HUD approval and letters of intent from the Lakeview Housing Authority, city politics and neighborhood political pressure stopped progress on the initial proposals. The city council failed to approve the necessary high-density zoning for the proposed sites, forcing the LHA director to withdraw the letters of intent to the three contractors.

In a city council meeting later that month, a resolution was adopted which stated:

> the city council is on record against the construction of 150 to 200 units
> on any one site and the city council prefers complexes of 25 to 50 units
> located in all sections of the city.

Accompanying this resolution was a city committment to "rezone whatever land is necessary and suitable for construction of turnkey housing units."

With these added restrictions to turnkey development in Lakeview, local developer participation was all but eliminated. It weeded out even larger contractors who operated profitably on large-scale housing projects at one site using stick-built construction methods. Scattered-site housing, while socially desirable, is expensive. After the city council's fifty-unit limitation, a spokesman of Turnkey Proposals, Inc., of Freeport, New York, stated that "the smallest economical quantity of units at one site would be 75."

In light of the council resolution, the Lakeview Housing Authority circulated another notice to developers for turnkey construction bids, this time requiring that no site or site area shall contain more than fifty units.

Because of the federal statutory limitations on cost per unit and the new council restriction limiting low-income housing construction to fifty units, the turnkey program for Lakeview began to flounder. One out-of-state firm (Penn-Erie Corporation) was working on a 100-unit proposal for two sites, but that was the extent of developer interest. There was thus no construction under turnkey in 1969. While the city council had somewhat pacified the neighborhood fear of low-income public housing with the fifty-unit rule, it was now faced with a critical need for housing and a mounting dissatisfaction among low-income families. In the first months of 1970, no less than three councilmen called for the removal of the housing director, blaming him for the lack of housing construction and problems arising with the leased-housing program.

In March, 1970, the mayor, in a calculated move to silence his critics, threatened "major changes for the housing authority if new housing isn't forthcoming," yet rejected the called-for dismissal of the director, calling him a "good organizer." A month later, following an emergency meeting of the housing authority, it was announced that approval had been given to two proposed projects of fifty units each to be constructed by a Baltimore firm. At the same meeting, the mayor "told the authority that meetings next week should solidify another 50 unit project . . . and pave the way for the beginning of the 200 independent scattered site units." The mayor's statement is deserving of attention at this point, for the units he referred to were all to be modular or factory built.

The fifty-unit project the mayor spoke of involved the Stirling Homex Corporation of Avon, New York. Stirling Homex was one of the original twenty-two firms contracted by HUD for the R&D housing program connected with Operation Breakthrough. The firm gained notoriety in 1968 when it assembled 275 dwelling units in Rochester, New York, in just thirty-six hours using factory-built modular units. One might suspect that the speed of construction was a key element in obtaining its contract with the Lakeview Housing Authority. Stirling Homex, however, never negotiated a proposal with the LHA. Its initial involvement in Lakeview's turnkey program was described by the housing director as "a political matter."

In mid-1970, Stirling Homex purchased a site in Lakeview for the purpose of erecting fifty modular units for low-income public housing. With neither local LHA nor HUD approval, the company began development. On October 30, 1970, HUD ordered Stirling Homex to stop construction. But as the housing director noted:

> Neither HUD not the city had the jurisdiction or the power to stop construction at the site. The point is that there is nothing particularly that we or HUD could do. Neither the city nor HUD has a contract with Stirling Homex and the company was doing all the work on its own initiative.

On November 6, the Lakeview Building Inspection Office issued permits for the construction of modular units despite the fact that they failed to meet city plumbing codes. City administrators at that time, however, were planning to revise the plumbing code so that the modular homes would meet the new requirements. This was more in keeping with its contracted commitment to another modular firm than it was for Stirling Homex. The latter, nevertheless, benefited from the entrance of the other modular firm.

There really never appeared to be any doubt on the part of the housing authority nor of the press that the Stirling Homex project would be part of the 500-unit turnkey program. It was more a matter of disregard of HUD procedure that caused a controversy. But as the LHA director recounted, Stirling Homex was a firm of bright lawyers. They were not breaking any law as they owned the land they were building on and had signed no contract with Lakeview and were consequently not under its supervision. When the director did attempt to inspect the project, he was met by security men who informed him that he was trespassing on private property.

At about this same time, Stirling Homex was issued another building permit for a twenty-six-unit site, a site that had been approved sometime ago by the city council as an appropriate turnkey site. In December, HUD again advised Stirling Homex to temporarily halt construction of the fifty-unit project pending a review of complaints raised by neighbors. HUD advised Stirling Homex that an on-site inspection was required and that construction should be temporarily halted. The housing director again stated that contracts would not be signed until final plans were submitted by the developer. Nevertheless, Stirling Homex proceeded with construction.

On March 4, 1971, Stirling Homex took out $980,000 in building permits for the construction of another seventy-one-unit project, this time presenting its plans to the housing authority. Though it continued construction of the original fifty-unit project without HUD or LHA approval, a spokesman this time insisted that the company would "seek Housing Authority and HUD approval before beginning construction." As the director stated, the first modular project was an embarrassing situation, but it was their land and money, and they could build anything they wanted. Three months later a contract with Stirling Homex was approved, and the fifty-unit project was purchased for $1.3 million.

Lest one suspect preferential treatment was given to Stirling Homex by the LHA or the city council, it might be noted that the Avon, New York, firm could be fairly certain, even without a contract, that its project would be accepted as part of the 500-unit turnkey authorization. This was not the modular firm's first encounter with HUD or LHA regulations, but it was only one of many projects Stirling Homex was involved in nationwide. It had been one of the original Operation Breakthrough firms and had worked with HUD regulations and specifications from the start. Perhaps it might be best to consider the Stirling Homex involvement in Lakeview as a bold and calculated move by an experienced entrepreneur in the housing industry. Recognizing the deadlocked situation of the turnkey program in Lakeview and well aware of all LHA and federal specifications required of turnkey housing, it appears that Stirling Homex was confident that its fait accompli would be begrudgingly accepted by an authority in dire need of progress. Such was the case with the first introduction of modular units in Lakeview. Further evidence of the bold attitude of Stirling Homex may be seen in its second Lakeview project.

Recall that in March, 1969, the city council passed a resolution in favor of limiting low-income housing projects to fifty units. In substance, this resolution meant that the city fathers would refuse to rezone any turnkey site for high-density residential use. Concerning the seventy-one-unit project, however, Stirling Homex secured a site already zoned high-density residential. It violated no city ordinance, and the approval of city hall was not required as the site did not need to be rezoned. Within a year the seventy-one-unit project had received the necessary HUD and local LHA approval. However, in September, 1972, Stirling Homex filed a bankruptcy petition claiming more than $26 million in losses in that fiscal year. According to a number of sources[9] Stirling Homex's method of accounting was to designate every module "sold" as it left the factory gates, when in fact, only a small percentage had actually been purchased. In Lakeview, for example, 400 modules were stored at a rented site for two years, their ultimate destination unknown.

Stirling Homex thus accounted for 121 modular units of the 321 to be constructed for the Lakeview Housing Authority. At no time, recalled the housing director, did modular construction influence the LHA decision to contract with this firm. The first fifty units were presented as a fait accompli, and the latter seventy-one as an acceptable proposal for the Lakeview housing shortage. What of the remaining 200 modular units?

From the onset of the turnkey program, Lakeview sought 200 scattered-site, low-income housing units. Although the mayor and housing director appealed for local builder participation (April 24, 1970), the minimum proposal of at least five units served as a constraint. But as the mayor noted, "cost would be prohibitive if we tried to get 100 developers each building one unit . . . we wouldn't be able to stay within the economic guideline." Lakeview therefore had to turn to any proposal that would offer the maximum number of scattered-side units.

In September, 1970, Lakeview received a $4.8 million commitment from HUD for 200 scattered-site homes to be supplied by Alco, Inc., of Lansing, Michigan, parent company of the Prestige Homes Modular producers. In cooperation with a local developer (First Allegheny Corp.), 200 sites were to be built in six stages. Working on a 50/50 basis, Alco, Inc., was to produce and supply the module units while First Allegheny would be responsible for securing the site, laying the foundation, and setting the units into place. On October 8, 1970, a contract was awarded to the firms by the city. The director recalled that perhaps the greatest reason for the selection of these firms was that they had obtained the sites throughout the city and that their modular units met all the specifications he desired for a low-income housing unit. A representative of the First Allegheny Corporation, although not disagreeing with this, noted that the sales pitch emphasized the speed factor as being the main enticement. He also pointed out that HUD considered Alco, Inc., one of the top five modular producers in the housing industry.

The project was initially stalled when the modular units did not meet the city's plumbing code specifications, but after modifications made by the firm and a visit by city representatives and plumbing inspectors to the modular factory in Michigan, construction started in the fourth week of November, 1970.

Although the fate of Sirling Homex was to befall Prestige Homes, the bankruptcy of the latter was not comparable to the scandal generated by the former. There was little delay in the First Allegheny firm's total assumption of responsibilities as 175 homes had already been finished and occupied, with only twenty-five remaining for completion on the contracted terms.

The decision-making process focused not on the choice of modular construction over conventional methods, but rather on those proposals that offered to meet Lakeview's requirements and restrictions. In the case of the 321 units, it happened that the proponents were modular firms. The turnkey method, indeed, may be seen as the underlying factor for modular use. The housing director, an individual who held that post since 1940, looked disdainfully upon the turnkey method. He noted, with dissatisfaction, how "foreigners" come in, not knowing the community, its zoning laws, neighborhood attitudes or needs, and purchase the available land with their substantial resources. Under the conventional method, he continues, the housing authority integrates social consequences with the basic economics of housing construction. Such consideration is lost when development and construction are placed in the hands of outside firms.

Easton. The introduction of modular units in Easton is not dissimilar to the situation in Lakeview. Here, however, 100 percent of the units built in the last ten years were modular although this amounted to only fifty-five units.

In 1968, Easton held 100 reservations with HUD for low-rise public housing for low-income families. HUD specifically "asked" Easton to go turnkey in the construction of these units. In compliance with turnkey procedures, a notice similar to Lakeview's asked for proposals for turnkey projects. Three proposals were received and studied, and a contract for fifty-five units was awarded to Stirling Homex.

According to the housing director, the contract was awarded on the basis of speed, quality, and price. In that the other bidders were rejected on the basis of price, one may assume that the latter carried the most weight. Unlike their initial involvement in Lakeview, Stirling Homex formally contracted with Easton prior to beginning construction. Three sites were approved, one for twenty-six units, one for fifteen, and one for fourteen. In October, 1970, the twenty-six-unit project was completed and turned over to the LHA. The remaining twenty-nine units were finished the following summer, one year prior to the firm's bankruptcy.

There appears to be a factor common to modular use in both Lakeview and Easton. Were a housing authority to construct low-income housing using the conventional rather than turnkey method, it might very well be concluded that modular construction would find no role in project development. Recall that in 1969, HUD initiated Operation Breakthrough, seeking to involve private industry in the national housing market. The method by which Washington hoped to shift from the local to national markets was already established through the strongly endorsed turnkey method. The method did not cater to modular firms but rather to firms oriented to national competition and profit-based on quantity, characteristics possessed by modular firms. Inasmuch as Easton's housing authority sought less concentrated housing projects, it is not surprising that Stirling Homex was able to underbid the conventional developers in the construction of three rather small projects. As was the case in Lakeview, a project of fifty units or less became financially prohibitive for developers using traditional construction methods.

River City. In July, 1974, River City neared completion of what was called "a public-housing era." Since 1953 when the first project was built, River City spent $3.5 million clearing slums and erecting 2,276 units on those sites. Then for a number of years, the LHA put off any further development. As the director at that time stated, "We want to take stock and see what the need will be before going any further." He added, "the one reason no more public housing is being planned is that there is a substantial vacancy rate in private housing." After ten years, the River City Housing Authority had progressed little beyond its position in 1964. Despite a recognized need since 1968 for low-income public housing for families, the LHA was unable to move forward with actual construction until 1974 and then only with housing for the elderly. A review of the River City LHA development attempts from 1968 to the present not only explains the absence of modular housing but further substantiates the findings of the other case studies concerning the degree to which turnkey construction influences LHA planning.

Turnkey, in essence, takes the actual decision-making concerning the construction's *where* and *how* out of the hands of the housing authority and puts it into the realm of the private contractor. This is not to say that a contractor must not meet certain specifications of both the LHA and HUD. Obviously, it is understood that a contractor must meet zoning and construction requirements and that site selection must be satisfactory. But turnkey places the responsibility for locating and developing a site and determining the actual method of construction in the hands of the contractor. With turnkey, the housing authority's basic decision comes down to the issues of price and site.

Of the sixty-five low-rise public-housing units constructed by River City in 1974 using turnkey, none were modular, nor were they family housing. Modular construction was not prohibited by local building codes. River City recognizes the third-party inspection process and thereby allows prefabricated homes.

In October, 1968, the River City LHA sought bids on 500 units of low-income housing. By February, 1969, the LHA had received sixteen proposals offered by eight developers, the majority of which were for one-family housing units. No modular-producing firm submitted proposals at that time. Two hundred units were to be constructed at two separate sites. One project with sixty-five units was to be a low-rise garden-type project and the other a high-rise, 135 unit project for the elderly. In addition, a turnkey proposal was accepted for the rehabilitation of an existing ninety-unit building. To this date, these 290 units remain the only addition that the River City Housing Authority has made in public housing since 1964. Inasmuch as the concern in 1969 was for more low-income public housing for families, an explanation is needed of why the 290 additional units were to serve only the elderly.

In 1972, the former housing director offered the explanation:

> We're frankly running into brick walls because the developers are not willing to run the risk of locating family-type, 4 and 5 bedroom apartments in suburban areas where HUD would like to see them put . . . HUD approved two 50 unit projects for poor families, but the developers were unwilling to build them for the price HUD was willing to accept.

The River City LHA therefore opted for a drive toward increased housing for the elderly for which there was also a recognized need. The chairman of the housing authority's board of commissioners stated:

> The whole country is in a turmoil as to what to do about family public housing. We had lots of things to do to get moving again in public housing in River City without trying to be guessing as to what the best way

to go would be on family housing. I think there is clearly a desperate
need for family public housing in River City, but it made no sense for us
to flail out in this area with it in such turmoil nationally. We have spent
our time getting on the go in existing housing and in elderly housing.

The standstill reached in River City for family public housing reduced significantly the possibilities for introduction of innovative construction programs. It is a
standstill that continues to the present day. Inasmuch as only sixty-five low-rise
units were built in the last ten years, on a single-site project, there need not be a
lengthy analysis concerning the absence of modular housing. One firm, using
conventional construction methods, was selected for the desired project. As
no modular firm submitted a proposal, selection remained only a choice between
conventional construction designs that met the specifications and price ceiling
of the LHA and HUD. One might argue hypothetically, however, that had a
modular firm submitted a proposal, the chances of its selection would have been
high. It will be recalled that in the case of Lakeview the fifty-unit limit per project established by the City Council eliminated a number of developers because of
financial cost. Similarly, the two 50-unit low-income family-housing project
proposals accepted by HUD for River City were never followed through because
of the high cost associated with traditional construction methods. Where it may
be argued that modular housing is no less expensive than traditional stick-built
construction, modular firms are capable of developing profitable projects of fifty
units or less. One could therefore conclude that the reason for the lack of
modular construction rests with the simple fact that no modular firm submitted
a turnkey proposal. Another reason may be found in the absence of low-income
family-housing construction.

    While the current housing authority director concurs with the reasoning
offered by his predecessor that "developers could not meet the cost limits set by
HUD," he expounds on the explanation given by the former chairman of the
board of commissioners. Where indeed the whole country was in "a turmoil as
to what to do about family public housing," the director noted that the question
can be narrowed down to the turmoil caused in River City. In the late 1960s a
national consensus had been reached by LHAs that high-rise family-housing
projects were disastrous and should be discontinued. The answer to public housing for low-income families was with the scattered-site approach. The "turmoil,"
so to speak, was caused by the neighborhoods which were to be hosts to the
scattered sites. The poor image held of public housing frightens any neighborhood,
noted the director. Rather than come to a standstill on housing development,
therefore, the River City LHA proceeded with low-income public housing for the
elderly, "which is safe politically in any neighborhood."

    Free City. While modular use/nonuse can be explained largely through the
method of contracting, what about the use of prefabricated components in

high-rise construction? In Free City, in the construction of twelve high-rise projects containing 1,953 units, little utilization of prefabricated components was noted. Only on a few projects was some type of precast concrete exterior used. Kitchen/bathroom utility cores, precast interior panel walls and precast panel floors, however, found no place in the construction of Free City's high-rise public housing. Inasmuch as contracting for these projects was done on an equal conventional and turnkey distribution, one would suspect that a decision on the part of the housing authority was involved concerning prefabricated-component use. However, upon contacting a representative of a local firm that has been involved with construction of several of the city's high-rise public-housing projects, this does not appear to be the case. City building codes, for example, prohibit the off-site construction of any component that involves the installation and sealing of, for example, wiring and plumbing and therefore prevents the on-site inspection of them. In most cases the off-site construction of utility cores, panelized interior walls, and panel floors prohibits their use in Free City. Another reason behind their nonuse, however, remains with the newness of the innovation to contractors. As the representative of the local construction firm noted:

> Construction firms without the financial stability and resources can't afford to go into experimentation. We did so this summer and lost our shirts on precast floors. The advantages are certainly there in the time element and through that costs savings. I'm favorable towards prefabrication but a company has to have the resources to absorb the loss from a setback caused by experimenting with something new, resources we just don't have.

It would appear therefore that, in addition to local building-code restrictions, the newness of the innovation acts as a barrier to its wide diffusion—especially among smaller contractors and developers.

Convention City. Between 1964 and 1974, the Convention City Housing Authority constructed six high-rise housing projects containing 855 units—all for the elderly or handicapped. Of these, one project, a fifteen story high-rise building, containing 153 units and completed in 1972, was the only project containing precast or prefabricated components. The project (Lakeview) utilized both precast concrete exterior panels and precast interior walls as well as precast flooring.

Of the six high-rise projects, one was built utilizing conventional bidding procedures while the other five were turnkey projects. Lakeview was one of these turnkey projects. The idea for the project, or at least the design portion of it, was first suggested by the project architect William D. Smith of Convention City. Smith, together with a local developer, approached the executive director and the assistant director of the Convention City Housing Authority with the idea (precast components) and with several site suggestions. In "selling" the project to the housing authority decision-makers, Bill Smith used three basic arguments: (1) the use of the precast components would considerably decrease construction time; (2) construction costs would be lower than with more conventional methods; and (3) the building would be highly fire-resistant.

Smith noted that both the executive director and assistant director were "highly enthusiastic" about the innovative nature of the proposal and gave the go-ahead to the architect/developer team. While there were some doubts about the project expressed by the local HUD office, project approval was obtained. Smith called it a "grudging acceptance." This all occurred in the early years of the Nixon Administration and during the time frame of "Operation Breakthrough" although this was not a Breakthrough project. Nevertheless, the emphasis in Washington was on innovativeness, and while the local HUD office was not particularly pleased with the project, they were directed to support innovation—and they did.

The decision to accept new methods was unusual for another reason—no other precast high-rise structure had even been built in Convention City, so the project was a first for the city as well as for the housing authority.

Unfortunately, the project didn't work out as well as had been hoped. The architect said the project "took years beyond what it should have taken" and believed that the housing authority paid a "bigger price for the building than they should have." Smith is still a believer in the method and says that evidence of its success can be found in cities like Denver where they have been using precast techniques for years. As this is not a study in problems associated with the building industry, no attempt will be made to document the tangled web of events involving the developers (they changed), builders, architect, and housing authority inspector which delayed project completion. Bill Smith, however, believes that if a "seasoned and mature contractor" (in the use of precast components) had been selected by the developer, most of the problems never would have occurred.

The comments of the executive director concerning HUD may be indicative of why there has not been more project innovation in public housing. He believes that the decentralization of HUD offices has been a serious mistake. He claims that his authority had a good working relationship with HUD officials when they dealt with the regional office. At that time, he said, HUD housing officials were helpful, competent, and experienced in public housing. With decentralization (there is now a HUD office in Convention City), the public-housing decisions are made by "FHA types." The director claims that innovation is no longer possible in project construction due to the extremely conservative nature of local HUD administrators. He attributes this to their FHA background and lack of experience in public housing.

This, however, cannot be entirely correct as decentralization occurred prior to Lakeview. It was the Convention City HUD office that approved the project.

The assistant director couldn't remember any particular problems associated with HUD approval of Lakeview either. While the project proposal was initiated six years ago, she believes that she would remember any major difficulties in obtaining HUD approval, had they occurred.

On the surface, then, there are no clear-cut reasons for the adoption of new techniques in high-rise construction by the Convention City Housing Authority. In fact, innovation in public housing is probably hampered by the fact that there are numerous decision points in the adoption process—any one point being enough to thwart an innovation. First, the architect/developer team might have decided not to "risk it" by proposing the use of techniques not only untried in Convention City public housing, but untried in the entire city. The authority administration could have killed the idea as could the board of directors. HUD officials could also have been actively hostile to the idea and might have killed the proposal.

It is believed, however, that the administration, specifically the executive director, is most responsible for innovation. It is the executive director whose influence is felt throughout the project. Bill Smith characterized the Convention City executive director as "innovative" or "receptive to new ideas." These descriptions are part and parcel of the concept of professionalism. It is thus suggested that the "outward looking to his peers" orientation of the director contributed directly to willingness to experiment or innovate. In a recent *NAHRO Roster*, for example, the executive director was listed as a member of the NAHRO Housing Divisional Committee, the Legislative Committee, and as Chairman of the Housing Subcommittee of the Legislative Committee. In addition, he was listed as a member of the Executive Committee of the Southwest Regional Council. Thus active participation in NAHRO is a major part of the director's professional life.

While no concrete evidence is available, impressionistic data suggest that the professional nature of the executive director's orientation probably contributed to his willingness to innovate. His NAHRO activities are indicative of his attitudes as well as his status in the profession. It is likely that he was receptive to Bill Smith's ideas because it was "good for public housing" as much as because it might be "good for the Convention City Housing Authority."

Summary

As was the case with the housing process innovation, the product innovation case studies substantiate the quantitative findings. The case studies emphasized the importance of turnkey as a vehicle for product innovations in public housing. In every instance of innovative behavior, in terms of modular or prefab use, turnkey provided the vehicle for innovation. The modular construction in Lakeview and Easton were turnkey projects as was the prefabricated high-rise in Convention City. Product innovation thus is really a product of the private sector and not of the housing authority. This is amply illustrated by the miniscule number of conventional projects utilizing either modular or prefabricated components.

A second factor was brought out by several of the case studies. The political trend away from large-scale housing projects and their built-in economies, is a trend that favors modular use. Thus the smaller developments in keeping with the scattered-site concept are amenable to factory-built housing.

In Free City, restrictive building codes prevented modular and prefab use in public housing as well as in private-sector homes and apartments. It is quite likely that similar restrictive codes are in force in many other heavily industrialized (and unionized) areas. The building trades have been very successful thus far in blocking action to allow much innovation to take place.

Finally, in Convention City, the professional orientation of the executive director was probably a contributing factor to the use of prefabricated components in one high-rise project. His willingness to try something new for the benefit of public housing in general can, in part, be attributed to his outward-looking attitude.

It thus appears that intergovernmental influence was, in the long run, responsible for innovative behavior. It was the turnkey program that opened the door for developer influence and innovation. The trend toward smaller scattered-site projects also contributed to innovation adoption as many of the builders and developers utilizing more traditional construction methods could not compete satisfactorily for scattered site projects due to cost constraints. Turnkey contracting then appears to hold the key to product innovation in public housing.

Conclusions

In summarizing the adoption of innovation by public housing authorities and in attempting to reconcile the differences between the process and product innovation models, it was first necessary to examine the interrelationships between the innovations. Table 2-8 shows these interrelationships. It is apparent that the product and process innovations are completely unrelated. In fact, there is only a slight relationship between the two product variables. It thus appears that we are dealing with very different kinds of innovation. The fact that the adoption models of the two product innovations are so similar while there is such a slight relationship between the two tends to substantiate this conclusion. There are other, and perhaps better explanations, however.

First it is suggested that there is a predictable model of innovation adoption

Table 2–8

Interrelationships Between Technological Innovations in Public Housing

	Computer-use Score	Prefab Score	Percentage Modular
Computer-use Score	1.000		
Prefab Score	.084	1.000	
Percentage Modular	.086	.192*	1.000

*Significant at the .05 level.

applicable to public housing authorities. In fact, it is suggested that such a model emphasizes efficiency, need, and resource availability, and closely resembles Figure 2-2–the model for the use of computer-based information systems by public housing authorities.

There is nothing in the model to suggest, however, that public housing authorities are particularly innovative. Hayes and Rasmussen emphasized the fact that local governments devote little energy to change or innovation and are essentially hostile to new ideas.[10] Figure 2-2 does nothing to dispel these ideas. In fact, the overwhelming dominance of factors in the organizational environment as determinants of innovation support the contention concerning the conservative nature of the public bureaucracy. While demand and desire for efficiency are relevant, it is the organizational environment that has the major impact. Intergovernmental influences and resource availability are the prime determinants of innovation.

But what of the product model? Do the findings relating to the adoption of the product innovations *not* destroy the concept of a predictable model of innovation adoption in public housing? It is suggested here that the answer is *no*, that a predictable model for innovation adoption exists for both the housing process and product innovations. Furthermore, it is suggested that the model is influenced primarily by the variables of the organizational environment much as we have described it and that demand and efficiency, while important, are secondary contributors.

Why does the analysis of the product innovations not support the model? Does the model of rational behavior exist until it is upset by the influence of the private sector of the economy? Do housing authorities respond to their environmental influences in a predictable way until the dynamics of the private market intervene? In the product models, the decisions to innovate were made in the private sector and had little relationship to the behavior of the housing authority. These decisions were based on a variety of factors having little direct relationship to innovation by public housing authorities–decisions such as construction time and profits–decisions well beyond the scope of this study.

Thus a conservative housing authority constructing a project under turnkey operations is likely to appear innovative when it really is the project developer who is innovative. The answer then might be to examine the model of innovation adoption as it relates only to conventional contracting methods. Unfortunately, this is not possible as virtually all the innovation occurred in turnkey jobs. Of the sixty-four authorities using conventional (only) construction contracting for high-rise, only 29.7 percent, or nineteen, authorities had a prefab score of one or greater. In fact, twelve of the nineteen authorities registered a score of 1 with only seven authorities scoring 2 or greater. Concerning the use of modular or factory-built housing components, the results are very much the same as only two of the twenty-three modular projects were built by conventional methods. Thus when considering product innovations utilized by housing authorities without the direct contractor influence provided by turnkey, the n is so small as to render analysis meaningless.

Why have so few conventional projects utilized modular or prefab components? The study of innovation in public housing suggests that, for public agencies, there may indeed be two types of innovations: not process and product innovations as hypothesized, but "operating" and "nonoperating innovations." Operating innovations fall within the incentive system of the public organization. These innovations are predictable and are based largely on need. Incentive systems for operating innovations include efficiency, slack, and intergovernmental influence. The adoption of computer-based management assistance is a good example of an operating innovation.

Nonoperating innovations cover a variety of new inventions or innovations that fall outside the operating goals of the organization. Adoption of these innovations is not on a rational basis—they occur in the environment and in the organization on a random basis, strictly by chance. Nonoperating innovations may be good things, but they occur outside the incentive system of the organization. There is little direct incentive for a public housing authority decision-maker to want specifically to utilize modular or prefabricated components. The innovations are interesting, and in fact it was housing authority professionals who first selected prefab and modular construction as being one of the most important innovations in public housing during the past ten years. But they are not essential. With few exceptions (the time constraint placed on the Lakeview executive director being an exception), the use of prefab or modular construction did not fill a need. Authority executives had no reason to opt for something new. Housing authorities apparently actively seek out only innovations that will help them solve real or perceived problems.

This analysis thus suggests a behavioral model for the other innovations considered in the following chapters. It appears that a predictable model for innovation adoption exists but that it operates only when the proper incentives are presented.

3

Innovation Adoption in Public Schools

The organization of this chapter is virtually the same as that of the preceding chapter. The chapter is divided into three sections—process innovation, product innovation, and conclusions. Again both quantitative and qualitative analyses are used.

Process Innovation

The general innovation model (Figure 1-1) again presents the model for the adoption of individualized instruction methods in public elementary schools. It was hypothesized that the community environment would be largely responsible for the success of the school system as measured by the demand variables— the percentage of students going on to college and the dropout rate. Demand, or in this case the perception of a performance gap, was expected to operate directly and through the organization and its environment to affect the use of individualized instruction. As in the housing model, the organizational environment was expected to determine innovation adoption, both directly and through the organizational characteristics. Thus the hypothesized model for innovation in public schools was much the same as the hypothesized model for innovation in public housing.

Data concerning school districts were taken from a variety of sources including the results of a mailed questionnaire. The school questionnaire was sent to the 309 school districts covering the 310 cities in the survey. A total of 289 districts cooperated for a response rate of 93 percent. As with housing, the high response rate limits concern with nonrespondents. No particular pattern concerning size, geographic location, etc., of nonrespondents was noted.

Quantitative Analysis

The percentage of elementary teachers using methods of individualized instruction was the dependent variable for the process innovation investigation. The variable is merely the sum of the number of elementary teachers in the school districts using any one of the three individualized programs described in Chapter 1 divided by the total number of elementary teachers in the system.[1]

The independent variables considered as characteristic of the community environment remain unchanged—that is, they are the same seven variables used in the housing model.

Demand variables include the percentage of students going on to college and the estimated dropout rate. Data for both variables were obtained from questionnaire responses.

Intergovernmental influence is represented by the total intergovernmental revenue received (by the school district) from the federal government, the total intergovernmental revenue received from the state government[2] and the total city intergovernmental revenue.[3] Availability of financial resources is the second major category of the organizational environment to be examined. Specific variables in this category include total school district expenditures,[4] per student school expenditures, and city per capita total general revenue. Also included was the city reformism score.

The question may be raised concerning the location of school district expenditures in the organizational environment. Would not these measures of financial resources be better included as organizational characteristics? Perhaps so—expenditures are a characteristic for the organization. Here, however, they are used as a surrogate for revenue as in public agencies, revenue and expenditures are (nearly) equal.

Four variables were selected to represent characteristics of the organization that might affect the adoption of individualized teaching methods. Organizational size is represented by one variable—total number of elementary teachers.[5] Professionalism is represented by the percent of teachers in the system without a B.A. degree and by the percent of teachers in the system with an M.A. degree or higher. And finally, a school board reformism score was developed in the same manner as the city reformism score. Reform measures include an elected school board, at-large representation, and nonpartisan elections. Data were obtained from the questionnaire responses. Values were assigned as shown in Table 3-1. The reformism score varies from 0 to 3 and is the sum for the three reform measures.

Initially, product moment correlations were computed between the independent variables and the dependent variable. The results are shown in Table 3-2. None of the relationships were significant. Thus the characteristics of the community show little direct relationship with innovation adoption.

Chapter 1 suggested that the nature of the innovation under consideration would determine the direction of the relationship between demand and innovation adoption. That is, the direction of the relationship will distinguish between "amenity" and "need" innovations. The two innovations considered in this chapter—individualized instruction and videotape recorders—lend themselves to testing this concept. It was expected that communities would adopt individualized educational methods based on need and videotape recorders based on amenity value.   Thus we expected to find a negative relationship between individualized instruction and percentage going on to college and a positive

Table 3-1
School Board Reformism

School Board Selection	
Appointed	0.0
Both	0.5
Elected	1.0
Representation	
Ward	0.0
Both	0.5
At-large	1.0
Type Election	
Partisan	0.0
Both	0.5
Nonpartisan	1.0

relationship between dropout rate and individualized instruction. For the product innovation, on the other hand, we expected to see these relationships reversed—that is, a positive relationship between innovation and percentage going on to college and a negative relationship between innovation and the dropout rate. Of the 270 school districts responding to the questionnaire item concerning the percentage of high school students going on to college, the percentage ranged from a low of 10 percent to a high of 85 percent with a mean of 49.6 and a standard deviation of 14.5. The mean dropout rate for the 253 respondents was 10.9 percent with a range from 1 to 50 percent and a standard deviation of 9.3 percent.

Despite expectations, however, there was no zero order relationship between the demand variables and the process innovation. It thus appears that the use of individualized instruction methods is not stimulated by demand in the manner hypothesized.

Two measures were selected to represent the influence of intergovernmental relations on innovation adoption—total IGR (intergovernmental revenue) received from the federal government and total IGR received from the state government. Neither intergovernmental variable was related to the percentage of elementary school teachers using individualized instruction methods, however.

Total school district expenditures and per student school expenditures were selected as indicators of financial resources. As the individualized instruction packages represent a financial commitment on the part of the school district, it was expected that resource availability would be an important determinant of program use. At the zero order level, however, this was not the case.

City per capita general revenue and city total IGR were selected as

Table 3-2

Zero Order Relationship Between School District Process Independent Variables and the Percent of Teachers Using Individualized Instruction in Elementary Schools

Variable	r
Community Environment	
Liberalism	-.032
SES	-.003
Suburb	-.032
Ethnic/Ghetto	-.114*
Size	-.039
Population Increase	-.029
Group Quarters	.021
Demand	
Percentage HS Going to College	-.036
Percentage Dropout	.061
Organizational Environment	
IGR from Federal Government	-.022
IGR from State Government	-.057
Total School District Expenditure	-.048
Per Student School Expenditure	-.038
City per Capita General Revenue	-.084
City Total IGR	-.035
City Reformism	.061
Organizational Characteristics	
School Board Reformism	.059
Total Elementary Teachers	-.042
Percentage Teachers without Degree	-.023
Percentage Teachers with M.A. or better	-.107*

*Significant at the .05 level.

indicators of financial resources of the city. Neither measure, however, was related to the dependent variable.

Nor was there any significant zero order relationship between city reformism and the dependent variable. As with housing, there does not appear to be any "spillover" of professionalism that stimulates the adoption of innovation in school districts.

There does appear to be a tendency, however, for reformed cities to have reformed school boards as well. A zero order coefficient of $r = .15$ (significant at the .01 level) was found between city and school board reformism. Unfortunately, in terms of innovation adoption, it does not seem to make much difference. School boards in general showed a high degree of reformism with scores ranging from 1 to 3 but with a mean of 2.69 and a standard deviation of .51. Most school boards were also elected at large rather than by ward. Of the 240 districts responding to the question, 82.1 percent reported at-large elected boards, 12.9 percent had board members elected by wards, and 5 percent used some combined system. Only 14.3 percent of the 237 respondents reported partisan elections. The vast majority (84.8 percent) elected the school board on a nonpartisan basis while 0.8 percent had a combination of partisan and non-partisan officials. Thus school board reformism, while slightly related to city reform, is actually much more common. School board reformism, however, did not show a significant zero order relationship with the dependent variable. Nor were the reformism components related to either of the dependent variables. Table 3-3 shows the zero order correlation coefficients between the school board reformism components and the dependent variable. There were no statistically significant relationships—even at the .05 level. It thus appears that reformism in both the environment and as a characteristic of the organization makes little difference in the adoption of individualized instruction in public schools.

The size of the organization as represented by the total number of elementary school teachers was also expected to show a positive relationship with innovation. Again, this was not the case.

Finally, professionalism in the organization, as measured by the percentage of teachers without a B.A. degree and the percentage of teachers with an M.A. or higher, was expected to be positively related to innovation. At the zero order level, however, the relationships did not materialize. Only the percentage of teachers with an M.A. or higher was slightly related to innovation—but in a negative direction. The relationship was so weak, however, that conclusions based on these zero order relationships are suspect.

As with housing, it was expected that professionalism would be related to publications emphasis in the education environment and thus might influence the adoption of innovation. To test this possibility, *Today's Education*, the journal of the National Education Association and *The National Elementary Principal*, the journal of the NEA Department of Elementary School Principals,

Table 3-3
**Zero Order Relationship Between Measures of School Board
Reformism and Individualized Instruction in Elementary Schools**

Variable	*r*
School Board Selection	.027
School Board Representation	−.103
School Board Election-type	.021

were examined for articles concerning individualized education. The results are shown in Figures 3-1 and 3-2. Figure 3-1 shows the percentage of articles in *Today's Education* dealing with individualized instruction and Figure 3-2 shows the same data for *The National Elementary Principal*. The data in Figure 3-1 show a rather constant interest in individualized instruction methods from the mid-1960s to date—at least in the NEA publication addressed to teachers. The percentage of articles rose to almost 3 percent in 1966, gradually declined during the late 1960s, and then rose sharply in the early 1970s so that by 1973 some 6 percent of the articles in the journal dealt in some way with individualized instruction.

Strangely, interest in individualized instruction in the journal for elementary school principals preceded *Today's Education* by a year or two. Three articles

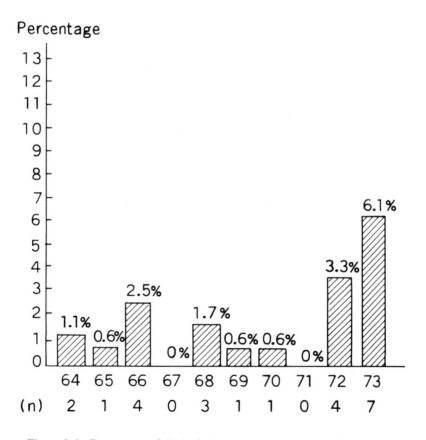

Figure 3-1. Percentage of *Today's Education* Articles Devoted to Methods of Individualized Instruction (1964-1973)

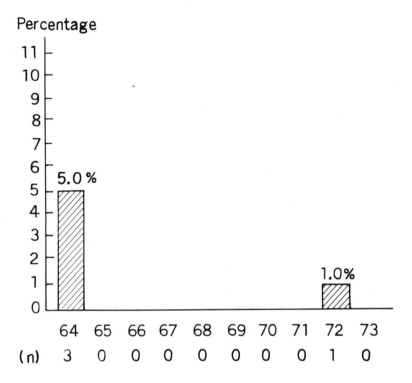

Figure 3-2. Percentage of *The National Elementary Principal* Articles Devoted to Methods of Individualized Instruction (1964-1973)

on the subject appeared in 1964 and one in 1972. These articles thus preceded the peaks in *Today's Education* by two years and one year respectively. Thus judging by the major professional association's publication, interest in individualized education peaked in the mid 1960s, declined until the early 1970s and then showed a rather substantial rebirth. Thus, as with housing, the major educational professional association showed substantial interest in the process innovation. Of course, the direct impact of such a series of articles has not been measured; however, such professional association interest undoubtedly stimulated some adoption.

As with the investigation into innovation adoption in public housing, it was necessary to use partial correlation coefficients to test the innovation model for public school districts. Partials were first computed between the organizational characteristics and dependent variable controlling for community environment, demand, and organizational environment. Only the relationship between organizational size (in terms of the number of elementary teachers) was related to a commitment to individualized instruction with $r = .19$. Thus a commitment to individualized instruction does not appear to be efficiency-related as was noted with the use of the computer in housing management. Other things being equal, school districts with high personnel resources were more likely to exhibit a commitment to individualized education than those with lower personnel levels. Neither reformism nor professionalism, however, was independently related to the dependent variable.

It should be pointed out that proponents argue that extra teachers are not needed for individualized instruction.[6] Nevertheless, the findings here suggest that while added personnel resources are not necessary for implementation of the innovation, those school districts with the extra resources showed a higher level of commitment to individualized methods than those without.

The fact that personnel resources are a major contributor to the adoption of individualized education suggests that slack resources in the organizational environment are necessary to provide the personnel resources. Thus partials were computed between total elementary teachers and the organizational environment controlling for the community environment and demand. Four of the seven variables were related to personnel resources with intergovernmental influences predominant. The independent relationship between federal IGR and the number of elementary teachers was $r = .35$ while the relationship between state IGR and teachers was $r = .72$. It thus appears that intergovernmental funding is extremely important in providing the personnel resources necessary for the serious adoption of individualized instruction methods. Similarly, the existence of slack resources in the school environment (total expenditures) provides the necessary funding for high teacher levels ($r = .70$). Surprisingly, however, slack as measured on a per student basis was not related to personnel levels. Thus it is total financial resources, not resources on per student basis, that provide the funds necessary for the personnel levels needed for a commitment to individualized education.

Surprisingly, the existence of slack in the city environment was negatively related to total elementary teachers with $r = -.23$. Thus cities with low per capita expenditures for city functions (excluding education) appear to have high school personnel levels with other things being equal. This relationship appears to reflect a trade-off in financial priorities in the city. A correlation of $r = -.28$ was obtained between city per capita revenue and total school district expenditures controlling for the community environment and demand. Thus low city per capita revenue is independently related to high total school expenditures when controlling for size and other ecological variables. The factor size, while computed from variable loadings of physical characteristics of the city, is also representative of the size of the school district. The zero order relationship between size and number of students is $r = .94$. Thus size also stands as a surrogate for the size of the school district. The partial relationship between city per capita revenue and total school expenditures, in effect then, also controlled for the size of the school district.

Neither total IGR received by the city, as a second measure of fiscal slack in the city environment nor the reformed structure of the city government showed an independent relationship with the total number of elementary teachers in the school district.

Computed next was the relationship between the organization environment variables and the dependent variable controlling for community environment, demand, and the significant organizational characteristic. None of the characteristics of the organizational environment showed an independent relationship with the percentage of teachers using individualized instruction. Thus in the case of the school process innovation, the influence of the organizational environment is through a characteristic of the organization rather than directly on innovation adoption. Since per student expenditures, city total IGR, and city reformism were not directly related to either the dependent variable or to the significant organizational characteristic, they have been removed from the model and are not considered in further analysis.

The impact of the demand variables on innovation adoption was also considered. It may be recalled that in the housing process mode, demand was related directly to innovation adoption as well as through the organizational characteristics. To test for an independent relationship between demand and percentage of teachers using individualized instruction, a partial was computed controlling for community environment, organizational environment, and total elementary teachers. Contrary to expectations, there was no independent relationship between demand and commitment to individualized instruction.

There was an independent relationship between demand and total elementary teachers, however. The percentage going on to college was positively related to the total number of elementary teachers ($r = .39$) under controls while the dropout rate was negatively related to the same organizational characteristic ($r = .19$). Thus it appears that individualized instruction is not the "need" innovation that was hypothesized. The model testing thus far suggests an "amenity" nature to the innovation. It appears that school districts with low dropout rates and a high percentage of students going on to college tend to have a large number of elementary teachers for the school population and also tend to exhibit a commitment to programs utilizing individualized instruction—relationships one would expect of an amenity innovation.

When the relationship between demand and the organizational environment controlling for community environment was computed, however, the picture became murky. The percentage going on to college was negatively related to state aid and to total school district expenditures ($r = -.22$ and $r = -.21$) while the dropout rate was postively related to total expenditures ($r = .18$). While these relationships are inherently satisfying (other things being equal, school districts with high dropout rates tend to have higher expenditures than those with low dropout rates—presumably to combat this and other educational deficiencies), they do not fit the model. For example, under controls, districts with a high percentage going on to college receive less state aid and have lower expenditures than their lower percentage counterparts. And yet it was shown earlier that high levels of state aid and a high total expenditure rate were necessary for the organizational condition stimulating commitment to individualized instruction. How can this be? Table 3-4 explains.

Table 3-4 shows the relationships between community environment and the variables of the organizational environment controlling for demand. Note especially the correlations between size and the four variables—especially between size and state aid and total expenditures ($r = .89$ and $r = .90$). Thus size is the overwhelming determinant of the availability of intergovernmental funds and of the financial slack available in the organizational environment. While the demand variables are related to the organizational environment variables in a way not concomitant with the model when controlling for size, it is size that is the primary determinant of intergovernmental funding and financial slack. This substantiates the zero order relationships, or more correctly lack of relationships, between the demand variables and community environment.

However, several variables in the community environment were significantly related to total elementary teachers when controlling for demand and the organizational environment. Again size was dominant with $r = .77$, but a low city socioeconomic status also contributed independently to high teacher resources ($r = -.21$).

Also computed were the relationships between demand and each of the community environment variables while controlling for the remaining variables in the community environment. Three of the variables were significantly related to both the percentage college bound and the dropout rate—and in the expected directions. Cities with a high socioeconomic status and with suburban characteristics generally had a high college-bound population ($r = .44$

Table 3-4
Relationship Between Community Environment and Organizational Environment Controlling for Demand

Variable	IGR Federal	IGR State	Total Expenditure	PC General Revenue
Liberalism	−.155*	.017	.067	.263**
SES	.010	.051	−.012	−.064
Suburb	−.114	−.028	.028	−.008
Ethnic/Ghetto	.066	.140*	.185**	.568**
Size	.475**	.889**	.903**	.234**
Population Increase	−.016	−.015	−.009	−.057
Group Increase	.019	−.031	−.032	.140*

*Significant at the .05 level.
**Significant at the .01 level.

and .17, respectively). These same cities also tended to have low dropout rates ($r = -.20$ and $-.31$). Liberalism also showed significant relationships in the expected direction with coefficients of $-.16$ between liberalism and college bound and .14 between liberalism and the dropout rate. Thus some of the community characteristics act as expected—that is, as determinants of the demand variables. As expected, the coefficients substantiate the work of Coleman and others.

Finally, the relationship between the dependent variable and the community environment controlling for demand, organizational environment, and total elementary teachers was computed. The results were virtually the same as for the housing process model. There was no independent relationship between any of the variables of the organizational environment and the dependent variables. Again the community environment has no direct impact on innovation adoption but rather generates demand and helps create the characteristics of the organization and its environment which lead to innovation.

Figure 3-3 presents a revised model for the use of individualized instruction in elementary schools. As with the housing models, the lines linking the different variables indicate the significant independent relationships at the .01 level. The model, like the housing process innovation model, is clearly a predictable model and points up some significant findings. First, there appears to be a substantial difference between innovations based on "amenity" and "need" as suggested by Oliver P. Williams and Charles R. Adrian.[7] In Chapter 2 it was noted that the adoption of computer-based management information systems was brought about, in part, by low personnel levels or a need for efficiency. In this model the opposite occurs—a high personnel level in terms of number of elementary teachers is indicative of a commitment to individualized instruction. Thus slack within the organization rather than the need for efficiency is the only direct determinant of individualized instruction methods.

Within the organizational environment, intergovernmental transfers appear to provide, or a least help provide, the financial resources necessary for high personnel levels. There is apparently no direct relationship between the organizational environment and the commitment to individualized instruction. The negative relationship between city per capita revenue and total school expenditures controlling for size, indicates a possible trade-off between city and school revenues.

The positive relationship between percentage of high school students college bound and number of teachers and the negative relationship between the dropout rate and number of teachers again fits the model of amenity innovation. Other things being equal, the school districts with the fewest educational problems are more likely to have a higher ratio of elementary school teachers and are thus more likely to adopt individualized instruction methods.

The measures of demand are both related to the same three factors in the community environment—factors which largely capture community wealth.

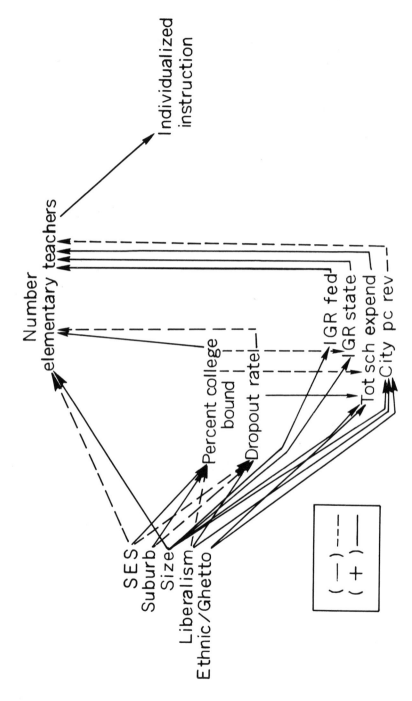

Figure 3-3. Revised Model for the Use of Individualized Instruction in Public Elementary Schools

Thus high SES, or wealthy bedroom-type communities, have fewer educational problems as measured by the percentage college bound and the dropout rate.

As expected, size was the most important determinant of intergovernmental assistance, school and city expenditure levels, and the number of elementary teachers. The environmental characteristics of the community, however, do not operate independently to determine the level of innovation adoption.

Qualitative Analysis

The use of individualized instruction methods in elementary schools was examined in detail in our cities. Two cities had a higher level of individualized instruction than predicted, one lower than predicted, and one city had a percentage use score less than 1 1/2 standard deviations from the mean. This latter city, Free City, was again used for field testing and to pretest the questionnaire. Thus Free City was not a deviant case but had adopted individualized instruction in elementary education at about the expected level.

Free City. The implementation of the IGE program in six elementary schools in Free City is of particular interest, for in this case it was the individual schools and not the administration that provided the initiative. Free City's elementary school district did not offer a formal presentation of the IGE program to its school principals but rather provided a source of general funds to the schools for the implementation of *any* innovative educational program. It was to be these slack resources and the amenability of the central administration to new educational practice that allowed for the introduction of individualized instruction.

In the 1969-1970 school year, Free City's school administration established a $2 million Program Improvement Proposal (PIP) fund for the purpose of promoting innovative approaches in education. Schools applying for the funds submitted proposals that were then evaluated for merit and either accepted or rejected on a competitive basis. According to one school administrator, the purpose of PIP was "to innovate on a broken front, with the individual schools assuming the initiative. Direction did not come from the administration." Once a program proved successful, the initial PIP fund allocation became part of the school's ongoing budget. Inasmuch as innovative approaches would not force a school to readjust its budget priorities, PIP served as a "nothing to lose" venture for progressive ideas.

The same year that the PIP was initiated in Free City, the Wisconsin Research and Development Center introduced its formal Individually Guided Education (IGE) program. In the spring of 1970, IDEA, of the Kettering Foundation, hosted the conference to introduce this new program to school administrators within the region. Although Free City's elementary and curriculum specialist attended that conference, it was more to keep in step with new educational approaches than as preparation for the formal introduction of the program by the central administration. Nevertheless, one school principal, who was cluster chairperson for a group of elementary school administrators, learned of the central administrator's visit to the IDEA conference and asked that she make a presentation of the different aspects of the IGE program to the cluster administrators. Following that address, the elementary and curriculum specialist was approached by the same principal and asked for more information. The principal was referred to the state IGE coordinator, who, in turn, directed her attention to a nearby city which had been a test site for the IGE program.

The elementary school principal subsequently approached her staff, explained the IGE program, and stated that if they were interested, she would endorse such a program. As this school administrator recalled:

> The majority were interested enough to warrant a group visit to the IGE test school. We agreed it was worth trying and immediately set about to writing a proposal under PIP which we submitted to the Administration in April, 1970. Even though we didn't have a judgment on our proposal, we proceeded as if we did, and began an in-service summer session for the training of staff. Now, the money for the in-service training was already available for the summer session teachers. It was optional for the staff who were interested—no one was being pressured. Well, our PIP proposal was approved the day before classes were to begin, but as you can see, we had thought it would. We've been an IGE school since that year (1970-1971).

When asked if implementation was as easy as that, if perhaps there wasn't some dissent, the principal recalled that:

> There were those who were opposed and were given the opportunity to transfer out. If I recall correctly, two of the three that remained who weren't interested became interested. Two transferred out, one because he thought IGE structured the individual.

As the proponents of IGE argue that additional funding is not necessary for implementation of the program, a question was directed to the central administration as to why IGE required PIP funds. Although they concede that, "it *could* be done without additional funds," PIP funds offered "added trimmings." The principal was more specific, noting that the PIP funds were used to increase the salary of the unit leaders and to secure a number of aides for the multi-unit school, as well as to purchase the instructional materials developed by IDEA. The explanation behind the adoption of IGE for this particular school, however, still does not explain why five other elementary schools in the district also opted for the innovative program.

Of the remaining five IGE schools, the two schools adopting the program most recently did not use PIP funds. Rather, the explanation behind their adoption of IGE stems from the fact that they were both newly constructed open classroom schools. Even before the schools were constructed, extensive community involvement went into planning not only the architecture, but the educational objectives and programs around which the construction was to be designed. Each school had a capital improvement committee chaired by two principals and composed of neighborhood leaders, teachers, and resource teams. It was under the direction of these committees that the decision to utilize the IGE program and design the buildings to serve the needs of the multi-unit schools was made.

Another Free City school adopted the IGE program after a new wing had been constructed with flexible walls for the open-classroom concept. Inasmuch as the new wing was architecturally innovative, the principal was asked by the administration to develop an approach that would utilize the open space. Drawing upon PIP funds, this principal saw IGE as a program designed for the use of such open-space classrooms.

Open-space architecture, however, was certainly not a prerequisite for the adoption of IGE as was noted in the case of the first school. Nor did it play any role in the adoption of IGE by an innercity school faced with unique problems. Because of the overcrowded pupil situation in this particular area, the school was converted from the traditional K-6 elementary school to a school for grades 5-6 only. Inasmuch as the school was already, for all practical purposes, a unit school rather than multigraded one; the principal saw a need for a special program to meet special needs. Having become familiar with the IGE approach in an urban education class at the University of Wisconsin in Madison (the developmental site of IGE), he latched on to the IGE program as a solution to the problems posed by a grade 5-6 school. With PIP funds, the individualized program was adopted "to meet the needs of the children."

Finally, recalls the district coordinator, there was one school that, though in a new building, had not undergone the careful planning witnessed in the case of the two recently constructed schools. The principal, who was appointed six months prior to the opening of the school, was asked to develop a new program, utilizing PIP funds. However, rather than initiating an annovative approach the first year, the principal opened the doors and sought to involve the community in the decision. The following year, IGE was implemented with PIP funds and with the endorsement of the school community.

Although the Free City school administration did not play a coordinating role in the adoption of this particular innovation by six of the elementary schools in the district, its commitment to progressive ideas in education, as witnessed by its creation of the PIP program, certainly serves as a general explanation behind IGE utilization. It was this general administrative support and freedom of action provided by the administrators of the Free City school district that appeared to serve as a prerequisite for the adoption of IGE.

Dutch Elm. Dutch Elm presents an example of a pioneering school district in the area of a formalized structure of individualized instruction. In the school year 1969-1970, five schools in Dutch Elm initiated the IGE method of instruction at the elementary level, joining three other school districts across the nation in what was termed "an experimental program" developed by the Kettering Foundation's IDEA. *How* the Dutch Elm school district came to be involved in this developmental program and, more importantly, *why* it chose to, are questions that merit consideration.

As far back as 1965, the school administration was concerned with "a humanized approach to child education." At that time the school district received a grant under Title I to conduct a "Humanities In-Service Institute." The institute was to be for a two-year period. The purpose of the program, according to one of the coordinators, was to point out to teachers the necessity of realizing the human potential of each individual student. Using such devices as a split screen, the teachers would be shown a student in the classroom and in his environment outside the classroom. Informal discussions would be carried on as to how to best approach teaching thirty-pupil classes without neglecting the individual needs of each of those students.

Essentially, the main purpose of the two-year program was to create change agents within the schools. The assistant superintendent of instruction at the time was strongly motivated in the area of humanizing instruction and had hoped that the in-service training would serve as an instrument in securing this goal. Through these small in-service sessions, a communication line was established from central administration to the faculty indicating that support would be given to innovative approaches designed to upgrade the humanized aspect of education. While the staff perceived a note of encouragement from the central office to upgrade its approach, the administration was, according to the director of elementary education, identifying those schools and principals that had "achieved a level of readiness."

In 1969, a team of four teachers approached the central office and, now fully aware that the administration was open to new ideas, asked that they be allowed to team teach. Administration approval was granted, and instructions were issued concerning the necessary physical alterations at the school—moves that caused a reluctant principal to request a leave of absence. One of the seven in-service humanities coordinators was then approached by the administration and asked if she might like to assume the vacant position. The new principal worked closely with the teaching team and attempted to develop new ways to "individualize" or "humanize" their program.

On the administration level, the assistant superintendent of instruction and the director of elementary education were assessing the level they had so far achieved and began looking for more developed approaches that could be implemented. In 1969, the two visited the "Goodlad School" at UCLA, a laboratory school that was renowned for its approaches to education. John Goodlad, whom the assistant superintendent of instruction termed "the most prominent in educational innovation," had introduced such innovations as the open classroom, team teaching, and the nongraded approach into the UCLA lab school. Goodlad was also the research director of IDEA.

The two administrators were impressed with what they saw in California and acted upon it. The assistant superintendent of instruction contacted Madeline Hunter, the principal of the Goodlad School, and asked if she would be interested in doing consulting resource work for Dutch Elm. Although she was unable to, she suggested that Dutch Elm contact Ken Shultz of IDEA at the Kettering Foundation in Dayton, Ohio. Ms. Hunter believed that he might have something that would be of interest to the searching administrators.

Mr. Shultz was thereupon contacted, and the two members of the central office flew to Dayton to investigate the program. IDEA was in the process of developing a league of schools across the country using the Wisconsin IGE model for the Multi-Unit School-Elementary (MUS-E). The Kettering Foundation funded IDEA on the condition that within two years the institute would effect a substantial change in education across the country. At this point, however, IDEA was in the early stages of developing the program and materials for implementation of IGE. They needed cooperative school districts to assist in refinement and debugging of their experimental package. The Dutch Elm administrators were interested enough to invite Mr. Shultz to Dutch Elm to address himself to those whose cooperation was necessary for success—the elementary principals.

In the spring of 1970, Mr. Shultz conducted two informative sessions in Dutch Elm. The assistant superintendent and the director of elementary education then asked for a written response from those principals interested in the IGE program. "There was not one negative response," recalled the director of elementary education.

> All responded favorably in one way or another. If they didn't want it for their school, they indicated the belief that at least someone should try it. Seven responded favorably for themselves, two with reservations. The five without reservations were chosen for their "level of readiness."

With the pledged cooperation of five principals, Dutch Elm applied to IDEA for participation in the experimental program. Of 800 applications nationwide, only four were selected, Dutch Elm being one. IDEA was to match funds with the school district for the experimental package with implementation of the program to begin the following school year. In the summer of 1970, the director of elementary education and the five principals attended a three-week in-service program in Dayton, fully utilizing the IGE model with a unit of students. That fall, with the director of elementary education acting as facilitator, the five principals introduced IGE to their respective schools.

It would appear that in the case of Dutch Elm, a "level of readiness" had been obtained long before any model or program of individualizing had been developed. Had no program come their way, one might well assume that this particular school district would have proceeded on its own, creating its own model through trial and error. The fact that the key administrative positions were occupied by professional individuals not content with a "wait-and-see" attitude certainly accounts for the progressive nature of the district.

It might be added as a footnote, that today only one school of the original five retains the IGE label. But as the assistant superintendent of instruction notes with a good deal of satisfaction, "the rest of the district is aware that this administration looks to them for new approaches." Though resistance is high to being labeled "one of those schools," different approaches and even parts of IGE are being adopted district-wide. For those opposed to the adoption of IGE, the challenge went out to come up with something better.

Rocky Mountain. The city of Rocky Mountain, unlike Dutch Elm or Free City, became involved with IGE because of a state-wide commitment rather than because of a localized experimental program or slack resource availability. One quarter of the twenty-nine elementary schools in Rocky Mountain are officially labeled IGE schools with a few others falling under the same type of instruction but without the label. Although the seven are all IDEA-affiliated schools, they received no financial assistance, either from the Kettering Foundation or from the state, in implementing the program.

In school year 1969-1970, the state department of education invited all school districts in the state to send representatives to the capital for a meeting with the Kettering Foundation and a discussion of the IGE program. The Rocky Mountain school district sent the director of elementary education and two elementary principals to the meeting as representatives. Despite their interest in the program, they decided against implementation that year. According to the director of elementary education, there were two reasons:

> First, we had expected an offer of financial assistance by the Kettering Foundation for implementation which was just not to be had; and secondly, our district was undergoing a transition from a very conservative superintendent to one more liberally oriented. It just wasn't a good time for experimentation.

The following year, however, the state invited all school districts to a second meeting on the IGE program. This time the director of elementary education was accompanied by the assistant superintendent of instruction and the assistant superintendent of schools. Upon their return, the superintendent, now established after the earlier transition, was asked if he might agree to some schools becoming involved. The IGE coordinator for the state was thus invited to Rocky Mountain to give a presentation to all interested elementary school administrators.

In that year, 1970, the district allowed five principals to implement the
IGE program, and provisions were made for transfers of disinterested faculty
members. If, after three years, the program appeared acceptable, other
schools would also be allowed to implement it.

Although the director of elementary education acted as the district IGE
coordinator, each school set up its own in-service workshops and programming
for IGE. There was no direction from the central administration, but this is
not to imply that there was no assistance or encouragement offered. After the
three years, four additional schools requested and received permission to
adopt the program. As two of the former IGE schools dropped out, Rocky
Mountain had seven IGE schools by 1975.

While some other school districts using IGE found that additional cost or
staffing were required, this was not the case in Rocky Mountain. According
to the director of elementary education, absolutely no extra money or extra
staff were required. As for staffing, the district maintains a ratio of twenty-
four students per teacher. IGE schools are allowed to differentiate staffing,
however, thereby allowing a trade of so many teacher aides per professional
teacher. The only drawback to the program, noted the director, is the number
of unit and hub meetings required of IGE participants.

> I am unhappy about all the support meetings required. They were
> designed to build morale among staff and exchange ideas throughout
> the state. But after having the program for five years, I can't see the
> necessity of so many meetings. I just don't have the money for sub-
> stitute teachers nor enough substitute teachers to cover the staff who
> are attending these support meetings. This is where additional expense
> comes in and we're attempting to taper off on unit and hub meetings.

While it is interesting to note that the director of elementary education had
Dr. Herbert Klausmeier, a leading developer of the IGE program, as an instructor
in college, this fact does not explain the high percentage of IGE schools in
Rocky Mountain. Certainly the background of this particular administrator is
important. Without a favorable attitude towards innovation on the part of
central administrators, it would be difficult for elementary principals to develop
and implement innovative programs. The Director's preference for the humanistic approach had, to a degree, ruled out "the behavioral approach of programs
such as Individually Prescribed Instruction (IPI)."

Thus a number of factors appear to be related to the fact that 25 percent
of the Rocky Mountain elementary schools utilize the IGE program. First, the
experience (fourteen years as an elementary principal) and humanistic background of the director of elementary education probably made him amenable
to IGE goals. But the director's background and favorable attitude towards
individualized instruction alone cannot offer a total explanation for the high
number of participating schools. Several other factors were involved. A strong

endorsement and cooperation by the state office of education towards the IGE program was obviously important. Also important were the liberally oriented superintendent of schools who placed the administration of the elementary schools totally in the hands of the director and the principals, and the cooperative attitude of the members of the board of education. The board's endorsement of individualized instruction, by formal resolution, also contributed to a climate of support for the IGE program.

Tumbleweed. In the lobby of the school administration building in the city of Tumbleweed hangs a 1957 testimonial to the objectives of elementary education:

> The educational program of the Tumbleweed City School District is directed toward the development of each pupil according to his abilities and capacities . . . . Our schools accept each child where he is, as he is, and provide opportunities for him to develop to his maximum growth.

Though one might suspect that the administration would thus be receptive to a formal individualized program to implement these objectives, such was not the case. Rather, formal programs such as IGE, IPI, and PLAN were looked upon with scorn by those administrators who would have the final say in matters of elementary educational programs.

The state in which Tumbleweed is located requires a course of study outline for all elementary schools. In addition to this required outline, Tumbleweed has composed a curriculum guide for each grade level (K-8) that supplements the outline. The eight volumes, each about four inches thick, list in separate columns: the objectives of the subject, the suggested approaches, and the available aids and references. According to the assistant superintendent, word of these curriculum guides has spread to such an extent that requests for copies of the guide have been made by school districts from around the nation. It would be difficult for one not to be impressed with the comprehensive approach applied to these curriculum guides. Studying the column of suggested approaches to reading in the third grade, for example, a number of approaches were found to be identical to those applied in IGE. There were, in addition, three pages suggesting approaches to individualized reading instruction. Thus the Tumbleweed City school district does not appear to be a tradition-entrenched educational organization. What remained to be answered, however, was the rigid and inflexible opposition to the three innovative programs being studied.

When a question was put to the assistant superintendent pertaining to a situation where a teacher or principal wished to implement an innovative program such as IGE and did not find it under the curriculum guide's suggested approaches, he responded:

If it's not here, they can use their own, excuse the expression, "innovative" idea by first writing it up and submitting it to us for approval. We look at it and if it has any merit, we put it on a pilot program for the district. The individual school runs it for a year or two and if successful, it will be included among the suggested approaches. We don't, however, encourage principals to go on without our approval.

The assistant superintendent and the director of instructional programs had their own definition of individualized instruction which they considered to be at odds with the formal programs. Essentially they looked upon it as, "taking each child as he is and moving him towards his highest level." When asked how that differed so greatly from IGE, IPI, or PLAN, the director of instructional programs responded:

We looked at all three programs and ruled out IPI and PLAN immediately. Neither met any of our needs or what we were looking for. They were so behavior oriented. I don't think individualized instruction is picking up where the student wants to go. In IPI and PLAN the student has too much say. IGE on the other hand is too strictly structured—there's no freedom, no leeway. I wrote the state coordinator for IGE for material and found that it just required too formal a structure.

At this point, the assistant superintendent interjected:

IGE requires a large amount of in-service training as well as a reallocation of teachers and funds. When you have teachers that have been with the district 18-20 years, it's hard to reeducate and train them. I would just hate to take a teacher who has shown great success with a tried and true method and condemn her for not changing to accommodate a formal program of less proven methods. An IGE school requires a total commitment, forcing those teachers who can't or won't change their methods, which more often than not are successful, to leave a school they've been at for ten years and transfer to another.

It was not difficult to detect a note of empathy on the part of the two administrators for those teachers who were being challenged to innovative approaches. Both had similar backgrounds with experience in the field including positions as teacher and principal. The assistant superintendent, for example, had a very strong opinion on what he called, "the attempts at progressive education in the past." He viewed Glasser's positive approach to education somewhat with disdain, noting that Glasser's experience was based on a girls' reformatory school, not elementary schools.[8] Though he did not go so far as to condemn

Glasser's method of positive reinforcement in the classroom as opposed to pointing out a student's negative qualities, he did consider the approach somewhat unrealistic and success-oriented.

Although the director of instructional programs had reviewed some literature on IGE, neither had attended a state conference where the program was explained in detail. An assumption appeared to have been made on the part of the two key administrators that the formal programs were just more attempts at packaging concepts to which they were already committed. Experience had convinced them that the concepts were not new; and they were wary of a formal structure or model.

The director of instructional programs had, however, visited the Goodlad Laboratory School at UCLA and had studied the approaches offered by principal Madeline Hunter. While the Goodlad School does not utilize the IGE program, it was a pioneer in developing a number of the approaches found in the model. If the Tumbleweed district was opposed to the formal model then, what of the features found within it, i.e., differentiated staffing, non-age-graded classrooms, open classrooms? According to one administrator, differentiated staffing is extremely difficult to implement in the state because of credentialling and staffing laws. Inasmuch as the law requires one certified teacher per thirty students for grades 1-3, an open classroom of ninety students would demand three certified teachers. Unlike the Rocky Mountain school district, a trade-off of two teacher's aides for one certified teacher is not allowed. In one district where a waiver by the state was granted for differentiated staffing, the director noted, "it was a total failure." While differentiated staffing is thus not considered by the administrators, they have given some thought to a K-3 nongraded unit. Under a state-sponsored early childhood program for grades K-3, funds are allocated for individualized attention to the students' needs, with a required daily progress and achievement report for each child. In addition, 27 percent of the students in Tumbleweed are bilingual, or have English as their second language. While one administrator notes that a nongraded approach might be warranted due to language difficulties, there presently are only age-graded classrooms in Tumbleweed.

It appears that individualized programs cannot be successfully implemented in a school without the commitment of a principal and the staff. Although one cannot cite the administration of the Tumbleweed elementary district as being intransigent to innovative ideas presented by individual educators, it is certainly fair to conclude that innovative programs requiring a large-scale commitment on the part of the present administration are quite unlikely.

Summary

In the case of individualized instruction, it is difficult to compare the results of the case studies with the quantitative findings—they are on different levels of analysis. The case studies do, however, add a new dimension to the study. In each case, the attitudes of top administrative personnel toward innovation appeared to play a key part in the use of individualized instruction programs.

In Free City, the administration took a laissez faire attitude toward innovation. They provided a stimulus to innovation with a "carrot" in the form of PIP funds. Thus Free City encouraged, but did not require, innovation in the local schools. Decisions to innovate were largely left up to the individual school principals and teachers. Diagrammatically, then, the process looked something like

slack ⟶ program search ⟶ adoption

Another factor contributed to the level of adoption in Free City—school construction. Instead of new schools or additions being designed around a teaching program, the opposite appeared to occur. Open-classroom schools and additions were constructed, and then a search was made to find an appropriate teaching program. Thus

open-classroom
construction ⟶ program search ⟶ adoption

Recall that in Free City the level of innovation in the public schools had been predicted with reasonable accuracy. Thus this case study merely adds insight into the process.

In Dutch Elm, however, the school district adopted a much higher utilization of individualized instruction than had been expected. It was, however, a top-down approach which was responsible for IGE use. Dutch Elm administrators were historically concerned with a humanizing approach to education—a fact that the school principals understood well. When Ken Shultz was brought into Dutch Elm to discuss IDEA with the elementary principals, there wasn't much question about the administration's position—"There was not one negative response." Unquestionably, then, the administrative position led to a high level of adoption

administrative position ⟶ adoption

Rocky Mountain was a virtual carbon copy of Dutch Elm with one exception—the state department of education took a more active role in promoting IGE than did the department of education in Dutch Elm's state. Here, the administration brought in the state IGE coordinator to explain the program to principals and faculty. Again, the administration asked for local school participation, and with some success—five schools were selected from the nine volunteering. Again, diagrammatic representation shows administration position────────► adoption

Administration attitudes in Tumbleweed were also of overriding importance. While state regulation made program adoption difficult, adoption was by no means impossible. Administrative satisfaction with present programs, coupled with perceived drawbacks to the three individualized programs under study, led to a resistance to individualized instruction. Administrators were familiar with all programs—there was no information gap. Two were too behaviorally oriented and the other was too strictly structured. Thus the "nonadoption" model looks strangely like the adoption models for Dutch Elm and Rocky Mountain:

administrative position ────────► nonadoption

In summary, then, certain patterns emerge from the two phases of study—quantitative and qualitative. First, individualized instruction is clearly an amenity adoption with teacher resources being the primary key. All things being equal, school districts with larger staffs are more inclined to adopt individualized instruction programs. These communities generally have a high percentage of college-bound graduates and a low dropout rate. They also muster the financial resources necessary to provide a relatively large staff. City size and socioeconomic characteristics are ultimately behind the demand and resource availability measures.

It then becomes necessary to explain the deviant cities. The case studies clearly show that the attitudes of the key administrators are responsible for deviant behavior. Strong administrative positions were clearly responsible for the deviant behavior of the three school districts examined in detail. It thus appears that the basic determinants in the quantitative model can be overriden by strong administrative attitudes—both pro and con.

Product Innovation

The dependent variable selected for analysis was the average number of video-tape recorders per secondary school in the school district. The data were obtained from the responses to the school district questionnaire. Responses ranged from a low of zero to a high of eighty-five VTRs. The mean was 1.9 with a standard deviation of 5.3 for the 273 usable responses to the question. While eighty-five VTRs per school seemed out of line with the normal response, telephone confirmation substantiated the questionnaire responses in this case and in those other cases that appeared out of line.

Quantitative Analysis

The model for the adoption of videotape recorders in secondary schools again follows Figure 1-1. There is essentially no difference between the school process and product models other than a few variable changes. In the area of organizational characteristics, three variables remain unchanged—school board reformism, the percentage of teachers without a degree, and the percentage of teachers with an M.A. or higher. As the product innovation is in secondary schools, the total number of secondary teachers replaces total elementary teachers as the indicator of organizational size. In addition, a scale was developed from question 11 of the questionnaire to indicate centralization/decentralization of the requests for audiovisual equipment. If the individual schools determined need, a score of 1 was assigned. If the central administration determined need, the school district was given a score of 3, while if both individual schools and the administration determined AV needs, a score of 2 was assigned. Of the 280 school districts responding, 67.9 percent had a decentralized system, 17.9 percent centralized, and 14.2 percent some combination of the two.

Similarly a decentralized/centralized scale for equipment purchasing was developed from questionnaire responses. If the central administration was responsible for equipment purchasing, a score of 1 was assigned. If each school was responsible for its own VTR purchases, a score of 3 was assigned, and again, a score of 2 was assigned if both arrangements were used. Of the 269 responses, only 5.6 percent of the schools purchased their own equipment, 91.1 percent had equipment purchased for them by the administration, and 3.3 percent used both methods.

Two additional variables were also added to the organizational characteristics in an attempt to measure the emphasis given to audiovisual equipment and programs by the school district. The first was simply the size of the audiovisual staff of the school system, and the second was the number of audiovisual staff members per 100 teachers.[9] Total AV staff size was selected as a measure of the district's total audiovisual emphasis while AV staff per 100 teachers attempted to measure relative emphasis. Total staff size varied from 0 to 112 with a mean of 2.6 and standard deviation of 8.3. Staff members per 100 teachers varied from 0 to 5 with a mean of .27 and standard deviation of .51.

Five of the variables included in the organizational environment for the process innovation were also included in the product innovation model: IGR from the federal government, IGR from the state government, per student expenditure, per capita city revenue, and the city reformism score. In addition, three measures of specific slack financial resources were included. Since VTRs are normally purchased from capital accounts rather than yearly expenditures, a new variable, total capital outlay, replaces total school district expenditures. In addition, two other variables were computed to determine emphasis by the school district on expenditures for capital items—per student capital outlay and capital expenditures as a percentage of total expenditures. Caution must be used in interpreting the results, however, as the bulk of the capital outlay is for new construction. Of the total capital outlay in all school districts, only 20 percent is for equipment.[10]

Variables representing the community environment and demand were unchanged. The specific variables used to operationally define these two areas are the same nine variables included in the school process model.

Table 3-5 shows the zero order relationships between the independent variables in the model and the average number of videotape recorders per secondary school. None of the relationships were significant at the .01 level. It thus appears that the school product model may be very similar to the housing product model—that is, influences outside the model appear to determine VTR use.

To check this possibility with more assurance, a series of partials were computed to more accurately test the model. Partials were computed in the same sequence as in earlier models. None of the relationships were significant. Thus a quantitative model for the adoption of videotape recorders in secondary school is a blank page. None of the selected variables showed any strong relationship with the innovation.

Did the major professional association give much play to videotape recorders? As with the process innovation, *Today's Education* was examined for articles concerning videotape recorders. Figure 3-4 shows the percentage of articles devoted to the use of videotape recorders as an aid to teaching from 1964 through 1973. Professional association interest in videotape recorders came much later than interest in individualized instruction. There were no articles relative to the product innovation from 1964 through 1969. In 1970, seven articles appeared followed by one in 1971 and one in 1973. It thus appears that professional interest in VTRs is a late development. Perhaps the lack of relationships noted in the quantitative model is indicative of the "newness" of the innovation.

Qualitative Analysis

Three school districts were visited in an attempt to explain VTR use. Free City again served as a test site rather than as a deviant case. The Indian Head School District served as an example of a district with very few videotape recorders while the Sunset School District in Tumbleweed had higher than expected adoption.

Table 3-5

Zero Order Relationships Between School District Product Independent Variables and Average Number of Videotape Recorders Per Secondary School

Variable	r
Community Environment	
Liberalism	.067
SES	−.055
Suburb	.031
Ethnic/Ghetto	.046
Size	−.045
Population Increase	−.014
Group Quarters	−.037
Demand	
Percentage HS Going to College	−.055
Percentage Dropout	−.118*
Organizational Environment	
IGR from Federal Government	−.012
IGR from State Government	−.049
Per Student School Expenditure	.009
City per Capita General Revenue	−.046
Total Capital Outlay for Schools	−.071
Per Student Capital Outlay	−.050
Capital Expenditure as Percent of Total	−.061
City Reformism	−.036
Organizational Characteristics	
School Board Reformism	−.076
Total Secondary Teachers	−.031
Percentage Teachers without Degree	−.005
Percentage Teachers with M.A. or better	−.060
Centralized Need	.061
Centralized Purchasing	−.027
Size of Audiovisual Staff	−.004
AV Staff per 100 Teachers	.038

*Significant at the .05 level.

In reality, there are two stages to the application of videotape recorders as an aid to instruction in the secondary schools. The first is the acquisition of the older half-inch, reel-to-reel tape system. It's application varies from recording student-teacher sessions to taping athletic meets or practice sessions for immediate playback and analysis. The second stage of VTR development was the introduction of videocassette equipment.

The degree of utilization of this innovative audiovisual equipment varies from school to school depending on the approaches taken by individual teachers

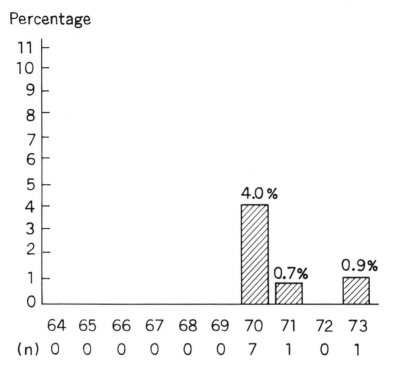

Figure 3-4. Percentage of *Today's Education* Articles Devoted to the Use of Videotape Recorders as an Aid to Teaching (1964-1973)

and staff and the quality of the audiovisual department within the school. However, most secondary schools have at least one videotape recorder, with preference given to the Sony port-a-pac portable variety.

Manufacturers and certain educators point out with enthusiasm the varied applications for VTR equipment. Rather than the entire class congregating around one table as the biology instructor attempts to display the procedure of dissecting a frog, VTR equipment allows the camera to be focused on the specimen as the class focuses its attention on the television monitor overhead. The tape can either be saved for the next class or erased and used for some other purpose. In speech or dramatic reading sessions, videotapes enable the teacher to constructively point out elementary flaws such as gestures and eye contact while the student can observe his or her performance. Certainly this is the case in the wide application of VTRs for recording student teachers in their first attempts as educators. The video recordings enable the new teacher to see the difficulties in reaching his first pupils. There are also special applications for VTR equipment such as recording field trips and interviewing city officials. While VTRs offer some special advantages, there are really not many occasions when a teacher desires the special attractions offered by the reel-to-reel equipment. Thus it is not surprising that the mean number of videotape recorders per school was less than 2 (1.8). In those cases where VTR use was high, for example eighty-five VTRs per school in one system, there were special circumstances. One school district responding to the questionnaire noted:

> We have just moved into a new 22 million dollar high school which includes grades 9–12. The school does not have the complete TV facilities we want. We will add each year. Presently there is a complete TV studio, manned by a TV technician obtained from a (metropolitan) TV station, for producing and "duping" our own tapes and programs. The building is wired for closed circuit TV in all areas, but only ten areas can pick up "off-line" TV as well as "on-line" TV programs this year. In addition there are ten mobile units.
>
> There is a Dial Access Retrieval system, with a total of 34 stations capable of receiving programs at any one time. Four carrels in the IMC are being rewired at this time to be used for videocassette only. We are merging into the system bit by bit and it will not be fully operational until February 1, 1975. Additional equipment exists in the district, but is used by federal projects or elementary schools.

Obviously, not all secondary schools have the resources for such applications and are limited to the basic functions provided by VTR equipment. For the most part, VTRs in secondary schools find themselves stored in the audio-visual closets along with the 16mm projectors, the slide and overhead projectors, tape recorders, and record players to be used only on special occasions and rarely in everyday instruction. For all practical purposes, the VTR may be considered an amenity product, which though nice to have, is certainly not a must, even for the most progressive schools.

Free City. In Free City, VTR use is somewhat limited to the basic applications. The director of instructional materials for the Free City school district noted that all of the fifteen high schools have at least one VTR. Although the instructional resource center sets certain guidelines for the secondary schools (e.g., a minimum of one 16mm projector per six teachers), the acquisition of audiovisual equipment is a decision made by each school and is funded out of the budget for that school. The center handles the actual purchasing of AV equipment and is thus able to assure standardization and guarantee the accessibility of service centers. Aside from the center's standardization activities, schools remain autonomous in deciding what they need and how they intend to use it. In special cases where a request for equipment would require additional funds above and beyond the school's budget, the IR Center must review the request and make a recommendation to the district administration. For example, should a secondary school request the purchase of ten VTR units because they wanted to offer a broadcasting and journalism course, the center would review the request for additional funds for the equipment. "In such a case," he adds, "I can see where it might be justified, but I believe we have reached the plateau on the acquisition of VTR equipment."

The older-type VTR equipment is limited in its application. To progress beyond such applications usually means advancing to the second stage of the innovation which is the acquisition of videocassette equipment. Videocassette recorders offer the additional possibilities of creating a cassette library—allowing for the transfer of slide and sound presentations as well as 16mm films onto the cassette tapes in addition to the recording of television broadcasts and local productions. As the proponents of this product argue, cassettes could ultimately replace 16mm film libraries, as well as slide projectors and trays, eventually becoming the mainstay of all AV departments.

When the director was questioned concerning the possibilities of cassette application within his jurisdiction, the obstacles facing the innovation became the topic of discussion. As the director noted,

> I can't think of a case when a teacher who tapes a classroom production would want to keep it on permanent record. The equipment we have now is suited for those cases when a temporary recording is desired. Cassette proponents argue that films and broadcasts can be recorded for a permanent cassette library. There is the one simple problem, however, of copyright laws forbidding such plagiarism. I'm sure you're aware of (Suburban) High School's wide use of VTR cassettes, but it's no secret they're stealing from others. I'm sorry, but I'm in a position where I can't advocate an illegal activity. Until the copyright issue is settled, I'm not about to encourage schools to use VTR cassettes for taping television broadcasts. As for obtaining permission to put a film on tape—are you aware of how much a copying fee can run for one film? We have over 8,000 16mm films in our own library and there are over 85,000 films available to teachers or schools who wish to rent them for a minimum fee. Why should we switch to this so-called innovation when we already have the equipment and films available? Personally, I think the screen size flexibility of 16mm shows has a distinct advantage over a television receiver.

It was further noted by the director that the Free City school system possessed a closed-circuit television system that provides point-to-point transmission from the central studio in the administration building. All secondary schools were wired to this closed-circuit system. This was an additional reason for his lack of enthusiasm for the videotape cassette application on a wide scale within the district:

It is far easier to obtain copying privileges on copyright material when the owner can be assured that it will not be misused. If a school or class wishes to view a delayed broadcast or program, we can assure the copyright holder that we will control the taping and limit the viewing audience to those within our closed-circuit system. It's not as if copies will be sent out to each school. A request need only be made and we at the center will tape the show and broadcast it at the requested time on the closed circuit television system.

It certainly would be unfair to categorize the IR director as a resistor to innovation. Having obtained a B.A. in Physics, an M.S. in Administration, and a Ph.D. in Curriculum from the University of Chicago, the director had, in the past eleven years, channeled his energy into creating a resourceful audiovisual and instructional resource center. The facilities possessed by the school district coupled with the obstacles remaining with the innovation itself, essentially explain the absence of a wide application of videotape cassette units within the Free City school district.

Indian Head. The case of VTR use in Indian Head school district is considerably different from that of Free City, if only for the fact that this district was somewhat lagging in the acquisition of videotape recorders. As was the case in Free City, the centralized media services department set standards and handled the purchasing of equipment for the two secondary schools in the district. There, however, the similarity ended. There was a distinct difference in professional attitude between the two administrative heads of the media services centers. While the administrator of Free City's audiovisual materials displayed an obvious familiarity with the innovation and was able to justify his opposition to its wide adoption by the fact that he had weighed carefully both sides' arguments on the educational product, Indian Head's administrator of instructional materials did not appear to be knowledgeable of the innovation's applications nor of the arguments for or against its adoption. As far as she was concerned, a school's audiovisual needs were totally met by the "Big Five": (1) 16mm projector, (2) 35mm filmstrip, (3) the reel-to-reel tape recorder, (4) the overhead projector, and (5) the record player. The cassette tape recorders had not yet become part of the center's minimum standard. The past performance of the AV center had been relatively noninnovative; a fact that might explain the reticence on the part of the administration to advocate the use of new equipment. On two occasions in the past (with the use of federal money), the center purchased equipment for the schools that became obsolete in a matter of years either because of irreplaceable parts breaking down or simply because of poor equipment. In the latter case, it was the purchase of two Ampex VTR units which became totally inoperative. As it became quite clear that acquisition of VTR units could not be credited to the media center, a visit was made to one of the two high schools in the district.

Of the three VTR units possessed by the secondary schools in Indian Head, two were used by Northern High School. Northern is a relatively new high school and boasts a student population of about 2,300. Although two VTR's is not exceptional for such a large student body, it is an accomplishment considering the attitude found in the media center and the "austere" budget of the Indian Head school system. The reason behind the acquisition of one of those VTR units was explained by Northern's librarian. Before being assigned to the library at Northern, she directed seven elementary school libraries. It was through her efforts that Northern had any VTR equipment at all. The librarian's decision to purchase a videotape recorder could not be characterized as any more than a desire to offer additional audiovisual aids. The technology had advanced beyond the earlier and imperfect models, and the only problem in her mind was the securing of funds for the purchase of equipment. In this particular case, money was secured by popcorn and candy sales within one of the elementary schools in addition to the library fine money she was allowed to keep for audiovisual equipment. When the elementary school was closed in a reorganization move by the district, the librarian took the VTR unit as well as other audiovisual equipment with her to the new assignment at the high school.

Most school districts provide a coordinator of audiovisual equipment who regulates the use and keeps inventory of AV material. In Indian Head the librarian usually has this responsibility. In Free City, one teacher per school is given a half load of teaching responsibilities with the other half being reserved solely for instructional-materials coordination. Though minimum standards are set by the Indian Head central administration (for example, so many 16mm projectors per number of teachers), it appears that most schools are autonomous in deciding their particular AV needs.

Funding AV material can follow a number of courses. As most school districts today allot so much money per student to each school, an individual school has both operating and equipment budgets from which it can draw funds. As Indian Head is a comparatively poor school district, it was not surprising that AV equipment acquisition ranks low in priority. Certainly this was the attitude of the administrative center for media services. Concern for minority-oriented films that had been lacking ranked considerably higher than advocating the use of videotape recorders. Because of the unusual situation in Indian Head, an unorthodox administrator was required to provide the motivating force in the progressive application of audiovisual equipment. Her attitude was that "a wheel that squeaks gets the most grease." For example, she was responsible for convincing departments in her school to pool their allotment of federal grant money so that an additional 16mm projector could be purchased. If money couldn't be obtained through a Title III or a National Defense Education Act (NDEA) Grant, or from school funds, she resorted to money-making sales and projects to purchase needed equipment.

In Indian Head, it was difficult to isolate the decision-making process of those responsible for VTR acquisition. That is to say, VTR units are looked upon by AV coordinators as simply equipment that serves a specific function, and belong with the other projectors, screens, maps, and tapes within the school. It appears that only when the application of VTR units offers an innovative alternative, such as building a cassette library, or transmission over closed-circuit television, are they revolutionary enough to cause an innovation adoption decision. Indeed, this was the case for Indian Head and certainly for the librarian who noted:

> VTRs aren't the only new thing available. I've pushed for and gotten
> microfiche, 3M copying machines and a number of small cassette
> tape recorders.

VTRs, she adds, are largely used by the athletic department as well as for student teaching and speech classes. She also noted that:

> Teachers don't have time. An AV head has to be there, listening to their
> problems and suggesting possible avenues of pursuit with library-AV
> equipment. That's their job. An AV head has to give new ideas.
> Teachers and kids don't read lists of what is available to them.

One might well conclude that Indian Head secondary schools are no less innovative than most in the area of AV equipment. Lacking a strong central media center, individual personalities play a more important role in determining the acquisition of AV equipment, particularly videotape recorders.

Sunset School District (Tumbleweed). The administration of secondary schools in the city of Tumbleweed is somewhat unique. The state in which Tumbleweed is located opposes separate administrations for elementary and secondary schools, but, because the twelve secondary schools in the Sunset district are so isolated from one another, the district has been allowed to maintain its independence from the local elementary school district. Although the Sunset district extends across the county, it nevertheless is a city school district separate from the county's. In addition to the twelve secondary schools, the Sunset school district administers an adult school and four other special schools. The student population of Sunset's high schools is about 18,000. Compared to Indian Head, the district is relatively wealthy. Of fifteen school districts of comparable size within the state, Sunset ranked second in funds allocated per student. This, however, is not to say that district wealth explains the high number (four) of VTRs per school, though indeed it is one of the factors.

Because of the separate administration accorded the Sunset high schools, the department of instructional materials was able to concentrate strictly on high school needs. With the absence of responsibility for elementary material, the department concentrates on more sophisticated avenues of instructional aids. The director of instructional materials appeared to be less a supervisory administrator, as found in the other school districts, and more an innovator or materials specialist. His doctoral dissertation lent itself to an explanation for the advanced applications of videocassette recorders in Sunset high schools. His dissertation concerned the application of instructional television in the state's secondary schools. Prior to his three years as director of instructional materials at Sunset, he had been assistant principal for curriculum at a district high school and a curriculum director for four years in another school district. The enthusiasm he had for applications of technology toward instruction were not lost in his assignment in Tumbleweed.

A second factor apparently stimulated VTR adoption—the installation of cable TV in all of the secondary schools about six years ago. Although the director noted that some schools had done a haphazard job in installing the CATV, nevertheless, they all had it. Before examining the actual decision-making process in the adoption of videotape cassettes, it is best to recall briefly the environment in which the decision was made. Because of the separate administration accorded secondary schools, the instructional materials department was able to focus all its attention on instructional resources for grades 9-12. This, coupled with the relative wealth of the district and the fact that cable TV had been provided to the district, appeared to be motivating forces for the professional and energetic director of the instructional materials department who was already oriented towards innovative applications in instruction.

As the director noted, "it is somewhat unique to find twelve high schools in a district so geographically far apart in a county the size of the state of Massachusetts." It was his opinion that this was one of the major functions behind the wide application of VTR units in the district. A few years ago, he recalled, the district had to make a decision concerning the application of instructional television within the schools:

> We had to decide whether we wanted a central lab and studio, lo-
> cated in the administration offices, that would transmit district-wide
> or whether each individual school should have its own studio.

Based on his previous experience and study, the director believed that a great deal more money was required in the central distribution of television than by locating studios in each of the individual schools. The district thus opted for the lower cost alternative—currently ten of the twelve schools have a permanent TV center while the remaining two have portable facilities. Therefore, in addition to having access to CATV, all twelve schools have the capability of making their own in-house broadcasts over closed-circuit television. One will note at this point that all television sets serve as receivers for VTR players, and consequently, Sunset secondary schools possessed a great deal of the necessary equipment for videocassette application prior to the VTR pilot program initiated in 1974.

Rather than establishing its own 16mm film library, the Sunset secondary school district had historically rented its films from the county. The films are delivered by truck at a rental cost of $1.70 per day. Because of the geographic distance of the schools and the limited number of prints per film, complications have arisen over delayed deliveries, unavailability of film, and in the opinion of the director, "the substance and quality of the films." Consequently, the district's instructional television (ITV) steering committee recommended that a pilot program utilizing cassette videotapes be initiated.

The pilot program was, in essence, the child of the director. The purpose of the program was to eliminate the complications found in the county film rental system by allowing each school to build its own videocassette library of films. The first year of the program saw 134 cassette tapes in the social studies area established in cassette libraries in seven of the twelve schools. Only seven of the schools initially participated in the pilot program as only seven had videocassette tape recorders and players at the beginning. Soon the remaining five schools will also have the necessary cassette units. As all of the schools are wired for closed-circuit television, the cassette players remain in the studio, and individual classrooms receive the film on the TV set in the room.

How did the Sunset district overcome the copyright barriers in obtaining the 134 tapes? After the pilot program received the recommendation of the ITV steering committee, the director leased 134 films from Encyclopedia Britannica and BFA, a subsidiary of CBS. A contract was signed with Encyclopedia Britannica that allowed Sunset to make seven copies of each of the ninety-one films at a cost of $125 for each school, or a total of $875. BFA allowed duplication of its forty-three films at a cost of 10 percent of the price of purchase of the film. As these arrangements only covered the "right" to duplicate the film, the Sunset schools were also faced with the cost of the actual duplication. As the director recalled with a detectable note of satisfaction, the Sunset school district was a member of a regional occupation center for the county which offered TV production as one of its satellite programs. Inasmuch as the center had the duplicating equipment, the cost of reproduction was limited to the price of a blank cassette. Considering that the entire district payed over $36,000 to the county in rental fees for films not of the caliber obtained from the two private educational firms, the director considers the application of videocassette recorders a worthwhile venture.

As in the other school districts studied, audiovisual costs are borne by each individual school within the Sunset district. In that the schools are autonomous in their decisions concerning where and how they use their funds, one might suspect that a difficult coordination problem existed in putting together the pilot program. Certainly the formation of the ITV steering committee gives credence to this belief. It would be difficult to understand how secondary schools within a district could implement such technology without the encouragement and coordination of the administration. The director of instructional materials at Sunset was indeed a proponent of the innovation and laid the groundwork before advocating such an approach. Having visited the Granite school district in Salt Lake City where the application of videotape cassettes in education is extremely high, the director had seen the most advanced applications of videocassette equipment. Salt Lake City, he noted, administered seventy-three schools (K-12), and all were actively applying videocassette technology in instruction. Unlike Sunset, none of the schools were wired for closed-circuit television, thus making all the video players rolling stock instead of stationary. Of the thirteen secondary schools, more than one third had over 500 titles in each cassette library. It became clear to the director that if Salt Lake City could apply videocassettes on such a wide scale, he should have little trouble applying the technique to only twelve schools.

While videocassette recorders retail for $1695-$1800, through competitive bidding Sunset was able to obtain them at a cost of $1,264 per unit, and similarly, to obtain videocassette players at $960 when the list price was quoted as $1,200. The cost, therefore, was not prohibitive when one considers that the Sunset secondary schools receive $10 ADA (Average Daily Attendance) for capital outlay, $30 ADA for instructional supplies, and $8 ADA for maintenance and repair. A school with a student population of 2,000, for example, would have $60,000 to spend at its own discretion. As the director stated, "They can sink it all into paper, supplies, etc., or they can purchase VTR equipment and cassette titles—it's up to them."

Despite the relative success of the Sunset schools with videocassette recorders, the director notes that they are still faced with a number of problems:

> We're still on the pilot program because we're just not ready to go one way or the other with videocassettes. My superior wants a decision by Fall, '75 as to whether we're going to pull out of the county film rental system. I really don't think we can as it's going to take at least three years to get the transition completed. There is also the question of obtaining further titles at a reasonable rate. I have a drawer full of letters here from companies charging exorbitant fees just for copying rights. And the question still remains to be solved as to whether you can take a broadcast directly off the air and delay it for a convenient showing to the class. Legally you can't, but that doesn't mean people

aren't doing it. Vendors of videocassettes for home use actually advertise the feature of taping your favorite television program. I would love to see how a judge would rule in a case against a school for "illegally" taping a program for educational motives. It would be interesting.

Although the director acknowledges the advantages of closed-circuit television within each school, he points out that there remain complications for videocassette application. Because the teacher has no control over the machine, the advantages usually found with VTRs such as frame freeze, stopping, and rewinding are lost. Furthermore, broadcasts from the studio are limited to one film at a time. The only way to get around these problems would be to establish a rolling stock of a number of videocassette players such as Salt Lake City's. Sunset's director, however, is apprehensive about the possible damage to the expensive equipment should they switch to rolling stock. Inasmuch as last year was the first year of the pilot program, he remains hopeful that these problems will eventually be resolved.

Considering the factors found within the Sunset School District, it was not surprising that VTR application was high. In a district of ample financial resources, unburdened with the considerations normally accorded elementary instructional materials, managed by an administrator enthusiastic about the possibilities technology offers secondary instruction, and forced to find an alternative to its complicated system of obtaining 16mm films, the application of videocassettes found receptive proponents.

Summary

While educators around the country were generally in agreement that videotape equipment constituted an important technological innovation in education, little of a positive nature can be said about the adoption pattern of the innovation.

The case studies suggest that levels of adoption may in part be based on the value placed on the innovation by local directors of instructional materials; thus there is probably a better explanation for the random adoption patterns found in the quantitative analysis. We suggest that the innovation has been "held in abeyance" pending the resolution of the copyright problems. Most secondary school districts have adopted VTRs, but on a limited scale—the athletic department has probably been the major beneficiary.

There is no question that administrators would enthusiastically back the innovation once the copyright problems are solved. At present, however, adoption is largely based on peculiar local circumstances such as those existing in Sunset. Sunset was able to move to a relatively high level of adoption because it did not have a substantial investment in a film library. Free City, on the other hand, was locked into its 16mm system with an inventory of over 8,000 films. Thus there is little incentive for Free City or Indian Head to move beyond the present equipment until copyright problems are resolved.

The VTR portion of the study suggests the random nature of innovation adoption with special problems. A predictable pattern of VTR adoption probably cannot be determined until there is a satisfactory resolution of the present copyright difficulties.

Conclusions

Both the quantitative model testing and the more qualitative studies suggest the independence of the product and process innovations. To test the independence, a correlation coefficient was computed between the product and process innovations. While both innovations appear to be of the "amenity" type, the resulting coefficient of $r = -.02$ indicates a lack of relationship between the two innovations. School districts showing a heavy commitment to individualized instruction are not necessarily committed to VTRs, nor are heavy VTR users committed to individualized instruction. As with the housing innovations, again it appears that we are dealing with two very different kinds of innovations although they both appear to be amenities.

The findings concerning the process innovation support the earlier contentions in Chapter 2—that is, that there is a predictable model for innovation in public organizations. In this particular case, however, the model is for the adoption of an amenity innovation. The model in Chapter 2 emphasized the mechanics of the conversion of need into innovation adoption. In the case of individualized instruction, however, the model emphasizes the conversion of slack and wealth into innovation adoption. Thus while proponents of individualized instruction emphasize that there is little if any cost differentiation between individualized and standard instruction methods within a school district, the findings presented here indicate that it is differences in need and resources between, not within, districts that determine adoption.

In the investigation of the housing product innovations, we suggested that prefab and modular use was random and unpredictable due to lack of incentive for adoption. In the case of the random adoption patterns of VTRs, however, the peculiar legal problems associated with equipment use are believed to be responsible for lack of predictive capability. The innovation is "held in abeyance" pending the outcome of the copyright difficulties. In the end, it may be that procedures such as those followed in the Sunset school district may be necessary for full adoption.

The findings of Chapter 3 thus substantiate, but also modify, the findings of Chapter 2, innovations were classified as operating or nonoperating. In the investigation of innovation adoption in public schools, it was possible to distinguish between need and amenity based on operating innovations.

It is also possible, although adequate empirical evidence does not yet exist, that there are several types of nonoperating innovations. Evidence thus far suggests (but only suggests) that there may be more than one cause for non-operating innovations. In the housing model, nonoperation was caused by lack of incentive while in the school model legal problems appear to be responsible for random adoption patterns. Further study is obviously necessary.

4

Innovation Adoption in Public Libraries

Public libraries posed a special problem for the analysis of innovation adoption in that there were 339 public libraries in the 310 largest American cities. Some cities, then, had two separate library systems, usually a dual system of city and county libraries. This forced us to develop a new unit of analysis—the "library city." Los Angeles, for example, with two libraries required two dependent variables in both the process and product innovation models. Since we hypothesized that city characteristics are determinants of innovation, it was expected that the characteristics of Los Angeles would, in part, determine the level of computer use in both the city and county libraries. Thus the "library city" was developed so that the community environmental characteristics of Los Angeles were associated with both major libraries located in the community. Instead of 310 cases or cities, this analysis covers 339 cases or library cities.

Process Innovation

The hypothesized model for the library process innovation once again corresponds to Figure 1-1. The dependent variable relates to computer use in library management. The dependent variable was operationalized by summing the *yes* responses to eight specific questions concerning library computer use. Data for the library computer-use score were again obtained by mailed questionnaires. Again, a response rate of over 90 percent was achieved (90.6 percent) with 307 libraries responding. The questionnaire sampled automation within five areas of library operations: cataloging, acquisitions, serials, circulation, and the selective dissemination of information. The specific questions are shown in Table 4-1.[1]

Library computer-use scores ranged from 0 to 7 with a mean of 1 and median and mode values of 0. Again, computer use in public libraries was far from a standard practice with some 177, or 57.7 percent, of the 307 libraries responding reporting no computer utilization whatsoever.

The variables shown in Table 4-2 are the independent variables for the library process innovation. In addition to the seven general community variables, four demand variables were expected to lead to computer use in libraries: number of volumes in the library, number of library branches, annual circulation, and the library population service area.[2]

121

Table 4-1
Questions Concerning Library Computer Use

1. In your cataloging function, is a computer used:
   a. for the listing or printing of output products such as catalog cards, book catalogs, labels, or new book lists? (Answer *yes* for any one function.)

2. In the acquisition of library material, is a computer used:
   a. for automatic control of funds that are encumbered and adjusted through successive input records?
   b. for complete production of the book-order form?

3. In the serials function, is a computer used:
   a. to produce current serial lists?
   b. to automatically reorder serials when subscriptions run out?

4. In the circulation function, is a computer used:
   a. to completely handle book charging by inserting book cards and identification badges into a computer terminal?
   b. to provide printed overdue notices ready for mailing?

In the organizational environment, financial resources were represented by the total library expenditures,[3] per capita library expenditures, city per capita total general revenue, and the city ADP score. City reformism was also included. In assessing the important of external professional influences, the Ohio College Library Center (OCLC) was found to be an external resource that might influence library computer use.

OCLC is a nonprofit corporation designed to foster greater cooperation among libraries in Ohio and regional library systems outside Ohio. The Center operates a computer network connected with hundreds of libraries across the country. The objective of the Center is to make library resources throughout the network available to users of the individual libraries and to lower the per unit costs in libraries.

As of 1973, the Center operated a shared cataloging system and produced catalog cards for members as requested. Also in process or recently operational are a serials control system, technical processing system, bibliographic information retrieval system, and a remote catalog access and circulation control system.[4]

Thus a dichotomous external variable indicative of OCLC influence, OCLC membership, was developed. A membership list was furnished by the OCLC.[5]

Two variables were selected to represent organizational characteristics of public libraries: the size of the library staff[6] and a scaled variable representing library organization. If the library was a city library, it was scored 1, a city-country library 2, a county library 3, and a regional library 4. The organizational information was obtained from the library questionnaire.

Table 4-2

Zero Order Relationship Between the Public Library Process Independent Variables and Library Computer-Use Score

Variable	r
Community Environment	
Liberalism	−.003
SES	.069
Suburb	.002
Ethnic/Ghetto	−.019
Size	.224**
Population Increase	−.032
Group Quarters	−.053
Demand	
Number of Library Volumes	.216**
Number of Branch Libraries	.321**
Annual Circulation	.295**
Population of Circulation Area	.306**
Organizational Environment	
Total Library Expenditure	.121*
Per Capita Library Expenditure	−.055
City per Capita General Revenue	.001
City ADP Score	.165*
OCLC Membership	.168**
City Reformism	−.064
Organizational Characteristics	
Size of Library Staff	.333**
Library Organization	.173**

*Significant at the .05 level.
**Significant at the .01 level.

Quantitative Analysis

As with the other innovations studied, the zero order relationships between the dependent variable and each of the independent variables in the model were first computed. Table 4-2 shows these relationships. Of the seven variables capturing the characteristics of the community environment, only size showed a significant and positive relationship with library computer-use score with $r = .22$.

The selected demand variables were all related positively to library computer use. While all four demand variables were size-related, each was selected to measure a specific management problem. Measuring need, however, proved to be somewhat illusory. In the area of library automation, Markuson, et al, distinguish between *genuine* needs and *artificial* needs for automation.[7] Genuine needs are derived from increased volume of activity, need for improved control over operations, need to prevent duplication of effort, and need for improved services to users. Artificial needs are, for example, derived from the availability of a computer the expense of which must be justified to management, or a desire for prestige in library management.[8]

Surprisingly, few of the variables in the organizational environment showed a substantial relationship with the level of library computer use. Two of the slack variables, total library expenditures and city ADP score, showed a slight positive relationship with computer use $r = .12$ and $.16$, respectively. OCLC membership was the only variable in the organizational environment to show a significant relationship with computer-use score at the .01 level ($r = .17$). While only fifteen libraries, or 4.4 percent of the total, were OCLC members, this membership apparently made some difference in library automation. Again, however, the correlation coefficient was not substantial. There was little difference between the coefficient obtained by correlating OCLC membership with the library computer-use score and that obtained by correlating the city ADP score with library computer use.

Both variables illustrating the influence of the characteristics of the organization on library computer use were significantly related to the dependent variable. The most prominent relationship was between another size-related variable, size of the library staff, and computer use with $r = .33$. Library organization, however, was also positively related to computer use ($r = .17$). Over the past years library leaders have given increasing support to larger units for library service. Data compiled in 1962 by the United States Office of Education of the 807 library systems serving populations of 35,000 or more indicated that 32 percent of these libraries were municipal, that is, directly or indirectly part of the municipal government. Another 24 percent were county operated, 19 percent were joint city-county, and 12 percent were regional. Furthermore, the ratio of library by type (e.g., city operated) did not vary significantly between different populations.[9] It was expected that this trend toward regionalism would lend itself to the use of the computer in library management—and apparently it does.

Our data for larger cities, however, did not show the strength of this trend toward regionalism indicated in the earlier Office of Education Survey. Of the 306 responding libraries, 58.2 percent were governed by the city or local school district, 17.3 percent were county libraries, 19.3 percent combined city-county libraries, and 5.4 percent regional. Nevertheless, library organization (the trend toward regionalism) was positively related to computer use. The independence of the organizational structure as a determinant of computer use, however, is still unknown and must be determined through the use of partials.

Partials were thus computed between the organizational characteristics and the library computer-use score controlling for community environment, demand, and the organizational environment. Both size of the library staff and library organization maintained positive relationships with the computer-use score under controls with coefficients of .16 in both cases.

Unlike the housing process model in which the size of the organization was independently related to computer use in a negative direction, here size was related to computer use in a positive direction. Thus larger library organizations tend to be more automated than smaller ones, even with demand characteristics held constant. Organization also appears to be an instrumental determinant of computer utilization. The more "regional," or less local, the library, the more likely it is that the library is automated.

Surprisingly, the variables selected as representative of the organizational environment did not contribute directly or indirectly to the library computer-use score. None of the relationships were significant. Thus the slack resources so important in the housing process model make little difference in the library computer-use score. Even OCLC membership loses its importance under control.

Nor do the variables of the organizational environment show any independent relationship with the organizational characteristics. City per capita general revenue showed a slight independent relationship with the size of the library staff (r = .15) indicating that, other things being equal, there is a slight tendency for cities with high per person revenue levels to devote some of their resource capability toward increasing the size of the library staff. This relationship was slight, however, and not significant at the .01 level.

What has been the attitude of the major professional association concerning computer use? To gauge this emphasis, the American Library Association (ALA) monthly publication was examined from 1964 through 1973. From 1964 through 1969, this publication was entitled the *American Library Association Bulletin*. In January, 1970, the title was changed to *American Libraries*. Figure 4-1 shows the percent of articles in these two publications devoted to the use of computers in library management from 1964 through 1973. Interest in computers has been constant, if uneven, with at least one article about computer use appearing every year between 1964 and 1972. Emphasis appeared to peak in 1967 with 8.9 percent of all articles in the *Bulletin* concerning computers in some way. Interest then decreased gradually through 1971, increased somewhat in 1972, and dropped to zero in 1973. In general, however, as Figure 4-1 shows, there was a continuing interest in computer applications by the American Library Association.

Since the variables of the organizational environment make no contribution to computer use, either directly or independently, they were eliminated from further consideration. The next task was to examine the relationship between demand and automation. Does such a relationship exist, or is it—as Markuson suggests—that artificial needs, at least in part, are responsible for library

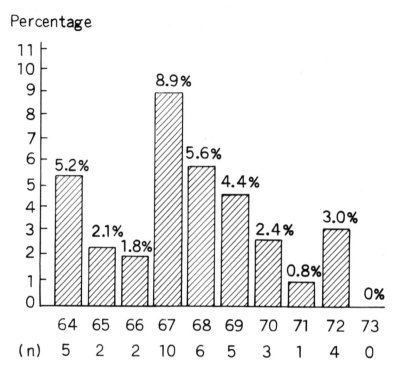

Figure 4-1. Percentage of Articles in the *American Library Association Bulletin* and in *American Libraries* Devoted to the Use of Computers in Library Management (1964-1973)

automation? To test the relationship between need and computer use, partials were computed between demand and the library computer-use score while controlling for the community environment and the organizational characteristics. It appears that Markuson may be correct. We did not find any independent relationship between the selected demand variables and the library computer-use score. Demand then—in terms of library size, decentralization, user demand, and library service population—does not independently influence the level of automation in library operations.

Perhaps the influence of demand is indirect. To test this possibility, partials were computed between demand and the organizational characteristics controlling for community environment. Table 4-3 shows the results of these computations. It now appears that demand is an influential determinant of automation—but an indirect determinant. All four variables showed a strong relationship with the size of the organization, irrespective of size and the other characteristics of the community. And yet demand was not strongly related

Table 4-3
Relationship Between Demand and Organizational Characteristics Controlling for Community Environment

Variable	Size of Library Staff (r)	Library Organization (r)
Number of Library Volumes	.644**	.042
Number of Library Branches	.478**	.198**
Annual Circulation	.776**	.093
Population of Circulation Area	.744**	.023

**Significant at the .01 level.

to the type of library organization. Only the relationship between the number of library branches and library organization was significant at the .01 level under conditions of control. Even this relationship is not causal. A large number of branch libraries is merely indicative of a county or regional library system.

Just as there was no independent relationship between the demand characteristics and library computer use, the community environment shows no independent relationship with the dependent variable. Partials were computed between the community environment variables and the computer-use score controlling for demand and the organizational characteristics. None of the coefficients were significant.

Apparently four variables in the community environment do affect the library computer-use score, but indirectly. As is shown in Table 4-4, size was positively and substantially related to all four of the demand variables while ethnic/ghetto was independently related to all of the demand variables except

Table 4-4
Relationship Between Demand and Community Environment Variables Controlling for Remaining Community Environment Variables

Variable	Volumes	Branches	Circulation	Population
Liberalism	.115*	.093	.125*	.071
SES	-.195**	-.022	-.012	-.131*
Suburb	-.041	-.045	-.060	-.079
Ethnic/Ghetto	.427**	.106	.220**	.328**
Size	.888**	.728**	.802**	.794**
Population Increase	-.026	-.028	-.034	-.005
Group Quarters	.000	-.028	-.049	.013

*Significant at the .05 level.
**Significant at the .01 level.

number of branches. Demand then is unquestionably a product of size and the socioeconomic characteristics associated with ethnic/ghetto. Interesting also was the significant negative relationship between SES and number of library volumes. Regardless of size and the other community characteristics, cities with low socioeconomic levels are more likely to have as large and complete a library as wealthier cities. While not particularly related to computer use, this relationship is nevertheless interesting. In terms of number of volumes, low SES cities seem to have an advantage over wealthier cities.

While the size of the organization was related to the number of library volumes which in turn was partially determined by the socioeconomic status of the city, there was no independent relationship between SES and size of the library staff. Table 4-5 shows the relationships between the characteristics of the community environment and the organizational characteristics controlling for demand. Only two relationships of substance were noted. Ethnic/ghetto was negatively related to the library organization scale ($r = -.17$) and suburb was negatively related to the library organization scale ($r = -.17$).

Figure 4-2 shows the revised model for the use of the computer in the operation and management of public libraries. There are a number of generalizations that can be made based on the model. The first concerns the relationship between library organization and computer use. The more "regional" the library, the more likely it is that the library has a high computer-use score. And yet it was not possible to identify the characteristics that lead to a sharing or cooperative approach. Of all the variables in the model—seven in the community environment, four in demand, and four theoretically relevant variables indicative of the organizational environment—none were related in any "causal" way to library organization. Only the relationships between suburb and organization and number of branches and organization are significant, but they tell us virtually nothing about

Table 4-5
Relationship Between Community Environment and Organizational Characteristics Controlling for Demand

Variable	Size of Library Staff (r)	Library Organization (r)
Liberalism	−.020	−.153*
SES	−.071	−.084
Suburb	.062	−.165**
Ethnic/Ghetto	−.169**	−.146*
Size	−.090	−.013
Population Increase	−.021	−.059
Group Quarters	−.042	.062

*Significant at the .05 level.
**Significant at the .01 level.

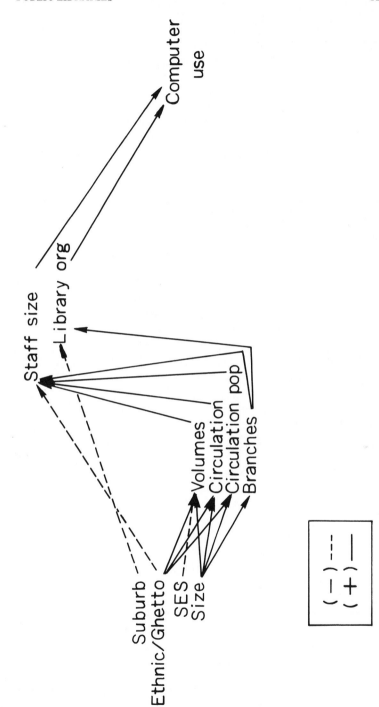

Figure 4-2. Revised Model for the Adoption of Process Innovations in Public Libraries

"causes" of a cooperative approach to library organization. The negative relative relationship between suburb and organization tells us only that the central offices of county and regional libraries are not located in the suburbs. The relationship between number of branches and organization is likewise devoid of theoretical meaning. The more "regional" the library system, the more likely that the system will have a large number of branches. And yet this may, in fact, lead to computer use. While number of branches was not independently related to computer use, it was related through both the organizational characteristics and at the zero order level. The fact that county or regional libraries have a large number of branches—irrespective of service area population, total number of volumes in the system, and the annual circulation—may be the key to the relationship between organization and computer use. It is thus suggested that county and regional libraries tend to automate because of the problems associated with a large number of branches.

Why is staff size positively associated with computer use? The positive relationship between staff size and computer-use score is obviously real as significant positive coefficients were noted for both the zero order correlation and under conditions of control. But why? In the housing model, computer use was negatively related to the number of authority employees, thus suggesting an efficiency model—that is, authorities utilize the computer to provide management information in lieu of higher employee levels associated with manual operations. The school process model, on the other hand, illustrated a case where organizational size was positively related to innovation adoption—thus suggesting amenity adoption.

However, unlike the school process model wherein staff size was negatively related to need, library staff size responds to size and the characteristics of ethnic/ghetto. The response of staff size to demand, even when controlling for size and the other characteristics of the community, is unquestionable. Partials ranged from .48 to .78 between demand and staff size.

Thus while the positive independent relationship between library staff size and computer use suggests an amenity innovation, the positive independent relationship between library organization and computer use suggests an efficiency model. Perhaps Markuson is correct. Perhaps library automation is the product of both genuine and artificial needs.

Another surprising finding was the sterility of the organizational environment in determining library computer use, both directly and indirectly. In other process models, the organizational environment was quite important—specifically those variables representing intergovernmental influences and resource availability. Surprisingly, these variables made very little difference. Weak relationships were noted between resources and computer use and between regional intergovernmental assistance (OCLC membership) and the computer-use score. With the introduction of controls, however, the effect of these variables on computer use (both direct and through the organizational characteristics) disappeared.

Apparently, resources provided by the organizational environment are not significant enough to have much effect on computer use in public library systems.

Qualitative Analysis

The application of computer technology to public libraries was examined in detail in three cities. Free City once again provided the researchers with an initial case study—although Free City's library computer-use score was not 1 1/2 standard deviations from the prediction. The city of Aqueduct provided the high deviant case study and Nouveau County the low.

Free City. The application of computer technology by Free City's public library finds its explanation in the dual city-county status held by the organization. While ADP applications were minimal prior to 1971, the creation of a county-federated library system in that year served as a catalyst for the development of sophisticated computer-managed operations.

In January, 1967, Free City established the central electronics data services department (CEDS) for the centralized management of all city ADP operations. Directives went out to city departments stating that, henceforth, all in-house data-processing tasks would be assumed by CEDS. Inasmuch as the transition of the city's data processing required conversion from a Univac round-hold card system to direct on-line computerization, the city library was instructed to phase out keypunch operations. The three million card file existing at the time required a three-year conversion time for this transition. While all city agencies fell under the jurisdiction of CEDS with respect to data-processing operations, a departmental request for a specific computer program, above and beyond those existing prior to 1967, had to be submitted to a separate city review board for justification. The director of the CEDS noted that the board's criterion for computer justification was cost. Therefore, even if a department decided in favor of adopting innovative applications of the computer in management, implementation of that decision was subject to cost justification by the city's overseeing board. Library administrators were thus to find centralization of ADP operations more a deterrent than an incentive to the adoption of computerized services.

Prior to 1967, Free City public library's data-processing activities were confined to punchcard files of the shelf list, patron registration, invoicing, fund accounting, and budgeting. With their own Univac computer, sorters, and keypunch equipment, the library compiled circulation statistics based on patrons per census tract. ADP operations were primarily directed, however, to the control of library inventory. When the directive concerning centralization was issued in 1967, the library began preparing for the transition. One library administrator offered his recollection of the transition, stating, "Three weeks after the city purchased the IBM 360, they came and pulled out the Univac." The director of central electronic data services disputes this, however, noting that the transition was not so immediate. Inasmuch as the conversion time required was three years, little thought was given to further ADP applications by the library until existing applications were operable again.

In 1970, the library hired, as supervisor of information systems, a "free lance programmer and systems analyst" who previously had worked for the CEDS as programmer for library operations. Normally, CEDS programmers work on a wide variety of tasks for various city departments. In library operations, however, the administrator recalls how he became fascinated with the possibilities of computer applications for the library and insisted on working only with their operations. In his new capacity as supervisor of information systems for the library, he began working on a systems design for book catalog information retrieval and internal distribution. But, as the director of CEDS noted, such a system would never have met board approval as the cost was prohibitive (over $100,000 per year).

An alternative was provided in 1971 when the state legislature enacted a Library Systems Law that provided financial support for libraries that cooperated in providing area-wide service. In 1972, Free City, in cooperation with eighteen suburban communities, formed the Free county-federated library system, with the Free City public library serving as headquarters. The county-federated library system's board of directors subsequently presented a plan to the state for financing a system-wide computer circulation control program, with operations being handled by the Free City public library. With state financial assistance granted, the library's supervisor of information systems began design and implementation of the circulation program.

While this system-wide circulation control was not in operation at the time of the field study, the initial phase of the program was to begin toward the end of 1975. Standard library cards, which are coded for light-pen reading, will replace the participating libraries own patron identification, and data from library card registrations will be input into a minicomputer located within the main library. The catalog listings of all member libraries are also being entered into the computer. Once the system is in full operation, every library will have access to the entire system's collection, with title, subject, author, number of copies, and location obtained from a terminal located in each library and tied into the central computer. When checking out materials, the code on the library card will be read by a light-pen and will register checkout immediately on the computer. If the patron has a delinquent record, the computer will be programmed to prohibit borrowing privileges. Because of the library's participation in the county-federated library system, it has assumed a "quasi-county" status and therefore has not received CEDS assistance with the internal distribution system. Library functions that are identifiable as functions of the city library are supported by CEDS. But as the CEDS director noted, it is often difficult to determine which is a function of the federated system and which is a function of only the city library.

Aqueduct. The application of computer technology in library management for Aqueduct proved to exceed our computer-use score prediction by 3. The explanation of this deviation rests on a number of reasons, the most important being the professionalism of the city librarian and the newness of the library facility.

In 1963, Aqueduct signed a five-year contract with the county library system wherein it was agreed that the county would continue to manage city library facilities until 1968, whereupon Aqueduct was to establish its own independent library system. According to the city librarian, there were three reasons for this move from county jurisdiction to city jurisdiction. The first was to provide a more diverse collection for local patrons as well as to allow for the immediate availability of that collection. Second, Aqueduct, in planning for the construction of a new civic center complex, wished to include library facilities as a resource for the city. Finally, it was the wish of the Aqueduct city government to assume local control over the fiscal management of library services.

On April 3, 1967, the city librarian was hired who began immediately to facilitate the gradual transition from a county to a city-operated system. Five library branches, in addition to the main library, had to be stocked with a minimum of 83,000 volumes to serve a population of well over 100,000. Financial assistance for this matter was immediately forthcoming. On April 15, 1967, a $2.4 million bond issue was passed for funding book purchases, construction of two new facilities, and physical improvements on two others. The city librarian was faced not only with the responsibility of directing a library system, but with the actual establishment of it as well. In addition to all the other problems, he faced the task of cataloging the thousands of volumes being acquired. It was in this area, he decided, that computer applications showed the most promise.

Prior to being retained by Aqueduct, the city librarian was director of technical services for another library system. In this position he became "convinced that computerization was going to be the trend." Having read much of the literature on the state of the art, he sought out the city's data-processing head. Together they began looking into the possibilities for on-line cataloging of the library's volumes. As he noted:

A primary reason for computerization is not to cut staff, but to release the staff for personal services. A library is supposed to be a place where a person will be assisted in obtaining information. They're certainly not going to get that personal attention if the majority of the staff is tied up cataloging books.

It is not surprising, therefore, that upon being named Aqueduct's city librarian, this administrator decided to computerize book cataloging. He persuaded the "powers that be" that computer cataloging was a practical step for a number of reasons, the most important ones being:

1. It would not require a large staff.
2. Inasmuch as the new main library had limited room, maximum space utilization was critical. Card catalogues would require a minimum of 2,000 square feet for the files alone, whereas computer-processed catalogs would be printed in book form requiring a minimum of shelf space.
3. Because of the number of branch libraries, wide circulation of "control information" was important. Computer-processed book catalogs would allow total access of the collection to every branch.

Although the decision to computerize was sound, the difficulties encountered in actually implementing the innovation were enough to discourage anyone less committed than the city librarian. While the city had its own computer facilities at the time, this administrator found a lack of "competence and in-house expertise" on the part of data-processing personnel. As he recounted:

The incapabilities of our own in-house system forced me to look to a professional vendor. I wanted a full output, as staffing problems would be less, but all our efforts came to grief. We signed with a prime vendor, but before we could get started, his company was bought out by Xerox. Now remember, this is November, 1967. We had started cataloging already and were buying books. We would be opening our doors in April, 1968. I went back to the City ADP Center and explained what I wanted. Their response was, "Sure, easy," a common fallacy of data processors who think there is nothing they can't handle with minimal planning. In January, 1968, the head of data processing up and quit. The programs were incomplete and the data was incorrect. She had all the programs in her head and had written nothing down. . . . I realized we had no system and began to look around again for a vendor that would at least do the systems design. Well I found one, but it wasn't approved by the city. It happens that the Chairman of the Board of another computer management firm was a friend of the mayor, so the young fledgling company that I wanted was shot down. The company which had pull in the mayor's office was given the task, but they weren't capable of running it. They looked at it as a simple accounting job. After seeing their first printout we had to have our typists redo the entire catalog.

This lack of initial success, however, did not discourage the city librarian.

Rather, it only convinced him that the problem was not with the concept of computerization but with the systems analysts who were limited in their ability to convert specific needs into workable programs. Coupled with the administrative difficulties in obtaining an effective systems design was the fact that the head of the library's technical services division at this time opposed computerization and sought a return to card catalogs. Most irritating to the director, however, was the lack of cooperation on the part of libraries nationwide that refused to share, sell, or lease their own systems design for computerization of catalogs. Additionally frustrating was the absence of communication among library administrators, despite their common goals. The administrator recounted how he

> talked to other libraries about using their system design but was forced
> to develop my own. It was costly because of the time and manpower
> used on a trial and error method. There is absolutely no cooperation
> among libraries in [state]. We've been stalled by 19th century thinking
> in the State Library Association, as well as lack of cooperation nation-
> wide. No one is talking with each other. There is no commonality
> sought, no common system. Where are the basics? Everyone develops
> all types of gobbledygook and no one shares. The cost, because of
> duplication, is absolutely ridiculous.

Frustrated, therefore, in his attempts to secure from the outside a proven systems design, the Aqueduct city librarian was forced to work with the city's systems analyst to develop an in-house program for cataloging. For four years they worked together, not simply on a cataloging system, but on a data base as well. The director of technical services, who was opposed to the direction being taken, was replaced by one who exhibited the same enthusiasm as the city librarian. Although the city had relative success in meeting the library specifications, it soon became apparent that a full commitment to ADP applications on the part of the city was lacking. As the current director of technical services recounted:

> Two years ago, the city reached a decision that it would be more
> efficient to secure a private vendor than to build up their own ADP
> facilities. They began phasing out their own operations and hired a
> computer management firm for the entire city's ADP applications.
> A decision had to be made on how to handle the expected develop-
> ment. Do you bring on more staff and equipment to meet the growing
> needs or contract with a vendor? They opted for the latter.

The contracted firm installed a CRT (cathode-ray tube) terminal in the library cataloging area that was tied into a minicomputer located in city hall.

Once a month, the data from the minicomputer is dumped into the main computer. Prior to the installation of the terminal, all catalog entries were keypunched, allowing for about sixty entries a day. With the terminal, the number of on-line entries per day progressed to 115, while the printout provided by the firm proved easier to read by the public.

While the city librarian acknowledges the added features provided by the vendor, he regrets the city's decision to abandon its in-house operations, in spite of the difficulties experienced:

> They mistakenly believed that a vendor would be cheaper, but did not allow for a projection of the future when ADP would increase tenfold.

Nevertheless, the Aqueduct public library continues in its development of data-processing objectives. The city librarian, in retrospect, believes that one of his greatest mistakes was that he started computerization at the wrong end, i.e., with circulation. He adds that, had they started with acquisition, they would have had a data base from which they could operate. Inasmuch as the book-catalog system is fairly close to meeting the desired specifications, the library plans to add a periodicals catalog in the very near future. They are also looking at the possibilities of a fully automated circulation system in addition to computerization of inventory control and acquisition.

The accomplishments of Aqueduct's public library in the ADP applications are certainly considerable, particularly when one considers the difficulties experienced over the seven-year period. It would be difficult to argue that the newness of the entire library system did not play an important role in the adoption of the innovation. The very fact that a conversion from an old traditional system to a new one was not required removed a major obstacle to library computerization. However, had it not been for the commitment and background of the city librarian, there certainly would be reason to question whether this new library would have instituted such a high level of computer use.

Nouveau County. The Nouveau County public library is fighting for its life. As the librarian noted, the "county government is in severe financial straits at the present time and our operations are severely curtailed." She further advised that they "are not planning to automate anything—just planning how we can manage to stay in operation until the crisis has passed."

There are two public libraries headquartered in Nouveau Riche—the Nouveau Riche public library, which is the library for the City of Nouveau Riche, and Nouveau County public library, serving the small communities in Nouveau County. The county library thus does not serve the residents of Nouveau Riche although the main library office is in the county courthouse in Nouveau Riche. The library office merely services the branch libraries by providing central

reference service, program planning, book purchasing, cataloging and services
for the blind and physically handicapped. County library services are provided
for the cities and towns in Nouveau County with populations of less than
25,000. There are currently thirteen branches in the system serving communities ranging in population from 1,100 to 20,000. The Nouveau County public
library is governed by a five-member library board with each of the five county
commissioners of Nouveau County appointing one member. At one time the
library system was much larger than it is today. In 1964, the seven largest
libraries were dropped from the county system, and the assets of each of the
branches were turned over to the seven communities.

The operation of the branch libraries is somewhat unusual. The county
pays for library operations in each one of the communities (the community owns
the actual building), but only for twelve hours per week. If the community
wants more library time (and most do), it must finance increased operating hours
itself—directly. The community does not pay the county for increased hours
but instead hires the librarians on a part-time basis. Thus most of the librarians
work for two employers—the county and the community.

In addition, most communities supplement the rather small county book
budget. Again, they do not pay the county for additional books but purchase
the books themselves. The county central office does not control or account for
these community-purchased books.

Thus the public library in Five Acres, a suburb of Nouveau Riche, has em-
polyees paid by two employers and a stock of books owned by two agencies—
some marked Five Acre public library and some marked Nouveau County public
library.

The present operating budget provided for the county library by the county
commission is less than the operating funds provided by the communities served.
In an effort to save money, the county commission is presently considering
abolishing the Nouveau County public library entirely. This would simply be
done by turning over the assets of each of the branch libraries to the communities
in which they are located and allowing the state to assume the responsibility for
the programs for the blind and physically handicapped.

In essence, then, on paper the Nouveau County public library appeared to be
an excellent candidate for automation. In practice, however, this was not the
case. While the Nouveau County Library system has thirteen branch libraries and
a substantial number of employees, the county library buildings are owned or
leased by the communities in which they are located, most library employees only
work for the county for twelve hours per week, and a large portion of the stock
of books in each branch is owned by the community and not the county. The
data were thus deceiving. While a large number of branches and county organization normally foretell automation, in this instance the peculiar nature of the
organization and operation of the Nouveau County public library clearly explains
the lack of automation.

Summary

The library process model of innovation points up the conflicting nature of innovation adoption. The model appears to indicate that adoption is based both on need and amenity value. The positive independent relationship between staff size and computer use indicates adoption for amenity reasons. As the Aqueduct city librarian noted: "A primary reason for computerization is not to cut staff but to release the staff for personal services." On the other hand, the positive independent relationship between library organization and computer use suggests a need-based innovation.

The case studies, while interesting, do not add much to the model. In Free City the move toward a regional library system obviously accounted for increased automation; but so did the lucky availability of expert help.

In Aqueduct, automation was obviously the result of the new independence of the Aqueduct public library and the immense cataloging task it brought while in Nouveau County, the strange nature of the library organization accounts for the lack of automation in the library system.

Product Innovation

The purchase of a theft-detection system by public libraries was the product innovation investigated. A survey of all of the manufacturers of library theft-detection systems (six manufacturers) revealed that only twenty-seven public libraries in American cities with 1960 populations of 50,000 and above had purchased such systems. This is only 8.2 percent of the libraries under study. The dependent variable, then, was a dichotomous variable—uses/does not use theft-detection system. Information concerning library theft-detection system use was obtained from the manufacturers of theft-detection systems for libraries and was confirmed by responses to the library questionnaire.[10]

Quantitative Analysis

Libraries having a theft-detection system were assigned a code of 1 while libraries without such a system were coded 0. This variable then operationalized the dependent variable for the quantitative analysis.

There were very few changes in the independent variables between the library process and product models. Two of the variables in the organizational environment, OCLC membership and city ADP score, were dropped as they were not theoretically relevant to the use of theft-detection equipment. The only other change in the model was the addition of a fifth demand variable, theft rate. One question on the library questionnaire asked that the library provide an estimate of the total number of books lost per year due to theft. Most libraries couldn't answer the question—176 or 51.9 percent of the responding libraries failed to answer the question. Other libraries found the question confusing. While the question specifically asked for an estimate of the annual theft rate, some libraries gave us the number of checked out, but unreturned, books. Even the libraries responding in the manner requested provided questionable data. The range was from a low of 33 (unbelievable) to a high of 100,000 books lost to theft per year with a mean theft rate of 4,973 books and a standard deviation of 11,511. Although 163 usable responses were obtained (and were used in the model as they were the only data on theft rate available), relying heavily on relationships between theft rate and other variables might be rather careless.

Table 4-6 presents the zero order relationships between the model independent variables and the use of theft-detection systems. No significant relationships are noted. The most sizable correlation coefficient was the $r = -.08$ between per capita library expenditures and theft systems—but even this was not significant at the .05 level.

Table 4-6

Zero Order Relationships Between Public Library Product Independent Variables and Library Adoption of a Theft-Detection System

Variable	r
Community Environment	
Liberalism	-.027
SES	-.007
Suburb	-.002
Ethnic/Ghetto	-.045
Size	.005
Population Increase	-.023
Group Quarters	-.051
Demand	
Number of Library Volumes	.049
Number of Branch Libraries	.019
Annual Circulation	.066
Population of Circulation Area	.019
Theft Rate	.071
Organizational Environment	
Total Library Expenditure	-.001
Per Capita Library Expenditure	-.082
City per Capita General Revenue	.027
City Reformism	.013
Organizational Characteristics	
Size of the Library Staff	.044
Library Organization	-.004

Partials were then computed between the two variables in the organizational environment and theft-detection systems controlling for the community environment, demand, and the organizational environment. No significant relationships were noted. The two variables representing organizational characteristics were thus eliminated from the model.

The four variables representing the organizational environment were also eliminated from the model when no significant relationship was found between any of the variables and the use of theft-detection equipment while controlling for community environment and demand.

Nor were demand characteristics substantially related to theft systems controlling for the community environment. A slight positive relationship between number of volumes and the use of theft-detection equipment (r = .13) and between annual circulation and theft systems (r = .12) was noted, but these relationships again were not significant at the .01 level.

Testing the library product model met with a singular lack of success. A rational model for the adoption of product innovations in public libraries does not appear to exist. Although there was a slight (.05-level) relationship between two demand characteristics and innovation adoption, the relationships were too weak to include in a formal model. Surprisingly (or perhaps it isn't so surprising, considering earlier concerns expressed about the variable), there was no relationship between book loss due to theft and the adoption of a theft-detection system.

Testing the library product model produced results similar to the housing and school product models—that is, there were no results. Thus there is very little that can be said about library adoption of theft-detection systems. The quantitative model tested here found no predictable basis for library adoption of theft systems.

Did the ALA advocate theft-detection systems through the *Bulletin* and *American Libraries* in the same manner as it advocated computer use? Not in the least. During the period 1964-1973 there was not one single article in either publication concerning theft-detection equipment. The only mention of such systems was a series of full-page ads in *American Libraries* by the 3M Company. The ads appeared monthly beginning in April, 1973, and advertised the 3M Tattle Tape detection system. There was apparently no concerted effort by the editors of *American Libraries* to influence library adoption of this innovation.

Qualitative Analysis

The public library systems of Lakeview and Dutch Elm provide examples of cities in which library theft-detection systems had been installed while Nouveau Riche exemplifies a large city in which the public library has not adopted theft-detection equipment.

Dutch Elm. What is it that convinces a library to install an automatic theft-detection system? In the case of the city of Dutch Elm, it was a crushing lack of funds coupled with an unexpected windfall. The combination of the two enabled the Director to justify, without hesitation, the installation of a theft-detection system.

Dutch Elm is broke, and has been for the last few years. The Dutch Elm public library found itself to be one of the first community services to feel the pinch; a pinch that has gotten tighter during each of the past five years. Where the library's operating budget was $400,000 a few years ago, the city now provides minimal operating costs. All money for other operations, such as book and equipment purchasing, must come from some other source, namely direct state aid.

State aid has, by law, provided libraries with an annual contribution of $0.05 per capita, or, in the case of Dutch Elm, about $4,000 per year. However, in 1973 and 1974 state aid was increased to $0.30 per capita by the state legislature. This $20,000 increase was to be a catalyst for the Director's decision to adopt a theft-detection system.

For the past five years, the Dutch Elm public library has not been budgeted for book purchases. It simply had to maintain what it already had. Therefore, any loss by theft or nonreturn was a nonrecoverable loss. The director had, obviously, been aware of theft problems and was familiar with the major theft-detection systems as a neighboring library was one of the first to install such a system (in 1965). At three American Library Association Conventions, she was also exposed to the manufacturers' literature on theft-detection systems. In the past, guards had been stationed at both exits of the Dutch Elm library for theft deterrence. Inasmuch as only $10,000 was allowed for security personnel, guards were employed at the doors only at the busiest times. "It didn't take long," recalled the director, "for everyone to figure out when the guards weren't around."

In 1972, she was overwhelmed by the number of manufacturers' representatives calling on her concerning their theft-detection systems. The "sudden scourge of book theft" was being proclaimed by all libraries. The Dutch Elm public library took inventory yearly, but in 1973 the inventory was aimed at determining just how great book theft actually was. The inventory indicated an annual theft rate of about 2,000 books, with a replacement cost approximating $20,000 to $25,000. The loss was something the city could not and would not replace. It was clear that if theft continued at such a rate, the library would eventually have to close its doors.

The 1973 inventory, together with the absence of funds for book purchasing and the unexpected windfall provided by the legislature's increase in state library aid, provided the conditions that made purchase of a theft-detection system the only logical solution.

Appearing before the library board of trustees, all of whom had been

appointed by the city manager, the director presented the following arguments.
Briefly, they ran as follows:

1. Money for book purchasing had been nonexistent for the past five years.
    Every theft was a nonrecoverable loss.
2. An inventory of 1973 indicated a yearly loss in theft alone of $20,000-
    $25,000.
3. The state-aid allotment for that year had been increased to $25,000, enough
    to handle the full cost of a theft-detection system, making any city funding
    unnecessary.
4. The cost of such a system would equal no more than the cost of replace-
    ment for one year's stolen books alone.
5. The city had been steadily cutting staff. Once the security guard went, so
    did what little deterrence they had against theft.

With no dissent, the Board approved the proposal and committed the library
to the planned purchase of an automatic theft-detection system. The decision to
purchase was firm; it now became a matter of selecting the product. Three systems were considered: Book Mark, Checkpoint, and 3M Tattle Tape. With the
latter two systems, major changes were required of the physical floor plan
ranging from redoing the entire lobby to sealing off a number of doorways and
stairwells. In that the library itself was a fairly new and modern structure built
in 1963, the director was seeking a system compatible with the existing architecture. Book Mark was finally selected as the system that best suited that library's
particular needs. In that architectural compatability was almost of equal concern with effectiveness, the representatives of the library bureau of Sperry
Remington obtained the original plans from the library architects. Beginning in
April, 1974, the installation proceeded in stages until completion in June, 1974.
The only alteration required of the floor plan was widening of doorways.
Although the city budget had cut the staff over the past five years from thirty-
nine to twenty-three, the Director and her staff were able to install the sensitiz-
ing book marks in their spare time without the addition of any personnel.

Despite the obvious need for immediate installation, the librarian related
her concern for the effect the system might have on older people and regular
patrons. The installation was therefore done in stages to familiarize the public
with the system and reduce possible alienation. Such a concern was not un-
common. In speaking with a representative of customer services in the library
bureau of Sperry Remington, we learned that this concern often deterred public
libraries from installing such systems. The Sperry representative noted that his
company and 3M, the largest systems manufacturers, do more business with
colleges than with public libraries because universities are more quick to innovate and are not hesitant about "alienating those students who are ripping off
library material." Public libraries, he points out, are reluctant to use a "gimmick"

or system that would be an affront to the public and an indication that books were being stolen. Libraries don't like to acknowledge that they can't prevent theft under normal procedure. The 3M Tattle Tape and the Sperry Remington Book Mark are more obvious to the human eye as a "Check Point Charlie Station," unlike the Checkpoint System that is discreet and more often used by public libraries. Only recently, he concludes, have public libraries accepted the necessity of using the new innovation with business, consequently, mushrooming as of late.

Lakeview.   Upon visiting the public library in the city of Lakeview, the distinction was again made by the Director between college and public libraries. College libraries, he notes, are more inclined to innovate in the area of circulation control because of their inability to deter theft.

As for his own library, the recognized need for a theft-detection system arose shortly after he became director in September, 1970. One of the responsibilities of the director was the compilation of the annual report to the board of directors, a committee of policy coordinators selected by the school board. Included in the annual report were the estimated totals of material lost through theft and nonreturn. Noting a considerable theft loss for 1970, the director instructed his staff to compile a ten-year composite of theft figures and an estimate of the cost of replacement of stolen books. Neither the director nor his staff were able, or if able, willing, to provide those figures; a protective secretary informed us that the figures had been misplaced or lost with not a single copy of the annual report to be found. Nevertheless, the theft rate was high enough to warrant an immediate solution. Discarding the possibilities of manual security provided by personnel or turnstiles, the director opted for an automatic theft-detection system. Before he went before the board for approval, however, there was the question of which system should be selected.

In mid 1971, very shortly after receiving the ten-year composite on theft loss, the director attended a workshop in a nearby metropolitan center hosted by the manufacturers' representatives of the different theft-detection systems. As far as he was concerned, the decision to purchase was firm; he was now shopping for the product. Looking back on the systems workshop, the director was most impressed by the Checkpoint system. Upon returning to Lakeview, he contacted a sales representative of the firm and asked him to visit the library and make a presentation to the board. Quoting a cost of about $20,000, the representative explained his product, answered questions, and departed.

One board member then questioned the director about other systems. As vice president of a small local college and a member of that college's library planning board as well, this trustee was curious about other systems, in particular, the 3M Tattle Tape system. As the college administrator recalled:

I was at that time serving on the committee that was planning the new library for the college. We had planned from the beginning to use such a [theft-detection] system and it was a matter that had to be researched beforehand so it could be included in the physical planning. I personally played no part in the selection of 3M's Tattle Tape for the college library. I thought I ought to mention it to the director, nevertheless, as it must have had some merit.

Rather than making a commitment at that particular meeting, the director indicated that he would take another look at the 3M system before asking the board for a decision. There is a considerable difference between the Tattle Tape and the Checkpoint systems. The Checkpoint system is programmed to activate an alarm for all marked material passing through its detectors, whether checked out properly or not. It is what is called a bypass system that requires all material to be passed around the detection system and through the hands of library personnel. After walking through the sensors, the patron picks up the material. It might be compared to the security gate now found in airports. The Tattle Tape is, on the other hand, a full circulating system. Material is marked with a magnetic tape that can be deactivated when the book is properly checked out and reactivated when the book is returned. It therefore requires no library personnel at the detection point itself and sounds an alarm only when unchecked books are carried past it. The Sperry Remington Book Mark is a similar full-circulation system.

After calling a number of system-user libraries for their observations and visiting libraries such as the public library in Gary, Indiana, where he could see the system in operation, the director concluded that he "saw the advantages of a full-circulation system like 3M's over the Checkpoint bypass system." The 3M representative, who was asked to make a presentation to the board, "came across quite well." The director recalled how he did not talk down the other systems but only explained the differences between the products. As the cost was about $22,000, or only $2,000 more than Checkpoint, the advantages of a full-circulation system with installation and preparation of 60,000 volumes included, appeared to outweigh the advantages of the bypass system. The Tattle Tape system was accepted and installation was completed in March, 1972.

Nouveau Riche. The Nouveau Riche public library presents an interesting case of a rather large public library system which has not adopted a theft-detection system. There is probably no single reason for nonadoption, but rather a series of events that have served to delay or put off a final decision on the need for theft-detection equipment.

In the first place, library officials cannot yet estimate annual loss due to theft, although they believe that the number of thefts is increasing steadily. In May, 1973, the library director requested that the city provide security checkers for the two exits of the central library. Concern stemmed from reports by service librarians that important books had been stolen—the most popular targets being reference works and out-of-print material. While the theft problem has been recognized in Nouveau Riche, the scope of the problem was unknown and hence there was no accurate way to measure the cost effectiveness of a theft-detection system. Toward this end, the library began a complete inventory of central library resources, paid for, in part, by revenue-sharing funds. The project involved a two-year effort with twenty-one staff members working full-time on the project. The massive effort will also computerize all the holdings of the central library. When the inventory is finally complete, library officials hope to be able to more accurately estimate book loss due to theft. Decision-makers are aware of the three major theft-detection systems and have been visited on several occasions by various vendors. No decision will be made, however, until the inventory in progress is complete and the cost/benefits of a theft detection system can be fully studied.

A second probable reason for late consideration of theft-detection equipment by library officials is the fact that the library has been able to keep the overall book-loss rate, at least the known losses, down. Through the records associated with the computerized checkout system, library circulation officials estimate that the library losses due to nonreturned checkouts approximate 17,000 volumes or about 0.5 percent of the library holdings. While obviously the citizens of Nouveau Riche must be given some credit for returning checked out books, the library has taken a unique step to cut losses.

In 1966, about one year after the city completed construction of the present downtown library, the administration began an overdue messenger service to track down delinquent books. The idea has been so successful over the years that the library now has two overdue messengers who venture out six days a week in two vans, tracking down elusive books all over the county. Once a month a computer printout containing an average of over 1,900 books twelve or more weeks overdue is generated. Armed with this list, the two messengers make an average of 700 house calls per month in an effort to recover the volumes. And they are remarkably successful—locating and recovering an average of 392 books per month.

The chief of circulation services reports that this program recovers at least $40,000 in material every year. It thus appears that this service is responsible for a reduction in overdue book losses amounting to some 20 percent of what losses might be expected to be. Thus, while losses from theft are not yet determined, overall book loss in Nouveau Riche is not unusually high—due in part to this unique method of recovering overdue books.

A third factor that appears to have contributed to a delay in reaching a decision concerning theft-detection systems is the possibility of a new central library for Nouveau Riche. The present library is so overcrowded that in 1972 the library was forced to lease office space in a nearby commercial building for many of its administrative functions. This lease expires in 1979, and library officials hope to move into a new library at that time. While a bond election to provide the needed $18 million for library construction has still not been put before the voters, funding for the architectural work has been approved and plans are largely complete.

Library officials are hoping that a theft-detection system, if the inventory results show that it is needed, can be built into the construction costs. Officials hope that the inventory will not show a dramatic book loss due to theft and that it will be possible to delay purchase of a system until it can be included in the new library. So prevalent was this idea in the thinking of the library decision-makers that they invited several of the theft-detection system vendors to make presentations before the library architects. It must be pointed out, however, that a decision to include/exclude a theft-detection system in the final plans for the new library has not yet been made.

The director of circulation also hopes to initiate a self-charge system in the new library building. This adds another dimension to the problem—that is, attempting to tie in the theft-detection deactivation device with the self-charge system. While these possibilities are still in the thinking stage, they nevertheless pose additional problems to library decision-makers. If the two systems cannot be integrated, which system—self-charge or theft-detection—is the more important from a service or cost/benefit standpoint?

While plans in Nouveau Riche call for a new central, or downtown, library, there is another structural feature of the Nouveau Riche library system that appears to be a contributing factor in delaying adoption of a theft-detection system for the downtown library. This feature is decentralization. The city has fourteen branch libraries including three new branches opened during the past four years. Theft-detection systems, with their rather substantial fixed costs, are obviously not feasible in small libraries. While there are serious theft problems known to exist in some of the branch libraries, a theft-detection system is not feasible in terms of cost. It is very likely that continued emphasis on services for the branches tends to put off large expenditures for the central library.

While the director of administrative services points out the conservative nature of their decision-making process—"we don't like to rush into things"—it appears that a theft-detection system for Nouveau Riche is several years away.

Summary

Like the other product innovations studied, professionals in the library field were in general agreement that theft-detection systems constitute an important technological innovation for libraries. Little can be said concerning the reasons for adoption, however. The quantitative analysis was completely unsuccessful in terms of presenting a valid model of theft-detection systems adoption.

Nor was there any underlying motive common to the case studies to suggest reasons for adoption. In Dutch Elm, a theft-detection system was installed as a desperate measure to preserve library resources. The decision to adopt was based largely on decreased operating budgets and a need to preserve the existing book inventory. In Lakeview, on the other hand, a known theft rate made cost/benefit analysis possible and theft system purchase was justified. Nouveau Riche could not justify the purchase of a theft-detection system until the theft rate had been determined.

One factor, however, was common to both the quantitative analysis and the case studies—the difficulty libraries have in determining an accurate theft rate. About the only way to accurately determine losses is by taking inventory (either by random sample or full inventory)—and such inventories are very expensive. The Nouveau Riche inventory, for example, will take twenty-one staff members two years to complete. While such inventory problems may be a factor, there are obviously other considerations that stimulate or inhibit adoption. The availability of funds is obviously a major consideration. An unexpected windfall in terms of an increase in state aid allowed Dutch Elm to purchase the system. Nouveau Riche wanted to wait for the construction of a new library before installing the system so that system costs could be included in the construction costs of the new library.

Conclusions

Again, there was virtually no relationship between the two library innovations. As was the case with the innovations in public housing and public schools, when the library process and product innovations were correlated, the resulting coefficient was not significant. When the library computer-use score was correlated with the dichotomous variable, theft-detection system, a coefficient of $r = .07$ resulted (not significant at the .05 level). Once again, there was no apparent relationship between product and process innovations.

In the last two chapters—those covering public housing and public school innovations—we suggested that innovations were best classified as operating and nonoperating. In both earlier cases, it appeared that the fact that the process innovations were operating and the product innovations were nonoperating occurred by chance. This again appears to be the case. Again, the product innovation is nonoperating.

While it is possible to suggest all sorts of "reasons" why each of the product innovations does not fit the model, one empirical fact is clear. All three process innovations to some degree behave within the framework of a predictable model of innovation, and all three product innovations do not. In addition, the three process innovations did not require purchase from private firms. On the other hand, all three product innovations were the physical products of private firms. In addition, none of the product innovations were developed specifically for the local government adopting them. Prefab and modular components were not developed for the public-housing market, videotape recorders were not developed for public schools, and theft-detection systems were not developed for public libraries. This was not the case, however, with the process innovations. These innovations, at least as they were studied here, were largely developed for use by particular public agencies.

Thus the study of the adoption of technological innovations by public libraries has done more to muddy the waters than to clarify a possible theory of technological innovation adoption in local government. There are four possible explanations of the findings thus far. First is the operating/nonoperating classification based on incentives, presented in Chapter 2. The second is a process/product classification; the third is a classification based on public/private production of the technology; and the fourth is based on use.

Thus the explanation for a model for innovation adoption may be based on the incentive nature of an operating innovation, the fact that the innovation is a process innovation, the fact that the innovation was produced explicitly for a local public agency, or the fact that the innovation was adopted by the organization it was explicitly designed to serve.

Study of the library process innovation did, however, add to the understanding of the need/amenity nature of innovations. Need/amenity classifications are not mutually exclusive. The need/amenity nature of operating innovations (or whatever) is best seen as a continuum. Thus as library computer use illustrated, innovation adoption can be based on both need and amenity value.

The study of public library innovations thus served to clarify the need/amenity nature of innovation adoption. At the same time, however, it added little to a general explanation of innovation adoption by local government.

5

Adoption of Innovation in the Common Functions of City Government

In an attempt to provide as broad a basis as possible for the investigation of the adoption of technological innovation by local government, two very different innovations were selected for two very different common functions of local government. The process innovation, like many of the process innovations in other areas, was the adoption of computers as an assist to police operations. Contracting with Mainstem, Inc., for vehicle fleet-management services was the selected product innovation.

Process Innovation

The growth in the use of the computer in police departments throughout the country is widespread. Police first began utilizing the computer in the early 1960s; the first real-time police computer system started in St. Louis in 1964.[1] While computer applications vary widely, Colton groups their application into four basic systems areas: administration, operations, management, and planning and research. Data measuring computer applications in police departments were obtained from the International City Management Association. To develop a scale indicating comprehensive computer use, we summed the twenty-four ADP/computer applications examined by the ICMA—thus developing a police computer-use score. Of the cities responding to the 1971 ICMA survey forming the data base for this investigation, 213 of the 310 cities of interest responded for a response rate of 68.7 percent.

While computer use by police departments had undeniably grown since 1964, adoption of the computer to police work is by no means standard. Of the 213 cities forming our population of interest, 126, or 59.2 percent, did not use the computer at all. The computer-use score developed for each city ranged from 0 to 23 with a mean of 3.9 and a standard deviation of 5.7.

Table 5-1 shows the independent variables for the model of computer use in police department. The variables listed under community environment again include the seven variables used in all previous models. Demand is represented by crime statistics taken or computed from FBI crime reports.[2]

Intergovernmental professional influence was measured by two variables. First, a scale score for each city was developed by summing the number of training and selection standards for police candidates mandated by the state in which the city is located. These sources include: (1) mandatory training standards,

149

Table 5-1

Zero Order Relationship Between City Process Independent Variables and Police Computer-Use Score

Variable	r
Community Environment	
Liberalism	-.099
SES	-.005
Suburb	-.164**
Ethnic/Ghetto	-.132*
Size	.469**
Population Increase	-.039
Group Quarters	.016
Demand	
1969 Crime Index	.459**
1969 Homicides	.438**
1969 Assaults	.404**
1969 Burglaries	.504**
1969 Auto Thefts	.395**
Change in Crime Index 64-69	.429**
Change in Homicides 64-69	.394**
Change in Assaults 64-69	.331**
Change in Burglaries 64-69	.412**
Change in Auto Thefts 64-69	.431**
Organizational Environment	
Professionalism Mandated	.052
Mandated Hours Training	-.068
Total Police Expenditures	.358**
Per Capita Police Expenditures	.179**
Total City General Revenue	.360**
Per Capita City General Revenue	-.006
City ADP Score	.550**
Computer Solely for Police Use	.229*
City Reformism	.138*
LEAA Money	.073
Organizational Characteristics	
Minimum Salary for Police	.044
Unionism	.150*
Size of the Police Department	.346**

*Significant at the .05 level.
**Significant at the .01 level.

(2) interview required, (3) high school diploma required, (4) physical exam, and (5) background investigation. The second variable was the number of hours of police training required by state law. Data for both variables were obtained from the National Association of State Directors of Law Enforcement Training.[3]

Available resources again included the city ADP score—a dichotomous variable—computer used solely by police department,[4] total city general revenue, city per capita total general revenue, total police budget,[5] and per capita expenditure for police protection. City reformism was again included. Intergovernmental fiscal influence was measured by one variable—use of LEAA money in computer operations. Data were again obtained from the ICMA.

Organizational characteristics believed to be important variables determining the level of computer use in police departments included the size of the police department,[6] minimum police salary,[7] and the percent of the police department unionized.[8]

Quantitative Analysis

Table 5-1 shows the zero order relationships between the police computer-use score and the independent variables in the standard innovation model of Figure 1-1. Of the seven variables representing characteristics of the community, only two were substantially related to computer adoption. Confirming Colton's findings,[9] size was related to computer use among police departments with $r = 47$. The significant negative correlation of $r = -.16$ between suburb and computer use also substantiates Colton's findings that central city police departments are more likely to utilize the computer than are suburban departments.[10]

Table 5-1 also shows a positive relationship between all the demand variables and the police computer-use score. In the past, there has been some question about the use of crime statistics as an adequate measure of the crime rate. The crime statistics contained in the Federal Bureau of Investigation's yearly *Uniform Crime Report* are frequently considered weak indicators of crime—even of the limited crimes they purport to measure. While these statistics may be weak indicators of the crime rate in a given city, there is increasing evidence on their usefulness. While national surveys indicate that official statistics seriously underrepresent the amount of reportable crime in a given community,[11] a recent study by Wesley G. Skogan suggests that the FBI crime statistics may be useful indicators of the relative distribution of crime across cities. That is, they may underrepresent overall crime, but they are accurate measures of crime differentials between cities.[12] Skogan, for example, using a ten-city sample, found that the correlation between his survey and official rates for auto theft is .94 in spite of wide differences between survey and official rates.[13] He thus urges a much more optimistic picture of the use of crime statistics as measures of comparison between cities.

Although a number of specific crime measures and changes in these measures over a five-year period are presented in Table 5-1, the fact that the correlation coefficients between each of the demand variables and police computer use are so similar brings into question the need for so many measures. Correlation coefficients were thus computed between the selected specific crime measures and the overall indices. All the individual measures were closely related to their indices with correlations ranging from .73 to .99. For this reason, only the total crime index (1969) and the change in the crime index (1964-1969) was used in model testing.

In the organizational environment, two variables—professionalism mandated and mandated hours of training—were selected to represent the intergovernmental influence of the state in upgrading or professionalizing local police forces. Neither variable, however, was related to the computer-use score at the zero order level. Apparently the professional requirements imposed by state statutes on local police departments have little effect on decisions to adopt computers as an aid to police work.

Four variables represent the existence of available financial resources: total police expenditures, per capita police expenditures, total city revenue, and per capita city revenue. All financial variables except per capita city revenue were significantly related to computer use. As expected, financial resources seem to be an important determinant of innovation.

The city ADP score, as an example of the existence of equipment slack, showed a strong zero order relationship with the police computer-use score. The correlation coefficient obtained was .55.

Surprisingly, however, the variable, computer solely for police use, was not strongly related to the computer-use score with $r = .23$ (significant only at the .05 level). Caution must be exercised here, however. This question was answered by only seventy-five police departments. Those departments not utilizing the computer were coded as missing data.

Although again faced with the problem of a small n (75), response to the question "Have you received money from the LEAA to aid in the use of computers in your department?" was not related to computer use. Among those cities utilizing the computer, a wide variety of computer applications was not related to the receipt of LEAA money for this purpose. Surprisingly, then, intergovernmental fiscal assistance of this type appears to make little difference in the level of computer use police departments achieve.

The relationship of $r = .15$ between reformism and the dependent variable was significant at the .05 level. Thus there is a slight tendency for police departments in reformed cities to be more advanced in computer applications than those in unreformed cities.

Only one of the three selected organizational characteristics was significantly related to computer use. The size of the police department was positively related to the dependent variable with $r = .35$. Unionism also showed a slight positive relationship ($r = .15$), while minimum salary as a measure of department professionalism was not related to innovation.

To test the model of city process innovation, partials were computed between the organizational characteristics and the police computer-use score controlling for community environment, demand, and organizational environment.

When partials were initially computed, none of the relationships were significant at the .05 level; however, due to missing value problems, the n for the computation was only forty-five cities. To increase the n to a reasonable level, it was necessary to remove two variables in the organizational environment—computer solely for police use and LEAA money—from consideration. Partials were again computed, this time without these two variables. None of the relationships were significant at the .01 level, and only unionism was related to computer use at the .05 level with $r = .15$. This positive relationship, however, was not hypothesized. Under "normal" conditions unionism is expected to be related to the status quo—unions are believed to be hostile to innovation. In this case, however, police unions do not appear to be hostile to the use of the computer—probably due to the nature of the computer use. Police computer systems are not designed to replace personnel but to assist the officer in his daily work. There is thus no reason for union opposition, in fact, there is every reason for union support.

Surprisingly, there was no independent relationship between the size of the police department and computer use. While department size was related to the computer-use score at the zero order level, under controls the relationship disappeared. This was the first time that the size of the organization did not show a significant independent relationship with the dependent variable in testing the process innovation models.

Nor did the selected measure of professionalism relate substantially to the use of the computer. In spite of the fact that evidence links salary to professionalism,[14] the minimum salary for the police department was not a significant determinant of computer use.

The three variables examined representing the organizational characteristics were thus eliminated from further model testing. Only unionism showed a slight relationship with computer use. However, the r of .15 was not enough to meet the .01-level criterion established earlier for continued consideration.

The relationships between the variables of the organizational environment and the police computer-use score controlling for community environment and demand were computed next. Only two variables were significant at the .01 level. Of the three indicators of financial resources, only the r of -.49 between total police expenditures and computer use was significant.[a] Interestingly, total police expenditures correlated positively ($r = .36$) with computer use at the zero order level, but with the introduction of controls a substantial negative relationship was noted. Thus in cities of equal size and other environmental factors and with equal crime rates, the city with the lowest total police expenditure is most likely to have a highly developed computer capability. This again supports an efficiency-based model of technological innovation. This

---

[a]Due to the high intercorrelation ($r = .95$) between total police expenditures and total city general revenue, the total city general revenue was removed from the multivariate analysis.

relationship tells us that police departments with lower total expenditures are more likely to be heavy computer users than departments with higher expenditures.

The only other significant variable in the organizational environment was the measure of equipment slack. A positive coefficient of $r = .46$ was found between the city ADP score and the police expenditure relationship; the coefficient between city ADP score and police computer use changed little from the zero order $r = .55$ to the $r = .46$ under conditions of control.

This relationship again supports the concept of the efficiency model—a well-developed city computer system is supportive of the development of a sophisticated police computer system. Furthermore, there probably is a connection between the two variables. The relationships between the two significant variables in the organizational environment and the police computer-use score are supportive of the efficiency model. It is possible, for example, that under controls for city size, crime rates, and other environmental variables, that cities with well-developed computer systems are able to offer these services to the police department and that these services are in lieu of higher levels of police expenditures.[b] In fact, this appears to be the case. A partial was computed between the city ADP score and total police expenditures controlling for the community environment and demand. A significant negative coefficient of $r = -.47$ was produced. It thus appears that a well-developed city computer system is indeed related to lower police expenditures.

As with the zero order relationships, the intergovernmental influences— both federal, in terms of LEAA assistance, and state, in terms of mandated professionalism—showed no significant relationship to computer use.

Was there serious professional interest in computer applications in police departments? To answer this question the journal of the International Association of Chiefs of Police, *Police Chief,* was examined between 1964 and 1973 with the exception of the years 1965 and 1966.[c] Figure 5-1 shows the emphasis given to articles dealing with the application of computers to police work. As was hypothesized, interest in computer applications, as indicated by the percent of articles in *Police Chief,* peaked in 1967 with 7.6 percent of the articles devoted to computer applications. The years following 1967 showed a steady decline in interest until, finally, in 1973, only 2.6 percent of the articles were devoted to computer use.

The next set of partials examined was the relationship between the demand variables (the two crime-index measures) and the police computer-use score controlling for community environment and organizational environment. Both relationships were significant with $r = .34$ between the 1969 index and computer

---

[b]The fact that there was no relationship between the computer-use score and the variable, computer used solely by the police, also supports this hypothesis.

[c]*Police Chief* could not be obtained for the years 1965 and 1966.

Percentage

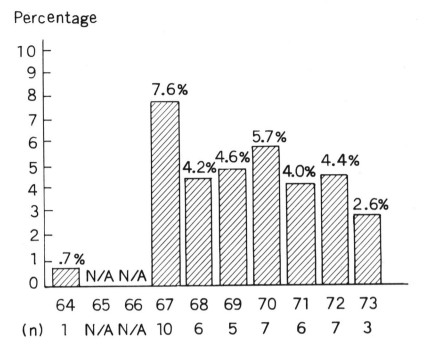

Figure 5-1. Percentage of *Police Chief* Articles Devoted to the Use of the Computer by Police Departments (1964-1973)

use and r = .24 between the change in the index and computer use. Thus demand—crime—is directly and independently related to the computer-use score, again suggesting a rational, demand-based model for innovation adoption.

The demand variable influenced computer use indirectly as well as directly. Table 5-2 shows the relationship between the two crime measures and the organizational environment controlling for the community environment. All relationships were significant with the relationships between police expenditures and the crime measures being particularly strong (r = .58 and .62). Thus among cities of equal size and socioeconomic characteristics, the crime rate and the change in the crime rate both directly and indirectly affect the level of computer use in police departments.

As hypothesized, some of the characteristics of the community environment were also related to demand (Table 5-3). Ethnic/ghetto and size were both positively related to the 1969 index and the change in the index when controlling for the other community environment variables. The strong relationships between size and the crime indices of r = .96 and .89 were expected. It was surprising, however, to discover very little relationship between SES and

Table 5-2

Relationship Between Demand and Organizational Environment Controlling for Community Environment

Variable	Police Expenditures	City ADP Score
1969 Crime Index	.582**	.193**
Change in Crime Index 1964-1969	.618**	.225**

*Significant at the .05 level.
**Significant at the .01 level.

Table 5-3

Relationship Between Community Environment Variables and Computer-Use Score Controlling for Remaining Community Environment Variables

Variable	1969 Index	Change in Index
Liberalism	.127*	.078
SES	−.111*	−.069
Suburb	−.131*	−.064
Ethnic/Ghetto	.535**	.318**
Size	.964**	.892**
Population Increase	−.005	.001
Group Quarters	−.078	−.024

*Significant at the .05 level.
**Significant at the .01 level.

crime. It is low SES characteristics that are normally associated with high crime rates. The same was true of suburb. Central city, or negative loadings of suburb, were also expected to be related to crime. Again, this was not the case, both SES $(r = -.11)$ and suburb $(r = -.13)$ loaded in a negative direction, (although the relationships were not significant at the .01 level).

Several variables in the community were also related to variables in the organizational environment controlling for demand. As expected, size was related to police expenditures. Three variables, SES $(r = .27)$, suburb $(r = -.30)$ and group quarters $(r = .18)$ were significantly related to the city ADP score. In the housing process model, the partial coefficients between the ADP score and these same three variables were virtually the same with $r = .26, -.28$, and .17 respectively. The relationships again suggest, as in Chapter 2, that central cities with high socioeconomic status are most likely to have a highly developed data-processing system.

Finally, the relationship between community environment and police computer-use score controlling for demand and organizational environment was computed. Two variables, ethnic/ghetto ($r = -.28$) and size ($r = .30$), were significantly related to the dependent variable. In all the previous models tested in Chapters 2, 3, and 4, none of the community variables showed an independent relationship with the dependent variable. Thus for the first time the community environment exerted an independent influence on the level of innovation adoption.

Perhaps it is the nature of the innovation (police related) that makes innovation directly responsive to the community. Or perhaps it is the fact that the innovation is in the city government itself that makes it responsive to the community environment. Analysis of the city product innovation may help to clarify these relationships.

Figure 5-2 presents a revised model for the adoption of process innovations by city government. Once again, the lines linking the various variables indicate the partial relationships significant at the .01 level. Translating the specific variables or operational definitions back into the system characteristics they represent, it is possible to describe the innovative process rather accurately.

As with the adoption of the other process models, the model for the adoption of computer systems by police departments is a model based on need and a drive for efficiency. Within the organizational environment, recall that the city ADP score was positively related to the computer-use score while total police expenditures were negatively related. Recall also that the size of the police department showed no independent relationship with the computer-use score although it was significantly related at the zero order level. The fact that slack resources in terms of a well-developed city computer system were available, coupled with the low-expenditure need for efficiency in police operations, appears to stimulate police interest in computer use.

Demand was again an extremely important determinant of computer use. Even under controls, crime definitely appeared to stimulate the use of the computer. Police departments in cities with high crime rates and/or a high increase in crime between 1964 and 1969 were likely to have high computer-use scores, regardless of size, community characteristics, or slack resource availability. Demand was also independently related to the two important variables in the organizational environment.

The community environment for the first time contributed directly as well as indirectly to the adoption of innovation with significant relationships between both ethnic/ghetto and size with the police computer-use score.

Thus this innovation adoption by police departments is based largely on rational considerations—efficiency, need, and resource availability. But which area was the more important? As shown in Table 5-4, the variables of the organizational environment appear to be the most significant determinants of computer use by police departments. Table 5-4 shows the results of a stepwise

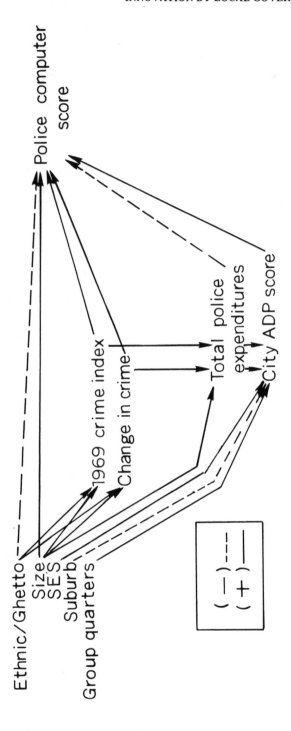

Figure 5-2. Revised Model for the Adoption of Computer Systems by Police Departments

Table 5-4
Summary of Stepwise Regression Explaining Police Computer Use

Variable	R	R^2
City ADP Score	.550	.303
Size	.613	.375
Police Expenditure	.655	.430
1969 Crime Index	.708	.502
Ethnic/Ghetto	.709	.503
Change in Crime	.711	.506

multiple regression including all the independent variables significantly related to the dependent variable in the model testing. The six variables explained 50.6 percent of the variance in the police computer-use score with $R = .71$. The city ADP score was the first variable added with $R^2 = .30$. Substantial increments were also added to the explanation of the computer-use score by the next three variables added. Size, the second variable added, increased the R^2 by 7 percent; total police expenditures added 5 percent, and the 1969 crime index added another 7 percent. Thus two of the first three variables included in the stepwise regression were the variables of the organizational environment. Surprisingly, demand added little to the explanation of computer use.

Qualitative Analysis

Only two police departments were visited in a search for information beyond that presented in the quantitative analysis. River City exemplifies a police department with computer applications well beyond expectation. Aqueduct, on the other hand, had a computer-use score substantially below that predicted. In fact, by 1974, the Aqueduct Police Department had been forced to abandon the use of the computer entirely.

River City. One of the most progressive applications of computer technology in the area of law enforcement is found with the River City Police Department. With a computer-use score of 15, River City exceeded our prediction by 6, a deviation explained by a number of unusual environmental and organizational characteristics. Together, these factors were to create not only an ideal environment for the implementation of ADP applications, but for a particularly advanced and progressive law-enforcement program as well.

The legal status of the River City Police Department is notably unique. It is one of only three police departments in the country that fall under state authority, a situation resulting from the local political machine and police corruption in the early 1930s. A board of police commissioners, comprised of four River City residents, is appointed by the governor, with the mayor serving as an

ex-officio member. The board, which serves as the policy coordinator for the
police, is responsible to the governor alone, and subject to few other controls.
The state legislature exerts some degree of control over police matters by its
empowerment to set police pay scales, retirement schedules, and other benefits.
Furthermore, state law requires that the municipal government set aside 20
percent of the city's operating budget for the police department, with special
elections called to pass on bond issues for any unusual police needs. The police
department of River City is therefore an autonomous organization within the
city, yet completely funded by city revenues. It is a unique environment that,
because of the absence of direct city influence, allows the police administrator
a large degree of freedom in organizational management.

In 1961, the board of commissioners appointed a chief of police who was
able to appreciate the opportunity presented by this unusual jurisdictional
arrangement for the police department. Having spent twenty-one years with
the FBI before assuming the post of police chief, Edgar Spence, a native of
River City, possessed the professional background and exposure to advanced
law-enforcement techniques that allowed for his total renovation of the RCPD.
However, Chief Spence's entrance on the scene was met with initial internal
resistance. As one police administrator recalled:

> When he arrived here to become Chief in 1961, he was automatically
> unpopular and remained so for a while until he overcame the resistance
> of internal political forces and cliques. They isolated him for the first
> two years and were able to do this because they had key people know-
> ing everything he was going to do in advance . . . . Spence helped over-
> come the resistance by changing the structure of the department . . .
> but in the first five years not much change was possible.

By 1965, however, Chief Spence had begun a total revamping of the police organization. In August of that year, the city allotted an additional $60,000
to the police for the Chicago-based consultants, Public Administration Service
(PAS), to plan the reorganization of the police department, a move which
met with strong but unsuccessful resistance.

Because River City is one of the nation's largest cities in geographic area,
covering over 300 square miles, administration of public services in the city
was historically decentralized. The police department was no exception—it
maintained a number of district stations across the city. With the recommendations submitted by the private consulting firm, however, the entire police
department began moving toward total centralization. Under the authority
of Chief Spence, coordination of department reorganization was directed by
Lieutenant Colonel Charles R. Newhouse, the department's number two man.
While this massive reorganization proved controversial, Spence and Newhouse
were successful in streamlining the department and making the force responsive

to central command, thereby eliminating the power cliques. While work progressed on physical renovation of the police headquarters, and reassignment of former district commanders, organizational change was also being introduced in data processing.

In 1966, the River City Police Department's data-processing functions consisted of payroll work on an IBM tabulating machine, with statistical reporting done manually on electronic accounting machines. All other files and records were maintained manually. Because of River City's large geographic area, however, the manual record keeping proved inadequate for police functions. The department found it impossible to hire the number of police officers warranted by the size of the city, which consequently "left the police with an unfavorable man-to-territory situation." When it required an average of thirty minutes for headquarters to search their files for information requested by a patrol car on a suspect or vehicle, police efficiency was recognized as having deteriorated to an unacceptable level. While the police budget increased from $7.1 million in 1962-1963 to $8.9 million in 1965-1966, the size of the police force remained at about 915.

PAS thus advised the city council that the police force should be increased by 250 officers over the next three years at an additional cost of $1.5 million. Chief Spence, however, was looking to alternate methods as well that would increase police efficiency. Inasmuch as the president of the board of police commissioners made it clear that "the boards have scrupulously followed the rule that the Chief runs the Police Department," it was not surprising that when Spence looked to computer technology as a means to maximize efficiency, he received the endorsement of the board.

In the same year that the entire police department was undergoing reorganization, Chief Spence hired Melvin Reiman, an expert in data processing, to direct a study of police information needs. Reiman, with twenty-five years of experience in ADP applications, had previously been connected with the Air Defense Command (USAF) at Colorado Springs, Colorado. In addition to possessing the technical expertise required for the design of a computer-managed information system, Reiman was equally proficient in departmental management. From the beginning, his attitude was "to fit the computer system into the existing police structure and operations and not fit the department into a computerized environment." As manager of the River City Police Department's computer systems division, Reiman was instructed by Chief Spence to "pick a site for the operations and tell me the cost." With financial considerations in the hands of the police chief and board of commissioners, Reiman was able to devote his entire attention to ADP systems design. This he did by asking the patrolmen in the field what their specific information needs were. It was to be "a result oriented, not technical oriented, operation," he recalled. Because the city's own computer did not have on-line capacity at the time, the decision was made to obtain a computer for the sole use of the police department. Spence was able to persuade the city council in August, 1967, that funds raised earlier from an approved bond issue for general police equipment needs should be used for the purchase of the police computer. He pointed out that a computer was needed for more efficient operation and department coordination with the FBI's computer system, adding that River City had a 16.9 percent increase in major crimes in the last year (1966) and ranked 24th among the top cities in the number of crimes committed. As one police administrator told this investigator, "Spence was the type who could talk you out of your last pair of pants." The following month, the board of police commissioners approved the selection of the IBM 360/40 computer and related equipment for purchase at a cost of $1,168,465, and within a year the computer was operational for police field inquiry services. The computer systems manager attributes the absence of strong resistance to the innovation within the department to the fact that the entire force was made a part of the decision-making and systems design. Their opinions were sought on what they considered pressing needs for information. "It's all a question of using psychology," Reiman remarked. "If a person thinks he had a say in developing an innovation, he's more likely to aid in its progress."

Inasmuch as the chief of police was determined to apply computer technology in maximizing efficiency, one might argue that River City's police department would be using data processing irregardless of whom they obtained as manager of the computer systems division. Nevertheless, it is questionable whether they would have obtained such a nationally prominent reputation without the professionalism displayed by Mel Reiman. A modest man of extraordinary administrative ability, Reiman balanced his time between managing the complex computer system and receiving national and international visitors investigating River City's police ADP operations. Prominent among his peers for his association with this innovation, his writings on the applications of computer technology in law enforcement have been published frequently. As one technical aide stated: "He's a genius. We'd be nowhere without him. Some may think so, but we wouldn't be where we are now."

Yet despite the progressive nature of the systems manager, the implementation of advanced computer technology in the police department would not have been initially possible without the commitment of Chief Spence, the direction of Lieutenant Colonel Newhouse, and the support of the police board of commissioners. The city council, although without say as to how the police spent 20 percent of the city revenues, was nevertheless vocal in its disenchantment with the lack of increase in police manpower. State law, the mayor pointed out, would place a desired police-to-population ratio at 1500 officers, and yet the city had a force of only 940 officers.

The police department, however, operated under a philosophy that gave priority not to more police officers, but to better police officers with the tools of education and technology. Because of this attitude, an attitude that pervaded the police administration, there was never less than full commitment to the application of computer technology to law enforcement.

By 1971, police department needs had outgrown the capabilities of the first computer, and consequently it was replaced with a more sophisticated IBM 370/155 computer, which in turn was replaced in 1974 by an IBM 370/158. In addition to the advanced applications of management-information systems for the RCPD, the computer had been expanded by 1974 to serve fifty-three other law-enforcement agencies with 233 terminals tied in directly to the department's computer.

The adoption of the innovative application of computer technology by the RCPD was, therefore, an ongoing process. That is to say, each year has brought an even more progressive utilization of the innovation. Currently, the department is ranked as having the most advanced computer-based police information system in the United States.

As has been noted, a number of factors were instrumental in creating this optimum environment for the adoption and development of the innovation. The fact that River City's police department is one of very few in the nation falling under state control certainly must be considered an important contributor to innovation adoption. Because of the absence of city governmental control, police administrators had a greater say in establishing their own priorities.

Additional factors, however, appeared to be equally important in the case of River City. The geographical size of the city alone required an alternative to the strict reliance on manpower for law enforcement within the city's 300 plus square miles. Inasmuch as it would have required twice the force of the police department to effectively patrol that large an area, the ability of a computer to "predict the number of calls for police service that will occur at a particular location at a given time" served as an alternative.

Chief Spence's professionalism and his experience with the FBI were also important factors in explaining the advanced stage of computer applications within the police department. His ability to overcome the resistance and power cliques he found on entering the department assured his success in managing the entire force with centralized control. One can assume as well that his experience with the FBI did not hamper his ability to secure state and federal assistance for further development of the computer system.

While the police chief's own administrative ability and perception of police priorities were major factors behind the adoption of ADP applications, the actual groundwork and development of the system must be credited to the marked professionalism found in the manager of the computer services division. It was his attitude that proved necessary for the effective implementation of computer technology in law enforcement. All factors considered, it is no wonder that the computer applications developed by the RCPD have become a standard of achievement for law-enforcement agencies across the country.

Aqueduct. In 1971, Aqueduct (population 130,000) was recorded as having a police computer-use score of 4, 6 less than predicted. Inasmuch as Aqueduct was selected as the low deviant city to be visited, another check was made of more recent data provided by the International City Management Association.[15] According to the ICMA's 1974 study of police ADP use, it was found that the Aqueduct Police Department had discontinued altogether its use of the computer and card-punch equipment. Therefore, two questions remained to be answered: (1) Why had computer application been less than predicted, and (2) why were ADP applications in police management abandoned?

The Aqueduct Police Department delegates responsibility for management information to its planning and research division. At the time they were utilizing ADP equipment, the planning and research division had four management functions automated: (1) a field interrogation report file; (2) police service analysis; (3) personnel records and payroll preparation; and (4) police vehicle fleet maintenance. As the current commander of planning and research notes, however, "They were the basic things, nothing we couldn't do manually."

The city at this time possessed an IBM 360 which fell under the city financial department's management. Consequently, most of the ADP applications within the city were oriented towards personnel and financial information. Each department within the city had its own keypunch machine with which to process the data destined for the city's computer. One administrator stated, with apparent justification, that "It was a rinky dink operation." Practically speaking, aside from the wants and warrants function provided by ADP application, all others were directed toward financial management.

The police department did not seek federal LEAA assistance to upgrade its management information system at this time, primarily because of "the absolute mayhem" being experienced at city hall. A police administrator recalled the situation as being one of confusion, stating: "We couldn't very well make a commitment when the city wasn't sure in which direction it was going to go."

There appeared to be general concurrence that the internal problems being experienced by the city with its ADP system hampered all departments in developing computer applications. One administrator stated:

> There was no in-house expertise in Aqueduct's ADP center—no competence. There was one time when the head of data processing up and quit. She was the type that never wrote anything down—kept all the programs in her head. It was a mess. A department that wanted assistance in developing ADP applications certainly couldn't find it there and there was no point in hiring outside consultants.

Faced with the inability to handle these internal problems, Aqueduct discontinued ADP operations in 1974 and began searching for a private vendor to manage the municipality's information systems.

Thus the city began anew in its automation of management information by hiring a computer management firm to handle all city ADP functions. Overseeing the entire operation was the city's data processing manager. However, a systems

programmer was provided by the contracted firm who worked with each department in developing desired applications. CRT terminals were located in each
department and tied in with a minicomputer located in city hall, with monthly
transfers of data to the private firm's central computer. In fiscal year 1974-
1975, Aqueduct budgeted $441,722 for data processing services.

The year 1974, however, still found the police department without any
ADP applications. The delay did not stem from a lack of commitment but
rather from difficulty in designing the system sought by the planning and research department. There was initial difficulty in deciding which approach to
take and a visit was made to the River City Police Department, internationally
prominent for its ADP applications, to gain some direction in how to best apply
data processing to police operations. A decision was made to give priority to
a management information system that would be followed in turn by a traffic
information system. By July, 1975, the Aqueduct Police Department planned
to have its first ADP system in operation.

While the police ADP score will still be lower than predicted, it is significant that department officials nevertheless remain committed to ADP application following the difficulties experienced. Had Aqueduct made an earlier
commitment to data processing, in both qualified personnel and funds, it is
likely that the police department would have been considerably more advanced
in ADP applications than was found to be the case.

Summary

Police computer use is unquestionably based on demand and operationalized
by high levels of available resources, although the resources were not necessarily
financial. The quantitative model clearly illustrates the demand basis of the
system. Two of the community characteristics, ethnic/ghetto and size, were
important determinants of the crime rate and the police computer-use score. The
crime indices, in turn, were both positively related to the computer-use score and
the variables of the organizational environment. Within the organizational
environment, the city ADP score proved to be the major determinant of the
police computer-use score. This relationship was again emphasized in the Aqueduct
case study. Police computer use was closely related to the city computer capability.

It is important to point out the fact that, for the most part, the case studies
were conducted by a researcher who had no knowledge of the quantitative
relationships found. The Aqueduct researcher thus "found" the relationship
between police and city ADP use without prior knowledge of the quantitative
results. The methodology of the study, the strict separation of quantitative/qual-
itative tasks, thus ensured the independence of the findings.

The River City Police Department proved to be a very unusual case. The strange structural arrangements brought about by machine politics and police corruption in 1930 led to a highly developed computer system. The unusual funding relationship and independence from city politics unquestionably aided computer adoption, especially in the face of council demands for increased police manpower. Again, the case study corroborated the quantitative findings. In this case, area of the city (one of the two major components of size) was one of the significant reasons for the development of an advanced ADP capability.

Product Innovation

The product innovation selected for analysis was the contracting with Mainstem, Inc., of Princeton, New Jersey, for vehicle fleet-management information. The Mainstem system was discussed in some detail in Chapter 1. Of the American cities with 1960 populations of 50,000 or more, some twenty cities had contracted with Mainstem for their vehicle fleet-management program. While this amounts to only 6.5 percent of the cities studied, the unique opportunity to study the diffusion of innovation in a virtual monopoly situation led to the examination of this particular innovation.

The city product innovation was a simple dichotomous variable—city uses Mainstem. If the city contracted with Mainstem for fleet-management service, the city was scored 1. If the city did not contract for the service, it was scored 0. Data were furnished by Mainstem, Inc., Princeton, New Jersey.

Concerning the independent variables, the seven standard variables again represented the community environment. Demand was represented by two variables, public works operating budget and per capita public works operating budget.[16] It was expected that high public works costs would generate an interest in Mainstem as a method to reduce vehicle- and equipment-maintenance expenditures.

Financial slack in the organizational environment was represented by total city general revenue and city per capita general revenue. Representing equipment slack was the city ADP score.

Intergovernmental influence was represented by two variables: intergovernmental revenue and a dichotomous variable, state allows collective bargaining of municipal employees.[17] Also included was the city reformism score.

Due to data available from an ICMA survey of public works departments, a large number of variables were selected as representative of public works organizational characteristics.[18] Initially included was the age of the public works department while size was represented by the number of employees in the department. Organizational complexity was represented by the number of divisions in the public works department and by a scale score representing the sum of a variety of functions performed by public works departments. Other structural characteristics include department centralization, the presence of an equipment-maintenance division, and the backlog of work with funds available.

Professionalism in the organization was measured by a variety of variables. Professionalism concerning the head of the department was measured by a dichotomous variable, department head a registered engineer, and also by the percentage of time the head spent in professional reading. Professionalism of the organization was also measured by the number of American Public Works Association (APWA) members working for the city, by the number of APWA Institute for Equipment Service (IES) members working for the city,[19] and by the number of graduate engineers on the public works staff.

Other organizational variables included civil service coverage, labor union contracts, and the presence of a collective-bargaining agreement.

Vendor influence was also believed to be important in Mainstem adoption. Thus a variable, percent of time head of public works department spends with vendors, was used as a possible measure of vendor influence.

Quantitative Analysis

Table 5-5 shows the zero order relationships between the Mainstem use dichotomous variable and a host of independent variables. The variables of the community environment remained unchanged from other models. As with virtually all the product innovations discussed in preceding chapters, there was no zero order relationship between product innovation adoption and community characteristics. None of the relationships were significant, even at the .05 level. In fact, the highest coefficient was only .07 between SES and Mainstem use.

The demand variables represent the cost/effectiveness nature of the innovation under study. Two variables were selected to represent pressures on the public works department to reduce costs: total public works budget and per capita public works budget. Following a rational model of innovation, it was expected that both measures would be positively related to Mainstem use. This was not the case. There was no relationship at all between the total PW budget and Mainstem and only a slight ($r = .14$) positive relationship between the per capita budget and Mainstem. While this second relationship is too weak for any generalizations at this point, it does suggest the possibility that Mainstem use may be based on need.

Within the area of the organizational environment, six variables were selected as measures of the availability of slack resources within the city as a whole. City total general revenue and city per capita general revenue were both selected as indicators of the availability of financial resources. Only per capita revenue, however, was significantly related to Mainstem use with $r = .14$. Thus the correlation coefficient between Mainstem and both city and public works per capita measures is virtually identical. In the case of per capita revenue, however, the

Table 5-5

Zero Order Relationships Between City Product Independent Variables and Mainstem Use

Variable	r
Community Environment	
Liberalism	.012
SES	.068
Suburb	−.064
Ethnic/Ghetto	.008
Size	.036
Population Increase	−.023
Group Quarters	.028
Demand	
PW Budget	.011
Per Capita PW Budget	.140*
Organizational Environment	
City per Capita General Revenue	.139**
City Total Revenue	.019
State Allows Collective Bargaining	.032
City ADP Score	.230**
Percentage Increase in PW Budget Since 1960	.090
Percentage Increase in PW Budget Since 1965	.091
Reformism	.026
Organizational Characteristics	
Age of PW Department	−.016
No. of Divisions in Department	.034
No. of PW Employees	.005
Percentage of Time with Vendors	.011
PW Department Centralized	−.030
PW Functions Score	.017
Performs Vehicle Maintenance	−.198**
Have Equipment-Maintenance Division	−.041
Backlog of Work	.102
PW Head Registered Engineer	−.032
Percentage of Time Reading	.019
No. Graduate Engineers on Staff	.004
No. APWA Working for City	.150**
No. IES Working for City	.016
Have Civil Service	−.030
Head Covered by Civil Service	−.027
Have Collective Bargaining	−.036
Have Union Contracts	−.039

*Significant at the .05 level.
**Significant at the .01 level.

higher n reduced the probability that the relationship might occur by chance to something below the .01 level. One other variable, city ADP score, was selected to represent the availability of equipment slack. Again a negative relationship was expected. Poorly developed computer capabilities within the city and/or lack of computer experience in the public works department was expected to generate pressure to "contract out" for services such as those provided by Mainstem. The city ADP score, however, was positively related to Mainstem use with $r = .23$. Thus cities with relatively sophisticated computer capabilities are more likely to adopt Mainstem services than those without.

The final slack variables were the percentage of increase in the public works budget since 1960 and since 1965. As might be expected, these variables were highly intercorrelated with $r = .76$. It was expected that pressures on the public works budget over the years might tend to force a cost consciousness that might stimulate Mainstem use. Such was not the case. Neither variable showed any substantial relationship with Mainstem use.

One variable, a scale concerning state legislation, was selected to represent intergovernmental influences that might be related to Mainstem. There was no significant relationship between state collective-bargaining legislation and Mainstem use. Of the 142 cities responding, 28.2 percent were in states with no state legislation, 15.5 percent were in states with mandatory collective bargaining, while 37.3 percent were permitted collective bargaining by state law. Ten of the Mainstem cities responded to the question on public employment. Four of the ten cities were in states where collective bargaining was permitted, two prohibited, two mandatory, and two in states with no legislation ($\gamma = -.06$). Thus again there was no significant relationship between the intergovernmental variables and Mainstem use.

The final relationship examined was the correlation between the city reformism score and Mainstem use. It was expected that the professionalism of the reformed city would manifest itself in a high level of Mainstem adoption. This was not the case at the zero order level, however. There was no significant relationship between reformism and Mainstem use ($r = .03$).

The eighteen individual variables within the area labeled "Organizational Characteristics" may be combined into six theoretically relevant categories: age, size/complexity, vendor influence, organization, professionalism, and civil service/unions. The theoretical relevance of these areas was covered in the review of the literature in Chapter 1 and for the sake of brevity will not be repeated here.

There was no significant relationship between the age of the public works department and Mainstem use. Apparently, when the department was formed has little relationship to Mainstem use.

Two variables, a scale of the number of divisions in the public works department and a scale concerning the number of public works employees, represent the size/complexity of the organization. Again neither showed a substantial or significant relationship with Mainstem.

Vendor influence was measured by the responses (by heads of PW departments) to the question: "Estimate what percentage of your time is spent with vendors." Once again, no significant relationship was noted.

Five variables were selected to represent specific organizational problems or characteristics of the formal organizational structure of the various PW departments. In response to the question: "Is your public works department centralized?" most directors (90.4 percent) answered affirmatively. Nine of these cities were Mainstem cities while one Mainstem city had a decentralized department. Utilizing both r and X^2 ($X^2 = .1042$), no significant difference in Mainstem use can be attributed to centralization.

The complexity of the task facing the PW department was also unrelated to Mainstem use. PW directors were asked which of sixty-four possible functions fell under the jurisdiction of their department. The total number of functions was then correlated with Mainstem use, but the coefficient obtained was only $r = .02$.

One factor within the distribution of PW tasks did appear to affect Mainstem adoption, however, and that was the location of the vehicle-maintenance function. Nine of the twelve responding Mainstem cities located the vehicle-maintenance function outside the PW departments. The $\gamma = -.67$ with X^2 of 5.077 (significant at the .05 level) suggests that locating the vehicle-maintenance function outside the PW department stimulates Mainstem adoption. The r of $-.20$ between these variables was also significant at the .01 level.

Surprisingly, however, there was no relationship between Mainstem and having an equipment-maintenance division in the PW department. Of the eighty-five cities reporting no such division in PW, seven were Mainstem cities. On the other hand, five Mainstem cities were among the eighty-two reporting the presence of such a division in the PW department ($X^2 = .0553$).

The final variable representing organizational problems was a variable representing the backlog of work in the PW department. Department heads were asked: "If you have a current backlog of work for which funds are available, but are unable to recruit engineers to carry forward at what would be acceptable normal pace, please indicate extent of backlog." Responses ranged from 0 to 4 years with a mean of .98 and standard deviation of .98. Of the 167 respondents 36.5 percent had no backlog of work, 38.9 percent a one year backlog, 18 percent two years, 3.6 percent three years, and 3 percent four years. It was thought that a substantial backlog of work might be stimulative of Mainstem use in an effort to "free up" scarce manpower resources. Such was not the case, however— no significant relationship was noted between the backlog of work and the contracting for Mainstem services.

Five variables were selected to represent professional influence within the organization itself. Two concerned the professionalism of the department head: the professional status (registered engineer) of the department head, and the head's estimate of the percentage of his time spent in professional study. Neither variable showed a significant relationship with Mainstem use with $r = .08$ and $.02$, respectively. Only thirty-eight of the 167 responding department heads were not registered engineers (four Mainstem cities) while the remaining 129 were (eight Mainstem cities). The computed X^2 was 1.006; not significant at the .05 level.

The number of graduate engineers on the PW staff was also selected as an indicator of professionalism. No significant relationship was noted, however, between this variable and Mainstem ($r = .00$).

Figure 5-3 shows the percentage of articles in the American Public Works Association (APWA) *Reporter* devoted to vehicle fleet-management systems between 1964 and 1973. A strange pattern is formed with declining interest in fleet management during the mid 1960s. Beginning with 1971, however, interest is revived with several articles extending through the period of interest. Not only is this interest general, however, but specifically concerned Mainstem.[20] It was thus expected that Mainstem adoption might be related to membership in the APWA. Two variables were selected to measure the possible APWA impact on Mainstem use: the number of APWA members working for the city and the

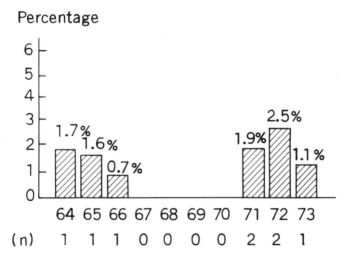

Figure 5-3. Percentage of Articles in the American Public Works Association *Reporter* Devoted to Vehicle Fleet-Management Systems (1964-1973)

members of the APWA Institute for Equipment Service (IES) working for the
city. APWA membership ranged from a low of 0 to a high of 147 with a mean
of 12.7, standard deviation of 15.9, and a mode of 1. This variable was correlated with Mainstem use and was found to be significantly related to innovation
adoption with $r = .15$. Professionalism then, at least as measured here, appears
to be related to innovation adoption.[d]

IES membership was not as widespread. Membership ranged from 0 to 10
with a mean of .63 and a standard deviation of 1.2. While only 4.5 percent of
the 289 cities had no APWA members at all, 61.2 percent had no IES members.
IES membership was unrelated to Mainstem use with a correlation coefficient
of .02.

The final area of organizational interest was that of civil service and unions.
Two variables were concerned with civil service influence and two with unions.
None of the variables, however, were related to Mainstem use. Almost 75 percent of the 167 responding PW departments (73.1 percent) had a formal civil
service system based on the merit system, although only 21.6 percent of the
department heads were covered by civil service. Most serve at the pleasure of
their appointing authority. Again, both Pearson's r and X^2 were used to test the
strength of the relationships between the two civil service variables and Mainstem
adoption. Neither variable was significant at the .05 level. The same held true
with unionization—the presence of collective bargaining and/or union contracts
was unrelated to Mainstem adoption when tested at the .05 level by both r
and X^2.

The zero order relationships, however, do not present a clear picture concerning the nature of the Mainstem adoption. The slight positive relationship
between per capita public works expenditures (remember, the figures are for
1969) and Mainstem adoption suggests that Mainstem may be adopted in an
effort to reduce costs. On the other hand, the financial slack-Mainstem relationship suggests that Mainstem adoption may be amenity based.

The relationship between the city ADP score and Mainstem was surprising.
It was expected that a low ADP score would be related to Mainstem adoption.
Perhaps, however, in this instance a high ADP score is indicative of more than
equipment availability. Perhaps the high ADP score indicates a familiarity on
the part of city administrators with sophisticated computer outputs. Perhaps
it is this recognition, based on experience, that Mainstem can provide a useful
management product that explains the positive relationship between city ADP
score and Mainstem adoption. Finally, the location of the vehicle-maintenance
function outside the PW department and APWA membership were both related
to the use of Mainstem services.

Again, however, there is a limit to the usefulness of reliance on zero order

---

[d]The relationship between size and number of APWA members working for the city
is $r = .69$.

correlations. Thus partials were computed in an attempt to isolate the contributions of the many variables in the model. Initially, partials were computed between each of the numerous organizational characteristics and the Mainstem variable controlling for the community environment, demand, and the organizational environment. Although limited by small n's, the results of the computations are very similar to the zero order relationships. Only one variable, PW department performs vehicle maintenance, was significantly related to Mainstem use at the .01 level. The negative coefficient of $r = -.28$ again indicates that cities in which the PW department is not involved with vehicle maintenance are more likely to utilize Mainstem services than are cities in which vehicle maintenance is a PW function.

To a lesser degree (the .05 level), the same appears to hold true with equipment maintenance. Departments with an equipment maintenance division are less likely to use Mainstem than those without. Does this then suggest that PW managers are less cost conscious than other department heads? Probably not. As will be shown in the case studies, it is suggested that a high degree of professionalism in PW coupled with an overlapping relationship between Mainstem, the APWA, and Public Technology, Inc. (PTI), have probably worked to the short-run disadvantage of Mainstem sales. It is most likely that the elaborate linkages between the three organizations and their cooperative and individual activities served to upgrade the vehicle-management function of city government without the specific purchase of Mainstem services. Thus Mainstem has been relatively more successful in cities in which the PW department is not responsible for vehicle or equipment maintenance.

While professionalism, as expressed by the number of APWA members working for the city, was related to Mainstem use at the zero order level, the introduction of controls reduced the coefficient from .15 to .09—not significant. It thus appears that APWA membership is a function of size or other variables. Caution must be used, however, before dismissing the possible influence of APWA membership on innovation adoption. The introduction of controls substantially reduced the n. In fact, the reduction was from an n of 289 at the zero order level to only 71 under controls. It is therefore possible, though not likely, that a change in the distribution of the variables brought about by the reduced n might account for the lack of relationship under controlled conditions.

In any event, following the precedence of the earlier models, all variables not significant at the .01 level were eliminated from further consideration in the model. Thus the revised organizational characteristics portion of the model consists of only one variable—PW department performs vehicle maintenance.

Next the relationship between the organizational environment and Mainstem use controlling for the community environment, demand, and the vehicle maintenance variable was computed. Only the computer variable, city ADP score, was significantly related to Mainstem use with $r = .29$. The positive relationship between city ADP score and Mainstem held up (in fact, increased) under controls.

The relationship between the organizational environment and the vehicle-maintenance function controlling for community environment and demand was next examined. None of the variables in the organizational environment showed a substantial relationship with the location of the vehicle-maintenance function. Thus, with the exception of the city ADP score, the variable of the organizational environment was removed from further consideration in the model department.

Recall that in the zero order computations there was a slight relationship between one of the demand variables and Mainstem. In computing the relationships between the two demand variables and Mainstem, controlling for community environment, the city ADP score, and the vehicle-maintenance variable, this same variable, per capita PW expenditure, was independently related to Mainstem with $r = .25$. This finding gives added credence to the suggestion made earlier that Mainstem, as now applied, is an innovation based on need.

Next the relationship between the two demand variables and vehicle maintenance controlling for community environment and the city ADP score were computed. Both total and per capita public works expenditures were significantly related to the location of the vehicle-maintenance function with $r = .28$ and .37 respectively. Thus other things being equal, higher PW expenditures are related to departments having the vehicle-maintenance function. This finding was obviously expected.

There was no reason to expect a significant correlation between the demand variables and the city ADP score controlling for community environment. In fact, no substantial relationship did exist.

Nor was there any reason to expect substantial correlations between the community environment variables and Mainstem use under controls as none of the zero order correlations were significant. As expected, there was no direct linkage between the community environment and innovation adoption.

There was, however, a direct relationship between several of the community environment variables and demand controlling for the remaining variables in the community environment. As expected, the coefficient between size and total PW expenditures was a substantial .61 (Table 5-6). This relationship was expected—large cities obviously spend more total funds on PW than do small cities. The other relationship between a community environment variable and demand again supports the expectation. The relationship between SES and per capita PW expenditures was $r = .19$. Thus high SES or wealthy cities spend a higher per capita amount on PW than do their poorer counterparts.

Next the relationship between community environment and the city ADP score controlling for demand was computed. There is very little difference between the relationship here and the same relationship in the housing, library, and city process models. SES again showed a rather strong independent

Table 5-6
Relationship Between Community Environment and Demand
Controlling for Remaining Community Environment Variables

Variable	Total PW Expenditure	Per Capita PW Expenditure
Liberalism	.149*	.102
SES	-.062	.191**
Suburb	-.160	-.017
Ethnic/Ghetto	.065*	.131*
Size	.611**	.049
Population Increase	-.032	.032
Group Quarters	-.030	-.066

*Significant at the .05 level.
**Significant at the .01 level.

relationship with city computer use ($r = .34$). Suburb was negatively related to computer use, and size showed a slight positive relationship, although neither was significant at the .01 level. These findings concerning the determinant of computer use are almost carbon copies of the earlier findings.

Finally, the relationship between the community environment and the vehicle-maintenance function controlling for demand and the organizational environment was computed. The highest coefficient obtained was only .06 between SES and the location of vehicle maintenance. It thus appears that community characteristics have only an indirect bearing on the location of vehicle maintenance within the city bureaucratic structure.

Figure 5-4 summarizes the finding concerning Mainstem adoption as indicated by the model testing. Three variables—representing demand, the organizational environment, and organizational characteristics—apparently influence the use of the Mainstem vehicle fleet-management program in larger American cities. The three variables explain approximately 15 percent of the variation in Mainstem use with $r = .38$. Table 5-7 summarizes a stepwise multiple regression including the three variables showing an independent relationship with Mainstem use. All three variables appear to contribute substantially to the variation in the dependent variable. The city ADP score, however, in that it was the first variable added, seems to be the most influential determinant of the adoption of Mainstem.

Based on the quantitative analysis and the model testing, it is now possible to summarize the model concerning Mainstem adoption. In this model, the socioeconomic characteristics of the community, as captured by the SES factor, appear to form the basis for Mainstem adoption. A high socioeconomic level in the city provides a high level of PW (and other) support on a per capita basis.

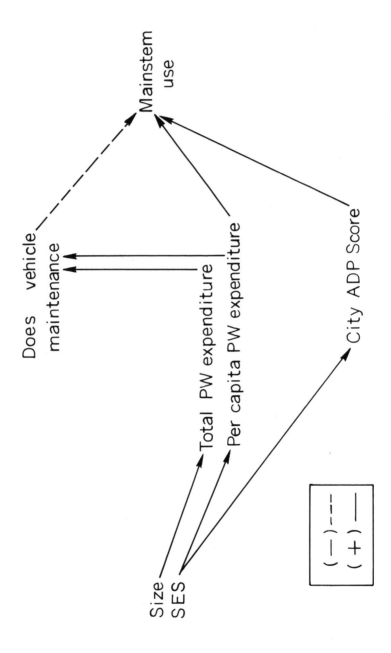

Figure 5-4. Revised Model for Contracting for Mainstem Services

Table 5-7

Summary of Stepwise Regression Explaining Mainstem Use

Variable	R	R^2
City ADP Score	.23002	.05291
Performs Vehicle Maintenance	.29790	.08874
Per Capita PW Expenditure	.37666	.14187

As we discovered in earlier models and affirm here, SES is also significantly related to a highly developed city computer capability.

Not present in this analysis, but again suggested in an earlier model, is the interrelationship between SES, reformism in city government, and the city ADP score. The zero order correlation between SES and reformism was $r = .27$, and between reformism and the ADP score was .16. Thus high SES cities tend to have the structural characteristics of the reform movement as well as to be high computer users.

Initially it was expected that cities with very low ADP scores would be Mainstem users based on the rationale that cities with low level computer capabilities would be forced to "contract out" with Mainstem to obtain the kind of management information necessary for effective vehicle fleet management. This was not the case, however—in fact, just the opposite was true. Cities with high ADP scores were the most probable Mainstem customers. This suggests an alternative explanation. It is quite possible that a high ADP score indicates that city officials are familiar with and use computer-compiled information in their day-to-day operations. It is perhaps this experience that makes local bureaucrats amenable and even enthusiastic about the type and level of information that Mainstem can provide. Thus the only satisfactory explanation of the ADP-Mainstem relationship is to assume that a high city ADP score is representative of a certain bureaucratic experience—an experience that can see positive benefit to the information that Mainstem can provide.

The relationship between per capita PW expenditures (1969) and Mainstem use was as hypothesized. It appears that high cost PW in 1969 shows an independent relationship with Mainstem use. That is, controlling for the vehicle-maintenance function and the other variables in the model, it appears that a high cost of PW in the late 1960s leads to the adoption of Mainstem in the 1970s—presumably as a cost-reduction mechanism. Again then the model for the adoption of the city product innovation supports rational considerations. Innovation adoption appears to be based on a desire to reduce cost. Granted, these high costs tend to be in high SES cities—but then there is no reason why wealthy cities should not be concerned about the high cost of the provision of municipal services.[e]

---

[e]Recall, however, that there was no significant relationship between SES and Mainstem either at the zero order level or with controls.

For our purposes, the positive linkage between the demand variables and the location of the vehicle-maintenance function was expected but adds nothing to the explanation of Mainstem use. Thus the model had not succeeded in isolating variables related to the location of the vehicle-maintenance function although the location of the function is unquestionably related to Mainstem use. It is in cities where the vehicle maintenance function falls outside the jurisdiction of the PW department that Mainstem adoption is prevalent. We found no "hard" data to explain this relationship. The case studies to follow, however, shed some light on probable reasons. As will be shown, the activities of the APWA and PTI have tended to supplant Mainstem contracts in cities with close PW professional ties.

Qualitative Analysis

While the quantitative analysis of Mainstem is unmistakably important, the small number of cities with populations of 50,000 or more contracting for Mainstem service has made generalization tenuous. Thus six cities were visited to examine Mainstem use. Free Too[f] and Convention City both exemplify cities adopting and still using Mainstem. Indian Head and Rocky Mountain had both used Mainstem in recent years but were now operating their own vehicle fleet-management systems. River City and Nouveau Riche, on the other hand, have never used the Mainstem service. The case studies may thus be useful in confirming or denying the quantitative findings.

Indian Head. In September, 1971, the Indian Head DPW hired a new superintendent for its equipment division and entrusted to him the management and maintenance of the city's 800-odd vehicles. The superintendent, with twenty-four years of previous experience in the area of management, considered the director of DPW's decision to hire him an indication of professionalism:

> I rank him (the Director) as a number one professional because of the fact that he went outside to get a manager who understood mechanics. Most cities lean on an internal system for promotion. Consequently equipment superintendents are usually mechanics, not managers. The director was unique in that he brought in a professional.

The DPW director at this time was also serving in the capacity of acting city manager, a role that possessed the political clout that would prove necessary in "persuading" the city to contract with Mainstem. Having been a member of

---

[f]The 1960 population of Free Too was less than 50,000. However, Free Too provided a case study close to Free City and could thus be accomplished at little cost.

the APWA since 1962, the DPW director had wide association with the organization and was consequently quite familiar with the Mainstem vehicle-maintenance system, a system endorsed by the APWA in 1970. Even prior to the new superintendent's employment, the director had approached the city council for tentative approval for a contract with Mainstem. When the new superintendent met with the director, the director informed him of the possibilities of a Mainstem contract, but he emphasized that the decision would be left to the superintendent. The superintendent thereupon contacted the Mainstem representative.

There was little question in the superintendent's mind that something had to be done. When he arrived, the PW 200 X 400 square foot garage was filled, with 150 pieces waiting outside for service. As the superintendent recounts: "Equipment utilization was zilch—everything was down." The police department's fleet was in dire straits. Of seventy-two police vehicles, fifty were either out of circulation or had requests for service. It was a particularly frustrating situation at this time, inasmuch as the police were hard pressed to quiet a racially explosive city that had just witnessed the bombing of school busses in reaction to court-ordered school desegregation. Yet maintenance of the police fleet was handled in a separate garage, manned by seven men on two shifts. Although this garage had three mechanics, only one qualified, in the superintendent's opinion, as professional. It was a frustrating situation with the question again being raised, "How can mechanics be managers?"

If the condition of the fleet was distressing for the superintendent, the record keeping managed by the finance department was to be his breaking point. As he recalled:

I had drawn my own conclusions from the information given by Finance—it was a complete farce! The financial problems faced were considerable. Their revolving fund was a "paper" entry with no monies for replacement of equipment. Financial reports were printed by the pound, but there was no semblance of any cost accounting. For example, after six months on Mainstem it was determined that cost was about $27.50 an hour per vehicle, where the budget had been built on $9.00 an hour. It was out of whack.

Nevertheless, as the finance department had a computer, the superintendent approached them with the request that they develop a management information system. Although they were opposed to having an outside firm come in, the finance department rejected the proposition. One administrator explained the lack of agreement as arising from "personality conflict." The superintendent, however, recalled that their excuse was rooted in politics. "They had built their empire on data processing," he stated, "and were not anxious to alienate other departments with an effective cost accounting system. As long as they balanced the budget, they considered it sound accounting." Whether it was "politics" or "personality conflict," (and it appeared to be both) there was to be no in-house management information system. Nevertheless, the superintendent waited until he saw the August records before making a decision. When they arrived in October, "two months late and with little semblance of record keeping on vehicles," he threw them out and contacted Mainstem.

Had it not been for the fact that the DPW director was also acting city manager, the Indian Head contract with Mainstem may have never taken place. Inasmuch as all the city departments were aware that Mainstem would establish cost accounting for their use of vehicles and consequently charge appropriate rental fees from their budgets, they opposed it. The finance department was particularly adamant in its opposition to an outside firm intruding in its realm of responsibility. It required political pressure, but as the director had already secured tentative approval from the council and was able to steer it through as acting city manager, Mainstem was contracted in the late fall of 1971. On December 20, 1971, the system input began, and by the first week of February, 1972, maintenance reports were being received with regularity.

The decision to adopt Mainstem and the steps required to implement it, however, are two different matters. Mainstem requires the completion of detailed forms as well as knowledge of vehicle codes, prerequisites demanding literacy on the part of the employees. Of the employees within the Equipment Division, however, the superintendent found thirty-five men who had less than a fourth-grade education and who were unable to comprehend what they read. As 50 percent of the employees were functionally illiterate, one full shift was invested to train the crews on completion of forms. A high school co-op program, a program designed to provide high school training for employees, was also provided. Further adjustment, however, was required as well.

While there remains no question that the superintendent's endorsement was necessary for the successful implementation of Mainstem, Indian Head's equipment supervisor notes that the cooperation of foremen was just as critical. A considerable amount of time and persuasion was required on the part of the superintendent for the successful adoption of the computerized management information system. It is worth it, he adds. Despite these apparent successes, the superintendent's days were numbered in his capacity as manager of Indian Head's fleet of vehicles.

In June, 1973, the city government was reorganized. In addition to switching from a calendar to fiscal year, each department assumed responsibility for its own vehicle maintenance, forcing the PW staff to be reduced by twenty-eight men. Among those slated to go was the superintendent of the equipment division, a post and department no longer in existence. Although the DPW continued to use Mainstem, it was only for an additional year and for a fleet of 200 vehicles. In June, 1974, Mainstem was discontinued by the

DPW. In its place, the DPW employed a management information system designed by the finance department that utilized the city's own computer. The DPW's superintendent of transportation noted that "the accounting people are cooperative now." Mainstem, he added, was dropped because

> We now have a system (MIS) that gives us all we need. Mainstem provided too much information—just volumes of paper. If you have no other way of doing it, Mainstem would be excellent. We didn't even know back then what preventive maintenance was. We do now and our own in-house system provides the info we need on repairs, maintenance and utilization.

As for the fate of the former superintendent, his experience with the Mainstem system induced the APWA to retain him as a consultant in a joint APWA/PTI research project designed to develop a standard equipment management information system. While PTI was to work on the actual software system design, the superintendent acted on behalf of the APWA, consulting with thirty participating cities and preparing "an updated management manual which would facilitate the implementation of current management techniques." It would appear fitting that one who so strongly endorsed the Mainstem system would find himself actively involved in the final stages of a project, which upon its completion, would provide a basic computerized vehicle-maintenance system for all PW departments.

Free Too. In a January, 1975, editorial in the *Free Too Gazette*, the city of Free Too was commended for having the lowest tax rate of all comparable cities in the state. This almost obsessive drive of the city to maximize efficiency and thus keep taxes at a minimum was, for the most part, the explanation behind the adoption of the Mainstem system of fleet management for PW.

Before the PW director outlined the 1973 decision to contract with the APWA-endorsed Mainstem Corporation, he sought to explain the environment in which such a decision was made. Free Too has used the council-manager form of government since 1924. It prides itself on its level of professionalism in city government, using what the city manager calls "the team management approach." While the separate departments are autonomous in their own right, there is a coordinated effort for all operations. Perhaps, after efficiency, the highest consideration in all operations is cost. For example, in 1964 the state department of natural resources ordered Free Too to improve its sewage-treatment facilities. As the PW director recounted:

> We were disappointed with the ultra-conservative approach offered by the first consulting engineers. They were so traditional, it was obvious they weren't keeping up to date. We studied all available material there

was on sewerage treatment and were well aware that the traditional approach would be obsolete in a matter of years. We found another consulting engineer who was aware of the advancements and ended up visiting Germany to investigate an innovative design in sewage treatment. Although the system would cost $50,000 more than the one offered by the conservative firm, we determined that it could be made up in three years. Actually it only took one to justify the additional expense. The German system needed only one shift of employees and utilized an alarm system for the rest of the day. The cost savings on manpower alone, not mentioning efficiency, were considerable.

The degree of professionalism displayed in the above case was found in what one might call "professional awareness." Rather than place the decision in the hands of consulting engineers, whose "expertise" in the area of sewage treatment might warrant an "experience knows best" attitude on the part of Free Too, the PW administration simultaneously carried on its own research. Although they did not have the "expertise," they did have the professional training needed to understand the technical journals on the subject and the ability to understand the need for advanced designs.

The Free Too DPW detests the image created during the depression of PW being the catchall of unemployment with a man leaning on his shovel as the national logo. They insist that PW must be run as efficiently and effectively as any private business. Consequently, Free Too's DPW cuts fat at every opportunity. They construct their own storm sewers and build their own roadbeds, contracting out only when necessary, as for excavation and pavement. Their winter road crews are utilized for maintenance or construction in the off season, thus eliminating all forms of seasonal or part-time employment. It is what the director calls, "a versatile labor staff."

Prior to implementation of Mainstem in 1973, the director recalled that the Free Too "cost accounting system was good but I wanted something better." For instance, on special assessment jobs, there was a need to pinpoint the exact cost to properly assess the taxpayer. Materials and labor could be accounted for, but it was impossible to set the assessment for vehicle use on a particular job.

The director first learned of Mainstem at a PW seminar at the state university. Before committing himself to anything, however, the director informed the city manager that a visit ought to be made to a city that had already implemented the system. In February, 1972, the director, the assistant director, and the superintendent of equipment of the DPW went to Indian Head to see Mainstem in operation. There they met the Indian Head DPW equipment superintendent who recalled how apprehensive the Free Too superintendent initially was of the system.

It is important at this point to understand the necessity of securing the superintendent's unqualified support before introducing Mainstem's computerized system of vehicle maintenance. As the assistant director of PW emphatically pointed out:

> The superintendent *must* be consulted as additional paper work is required, calling for much more organization and preparation on his part.

The former Indian Head superintendent only reinforced this, adding,

> The heart of Mainstem involves the total foremen cooperation and it is the superintendent who must manage them.

He further recalled that the apprehension of the Free Too superintendent was, in his opinion, a reaction to the additional paperwork and unfamiliarity with the system.

The trip to Indian Head convinced the participants that Mainstem was worth a try. With the backing of the superintendent, the director of PW began negotiations with the Mainstem representative while the assistant director proceeded to canvass by mail every city utilizing the system. Word came back from the various DPWs that indeed it was a good system, but preparation was an absolute necessity. After the director "had worked on him (Mainstem representative) for six months," a preliminary contract was negotiated and presented to the common council for approval. The vehicle-maintenance system became operational in September, 1973.

Free Too exemplifies a city without fear of innovating, provided that innovation serves a purpose and offers a saving to the city. When a disposal truck was developed that required a one-man rather than a three-man crew, for example, Free Too converted to its use only after a study guaranteed cost savings. When Free Too was faced with a parking problem that threatened the profits of local merchants, it was the city manager himself who invented a parking meter that offered a solution. As the bulk of sales were made by shoppers who knew what they wanted, rather than browsers and window shoppers, the city manager developed a meter that gave the first fifteen minutes free but hiked the rate for any time thereafter. This allowed the city to encourage "profitable" shoppers without losing any revenue itself, the long-term shoppers making up the difference.

In 1973, when bulk paper waste was being purchased at a premium by recycling firms, Free Too initiated a limited solid-waste recycling program that not only afforded the city a profit but answered a more pressing problem of limited space for solid-waste disposal. The rationale given at the time by the assistant director of PW lends itself to explaining the overall attitude of Free Too's city government. As he stated:

During the past two years the subject of solid waste recycling has been under close examination and while philosophically desirable, it has not appeared to be economically feasible. *By economically feasible, I mean a program which is financially self-supporting without tax dollars, and one which fills a real need other than a sentimental one.* . . . It is noteworthy that we have been able to develop this effort without going to the council for funds to get it underway. [emphasis ours]

Another "economically feasible" innovation was developed in November, 1974, when the city began recycling 90 percent of its petrochemical wastes with a state firm, thereby eliminating a hazardous waste-disposal problem. Not only was the city able to find a solution to a disposal problem, but at the same time it was able to use the recycled oil and antifreeze at a considerable cost savings in fleet operation. As the city manager remarked to this investigator, "We're always looking for a newer method."

If perhaps this lengthy heralding of Free Too's innovative, cost-saving practices has been taxing, it was done to illustrate more clearly the environment in which the decision to use Mainstem was made. Free Too is, needless to say, progressive, a trait equally characteristic of those managing the city. The present city manager is a professional brought in to manage Free Too with the experience he had accumulated in five other cities. Other participants in the Mainstem decision, notably the director and assistant director of PW, were no less qualified. The director (since 1970) had been with the city for twenty-four years—experience that no doubt contributed to his election as president of the Professional Engineers of the state. He was additionally honored in 1971 by being named a "Top Ten Public Works Man-of-the-Year" by the APWA. The assistant director, a protege of the director, was named the Outstanding Engineer in the state in 1973, no less a distinction than that held by his superior.

As has been noted, the decision to adopt Mainstem was made in September, 1973. It was a decision made on the precepts that it would furnish a tax savings to the city and assistance in management, factors that were carefully researched beforehand by Free Too's DPW. The evidence was to prove that their research had been justified. A 1974 memo written by the assistant director indicated that Mainstem information would save the taxpayers $14,500 in 1975.

Whether it involved a new sewage-treatment center, a lack of space for solid-waste disposal, a potential hazard in disposing of petrochemical wastes, a need for vehicle-maintenance data, or simply a municipal parking-space shortage, there was a recognized need for innovation by the city. Adoption of an innovation was based on need, not amenity. Though the city manager stated: "We're always looking for a newer method," he qualified that search by adding, "if it provides a time and cost savings." Once the city recognizes a need, it goes "shopping" for a solution, not necessarily selecting the first alternative that satisfied the goal. Whether it involved travelling to Germany or to Indian Head, final decision was delayed until all the possible avenues were explored. Experience of others ranked high in all deliberations, but "expertise" alone did not guarantee adoption. The adoption of innovation by Free Too is decided on only after it is determined with some degree of certainty that the innovation has been proven; that it would not be an additional burden on the taxpayers; and that it would serve a function in the future as well as provide an answer to the contemporary needs of the city.

Convention City. The adoption of the Mainstem fleet-management system in Convention City effectively had its beginning in a history of interdepartmental conflicts between the police and PW departments. As of early 1957, the DPW was largely responsible for city vehicle fleet maintenance—with the exception of operations pertaining to the airports and parks department. Late that year, after a series of complaints about the quality of service and maintenance of police vehicles, the police garage was removed from the control of the DPW and was made a division of the police department.

In 1959, the vehicle and equipment-maintenance and repair functions were removed from the control of the PW and police departments, were assigned to the city manager's office, and placed under the jurisdiction of the assistant city manager. Also in 1959, the city purchased the Convention City transit company, demolished its old facilities for repair of heavy equipment, and assigned this responsibility to the transit system garage.

Eight years later, in 1967, the superintendent of the police garage assumed the responsibility for all shop operations and coordination. In this capacity, however, he worked directly under the city manager.

In the late 1960s, a former assistant city manager, Gerald Howard, became city manager. Howard recognized the need for improved management in this area and operationally began transferring management functions to the department of purchasing and central supply. On August 1, 1971, formal reassignment was made of the vehicle-maintenance function to this department. On November 1, 1971, ownership of the passenger fleet was transferred to a special fund and in February, 1972, the city trucks were also transferred to this fund. At approximately this same time, the city contracted for vehicle fleet-management service with Mainstem.

These three events, all of which occurred at about the same time, were all interrelated and formed the basis for a new system of vehicle management. They formed the basic components that John Brock, the director of purchasing and central supply, had been working for years to achieve. In the past, in spite of the fact that the city had a council-manager form of government, fleet management had long been ignored. While maintenance was moved around from department to department, each operating unit in the city "owned" its own vehicles. Thus when vehicle replacement time came around,[g] the individual department had to request funds for replacement vehicles in its annual budget. And there was no assurance that the requests would be met. The police department, for example, might have 100 vehicles approaching 60,000 miles, yet the council might appropriate only enough money to replace seventy. Thus thirty vehicles would move into the high-cost maintenance cycle and would contribute to an overburdening of the vehicle-maintenance system. Such was the case year after year in Convention City.

While John Brock had been complaining for years about this situation, past city managers were not overly concerned with vehicle-management problems. In Gerald Howard, however, he found a sympathetic ally. Howard and Brock moved ahead.

The program in vehicle fleet service had three components. First, and probably the easiest, was finding a home for vehicle management. This was accomplished by gradually transferring functions to the department of purchasing and central supply. These actions culminated in August, 1971, when "reassignment was made of the Service Center shops, the Police Garage and the Victoria Yard motor vehicle operations to the Department of Purchasing and Central Supply."

The second component in the development of the program was the development of a functional vehicle-replacement system—a centralized leasing system. Mr. Brock was impressed by the "very good" manual leasing system operated in Nouveau Riche during the 1960s although he understood that "things in Nouveau Riche had gone downhill in recent years." Under the proposed system, all vehicles would be "owned" by the department of purchasing and central supply and would be "leased" to the using department. The department would then be charged a given rate for lease of the vehicle (less fuel). The lease rate was to be set so that when optimum vehicle-replacement time appeared (e.g., five years or 60,000 miles), the using department would have paid enough "lease" money to cover all the maintenance on the vehicle plus cost of replacement. Thus replacements would be "automatic" and the vehicle-replacement costs would not be a portion of the budget subject to the pressures of the city council. Such an effort did require an initial capital outlay, however, and the city council appropriated $1,000,000 in 1971 to start the system off and another $750,000 in 1973 to complete the program. This then was the basis for transferring ownership of the passenger fleet, and later the city-owned trucks, to the special fund.

The third component of the new system was the development of an adequate fleet-management system. If vehicles were to be "rented" out, it was necessary to keep accurate cost records and also to ensure that the vehicles were properly maintained (e.g., lubrication and oil changes, when required). With a fleet size

---

[g]At that time vehicles were replaced after five years or 60,000 miles, whichever came first.

approaching 2,000 vehicles, Mr. Brock recognized the need for an automated system. He requested staff help from the city manager to examine all alternatives. The manager assigned Winston Veller, one of his administrative assistants, the task of looking for alternative plans. Mr. Veller brought Mainstem to the attention of Mr. Brock. Mainstem representatives were then contacted and requested to make a presentation to Convention City.

As a CPO (Certified Public Purchasing Officer), Mr. Brock had no contact with the APWA, with PTI, nor had he ever heard of Mainstem. In their search for a system for Convention City, Mr. Brock or others on his staff visited a number of cities, most notably Los Angeles, but none using Mainstem.

Convention City does not have a centralized computer service for the city. To set up a computerized management system internally, then, the department of purchasing and central supply had only two alternatives as only two city-operated computer systems were large enough and/or had time available to satisfy the needs of the vehicle-management program. One was owned and operated by the Convention City transit system and the other by the city water board. The transit system was not anxious to make its computer available and the water board estimated that $200,000 was needed just to get the system started. On the other hand, the city could "buy in" to a proven Mainstem system for approximately $20,000 per year. This $20,000 not only included the cost of the services but provided the multitude of forms, work orders, etc., that the city would normally have to purchase. Thus Mainstem was the least expensive and best alternative for the city.

Most surprising was the seeming lack of influence of the professional associations in the process in Convention City. Mr. Brock was not familiar with PTI and its activities in fleet management nor had he had any personal contact with the APWA on Mainstem or on the subject of fleet management in general. However, it turned out that professionalism was present all along. While Mr. Brock had no APWA contacts, he is a recent past president of the National Purchasing Institute (NPI) and is a pioneer in introducing fleet-management information to municipal purchasing agents through his association. Mr. Brock says that there are three cities in the country that anyone interested in fleet management should visit—Los Angeles, River City, and Convention City. Through his association activities, he was instrumental in scheduling a presentation on fleet management by a Mainstem representative (although Mainstem was never specifically mentioned by name) at a recent NPI annual meeting. Thus professionalism was an important part of the Mainstem adoption in Convention City. Mr. Brock, however, is an innovator rather than a follower.

Thus, while we found a relationship between PW professionalism and Mainstem, it appears that our assumptions were too limited—we should have looked beyond PW.

Rocky Mountain. A study of the Rocky Mountain DPW proves most interesting, for in it one finds the transition from an extremely backward and inefficient fleet-maintenance program to a self-sufficient, in-house, and innovative operation with the Mainstem system providing the catalyst for change.

In 1969, after an extremely long history of city departmental complaints against the DPW's fleet-maintenance operation, Rocky Mountain's city government was forced to assess the situation. The disenchantment with the DPW's particular operation was no doubt justified. Maintaining a garage with only three mechanics and one mechanic assistant, the majority of fleet maintenance was farmed out to different private garages. Different service stations were used by the varying departments for gasoline and oil purchase, while the purchase of tires and parts was just as diversified. There was little, if any, synchronization of vehicle maintenance and control, and yet the Rocky Mountain DPW was, on paper, in charge of operations. As the streets superintendent recalled:

> Shop operations were just not producing. We were overwhelmed with dissatisfied customers from the other departments with equipment repairs. When budget time approached we were all faced with either making the recommendation to change or to get rid of it [DPW responsibility for fleet maintenance].

It took nearly two years for the city manager and director of PW to come up with a solution. In 1971, the city decided to contract with Mainstem to "clean up" the operations of the Rocky Mountain DPW fleet-maintenance program. It was a decision that everyone concerned still considers the catalyst for change. As the streets superintendent recalled, "We needed something. We had to show that we had to go forward." After a meeting of all department heads and division chiefs, it was decided to allow Mainstem, through the DPW, to determine the needs of shop maintenance.

Before Mainstem could even begin computerization of vehicle-management operations, however, they had to totally reorganize the disjointed operations, or as one administrator put it: "They brought everything together under one roof." An end was put to farming out equipment to other facilities, and all mechanical repair was put together under central control. The number of mechanics was increased, as was their supportive staff, and a service station was constructed to be the sole source of gasoline and oil. Parts and tire purchasing were centralized, and all maintenance was consolidated into one operation. The Rocky Mountain DPW contracted with Mainstem as a "tool used to clean up the program." After a degree of centralization was accomplished, the DPW and Mainstem were able to integrate their data-processed forms into the management program. To facilitate even further the efficient management of preventive maintenance, the city hired an outsider in 1973 who had both a background in mechanics and administration and who would serve as the assistant city manager for fleet maintenance.

The manager for fleet maintenance utilized the data provided by Mainstem to streamline maintenance operations. Gone were the days of poor management due to poor control. With stock and inventory, vehicle history, and preventive maintenance costs all data processed, the DPW was able to more accurately assess the various departments for costs. But, as noted earlier, Mainstem was, from the beginning, looked on only as a tool and catalyst for change and not a permanent fixture for DPW management. By 1974, the city manager, the director of PW, the fiscal officer, and the assistant city manager for fleet maintenance concluded that they were operating at maximum efficiency under Mainstem. They also determined that the time had come when fleet maintenance could be made a total in-house operation in Rocky Mountain. The assistant city manager for fleet maintenance was quick to add that

> Mainstem is good. It's an excellent system and an excellent company. For any city that doesn't currently have the direction or capability for an efficient fleet maintenance system, it is certainly worth the cost.

The assistant city manager went on to note:

> There are drawbacks with any batch processing system. Mainstem's data is always thirty days late and historical data is useless for immediate and corrective decision making. The system provides useful data if you're going to use it, but of all the reports provided, we only use the inventory, billing, and historical reports. At a cost of about $900.00 per month it becomes a question of whether you're getting your money's worth.

When Mainstem was first implemented, Rocky Mountain did not have a computer. They have since acquired one, and by May, 1975, the fleet maintenance division of PW expects to be on the system. As the manager recounted, "There was some talk earlier of dropping Mainstem, but as long as we didn't have another system equal to its capabilities, I opposed it." When the DPW was approached by the finance department and told that time was available on the city computer for their operations, the decision was made to go with the in-house program. The rationale for the decision was readily apparent. Whether the DPW used the city computer or not, it was being billed monthly for its operation. As the programmers in the finance department assured the fleet-maintenance office that those programs of Mainstem that they considered useful could be run by the city in a week's time, the opportunity to have near real-time data as opposed to historical data convinced the decision-makers of the DPW. Furthermore, the finanace department would now be able to assume responsibility for direct billing of vehicle costs, relieving the DPW of a two-day operation that was always thirty days behind schedule.

Although everyone concerned in the Rocky Mountain DPW considers

Mainstem the catalytic agent responsible for its transition to efficient vehicle maintenance, it could no longer justify the $900.00 monthly expense when it was now able to manage the system itself. From a totally inefficient and costly operation of fleet maintenance, the city had, in five years, advanced beyond what Mainstem could offer, an interesting metamorphosis.

River City. Inasmuch as River City's DPW was not a client of Mainstem, we expected to find the common manual operations of fleet and vehicle management in practice there. However, such was not the case. River City's DPW was one of the more innovative in the nation in applying computerized fleet management.

The DPW's motor equipment division is somewhat unique because of the city's geographic size. Because the city is one of the largest in geographic area in the country, covering over 300 square miles, it was physically infeasible to control fleet maintenance in one central garage. Consequently, the 825 pieces of equipment are dispersed across the city with five repair facilities responsible for their operation. Needless to say, this peculiar arrangement resulted in decentralized and inefficient management of vehicle maintenance. With each garage and foreman establishing his own quasi-independent form of administrative control because of geographical distance, there was little efficiency in vehicle-maintenance operations.

In late 1970, River City's superintendent of motor equipment retired and the director of PW began looking for a replacement. Coincidentally, the equipment superintendent, from Elmhurst, Illinois, had at this time written to River City's DPW for information on its system of job classification. Responding with the information requested, River City also included a job application for the superintendent.

In March, 1971, the superintendent from Elmhurst was hired as the superintendent of motor equipment for River City. He recounted how, at the time, he was wary of just how much authority he was being given:

> With most organizational decision making you expect the ladder of command approach. I was told that all decisions were mine and wondered, "What's the catch?" But that's exactly how it's been.

It did not take the new superintendent long to recognize the poor state of affairs in fleet management and maintenance. While there was limited cost accounting on the city computer, the reporting of fleet cost by type of vehicle was accomplished manually, an operation that took a minimum of three months to complete. There was little a superintendent could do under that system to keep tabs on the five scattered garages without travelling to each one, a practice made impractical by the city size. In September of that year, the director of PW was elected president of the APWA, an organization that was currently cooperating with Mainstem on vehicle-maintenance systems. Inasmuch as his boss was now president of the APWA, which had endorsed the Mainstem system, and recognizing the need for a system of management, the Superintendent invited Mainstem to send a representative to discuss the possibilities of utilizing its system.

The decision against the utilization of Mainstem by River City was based on the superintendent's opinion that it did not offer complete vehicle coverage. While the programs offered were to his liking, he nevertheless viewed the package as catering to the larger equipment rather than to comprehensive coverage of all vehicles. After seven years of experience as maintenance supervisor with a commercial trucking firm, the superintendent viewed Mainstem as a more commercial-oriented operation for long-haul vehicles than as one specifically designed with the necessary information for a DPW. The dollar value of what Mainstem would cost River City could not be justified, in his opinion, if they couldn't get the information they wanted. The superintendent consequently decided to develop an in-house system that would meet the particular needs of River City's DPW.

The same year (1971), under the Emergency Employment Act, federal funds were utilized to hire two programmers for the purpose of developing a computerized management program. One was assigned to developing a parts-inventory program, the other, a motor equipment-maintenance system. Because of complications, both procedural and personnel, the parts-inventory system was abandoned and all effort concentrated on developing the equipment-maintenance program. The superintendent at that time attended an IBM data systems design course to facilitate communication between himself and the programmers.

It took three phases to fully implement the new system, primarily because management was afraid of alarming the employees and wished to introduce the new method gradually. The prior record system could, in no way, tell what work an employee was doing while the in-house system was able to account for all employees' responsibility. Some veterans, near retirement, resigned because of the system, maintaining the old belief that, "a computer was a threat rather than a tool." Initially, management had considerable difficulty getting the shop personnel to write legibly or submit their reports on time, but, with biweekly meetings scheduled to iron out differences, a gradual tolerance was developed. In time, as the information came in, the benefits became so obvious that tolerant acceptance became enthusiasm. By 1974, the River City PW motor equipment system was in full operation. No longer did the city's geographic size prevent the centralized management of the outlying garages, for now the computer served as a monitoring device for all fleet operations within the 316 square mile city.

While it might be argued that any city's DPW could follow the same approach as River City, provided there were similar federal funds available for employment of programmers and an access to the city computer, the professionalism found in the motor equipment superintendent and his receptiveness toward innovation

certainly require recognition. As has been noted, the Director of PW was
president of the APWA in 1971, and had been vice president the year before.
As the APWA had been working on and advocating a motor equipment data
bank system, it is not surprising that the motor equipment superintendent
found only encouragement from the administrative officers of River City's
DPW in developing a fleet-maintenance system. In short, the development of
an innovative approach to vehicle and fleet maintenance was not revolutionary
in the eyes of the DPW administration but rather was to be expected in light
of the APWA commitment.

This, however, is not to belittle the credit belonging to the superintendent
for advancing beyond the innovative approach offered by Mainstem and
developing an even newer approach to computerized fleet management. For
where the director of PW was a recognized professional in his field, so too was
the superintendent a progressive professional, having been nominated as one
of the "Top Ten Public Works Men of the Year" in 1975. With an educational
background in both public administration and automotive engineering, combined
with thirteen years of motor equipment supervisory work, the River City DPW
superintendent was in a position to recognize the needs and direction required
in a motor equipment system. Having kept close professional contact with the
APWA through APWA institutes and seminars, he was also aware of the progress being made by the professional association on the APWA research project
developing a PW equipment data bank. After the APWA research project had
developed an eight-digit code for vehicle identification, for example, the
superintendent included it in his own data system. Perhaps the greatest indication of his recognized professionalism, however, can be found in his selection
in 1973 as chairman of a joint APWA/PTI steering committee responsible for
developing an equipment management information system that could be adapted
to any city DPW.

Whether it involved the development of a fleet-management data system, a
willingness to try a new product, the establishment of an in-service training program for employees in cooperation with a junior college, or the development
and presentation of a sound on slide program of training for the APWA motor
vehicle equipment management workshop series, the receptiveness of the River
City DPW to new ideas and innovations marks it as a progressive organization.

Nouveau Riche. When it was explained to the director of equipment
services that we were interested in the Nouveau Riche vehicle fleet-management
program, the director's initial response was: "We are probably as far behind as
any city in the country as far as automation is concerned." And this statement
is not far from the truth. The director, Mark Roberts, is making progress; but
progress is slow.

The former director, Mr. Trout, had been in the job for many years. He
was largely opposed to any computer-based system of cost accounting and was

generally quite satisfied with his manual costs system—a very simplified, but slow, system that had been used for years. During Mr. Trout's era costs were not a major problem. There was really very little reason to be concerned with costs as money was plentiful. The major task of the manual cost system was to set rental rates on the various pieces of equipment. With a slow and constant inflation rate, this could almost be done by adding 5 or 6 percent to the previous year's rental rate. Cost data were never used to determine vehicle replacement. Trout used a rule of thumb of "five years or 60,000 miles" to determine vehicle replacement.

Things have not been quite so easy for Roberts. With no city tax increase for the past three years, Roberts has been forced to abandon the "five-year" portion of the rule of thumb and also to bend the 60,000-mile replacement figure to take into consideration the general condition of the vehicle. Roberts does not have a data-processing background but moved to his job from another position within the city. He was formerly in the automobile business although he was not specific about his actual experience.

Roberts has had contact with a representative from Mainstem and is responsible for all the vehicles in the city's fleet except those assigned to the fire department and the parks department—a major responsibility in one of the twenty largest cities in the nation. His office is now completing work on an automated system of its own with a complete vehicle-inventory and an accounting system that will keep track of parts, labor, and fuel and oil costs for each vehicle. Once this is done, he believes that they will have a "pretty good system."

The director's assistant, Bob Smith, came to Nouveau Riche in 1969 as an intern from a neighboring state university where he just finished work on his M.A. in Public Administration. Smith spent several years in the office of the city manager before taking a position as Trout's assistant. He spent about a year under Trout before Trout's retirement and has been working for Roberts for the past two years. Thus, neither Roberts nor Smith are what you could call professional "PW types."

While Roberts stated that Smith was brought in from the manager's office with directions to automate, Smith stated that this was not the case. He applied for the job as he saw that it was a chance to "move up" to a better-paying job with more responsibility within the city. Smith, however, was the spearhead behind automation in fleet management in Nouveau Riche. He spent time with Mainstem representatives, PTI, and APWA officials. During the past several years he had been looking at fleet-management systems and visiting Phoenix, Long Beach, Los Angeles, and a number of other western cities. Smith and Joe Wilborn from the city data-processing section spent a week in Chicago as two of fifty participants in a PTI/APWA program on fleet management.

Nouveau Riche was originally one of eight cities scheduled to implement the PTI fleet-management system, but, as Smith put it, the "package fell apart." Smith stated that PTI initially approached Nouveau Riche asking if the city might be interested in working with them to develop a program. Smith said that "PTI wanted a test city," but that they wanted a definite commitment from Nouveau Riche in terms of personnel to implement the system so Nouveau Riche decided to go its own way.

Wilborn's objections to the system were based on the fact that the program was written in COBOL which he was unaccustomed to using and would therefor cause them a few initial problems, and a belief that the PTI system was geared toward smaller cities.

Smith watched carefully as Sun City, a neighboring city, implemented part of the PTI package, but he was unimpressed (and he claimed Sun City was unimpressed). He claimed that no matter what the input variable values were, vehicle-replacement time "always seemed to come out to be ten years." Smith complained that there were too many data people in PTI and not enough expertise or experience in fleet management.

But why didn't the city adopt Mainstem? According to Smith, the system provides too much detail for their decisions, and also he did not believe that it would be possible to train his mechanics to accurately record the input data Mainstem needed.

Smith claims that the summer workshop in 1973 that he attended in Chicago showed him what was important, what was easy, and what was difficult. He states that he was able to design a system "borrowing from PTI and Mainstem." He also stated that their system was very much like the system used in Sun City— in fact, that they had received a great deal of help from Sun City in designing their present system.

Smith also states that they do not "pay" or have to account for computer time on the city's computer and that the city furnishes a systems analyst or programmer when they need one. (Wilborn reports that city departments are charged a flat rate for computer services.)

There appear to be a number of factors relating to characteristics of the organization that probably contributed to a decision not to use Mainstem (or PTI) but to develop a system internally. Smith was probably right when he said that Mainstem provides "too much detail." It is our belief that the city probably would not know what to do with Mainstem's output at the present time. There is too much output at a level much too complex for use in the decision-making structure of the organization. In fact, the casual approach to management and cost analysis was quite surprising when one considers that Nouveau Riche is a large "reformed" or council-manager city. Apparently fleet management was never of much concern to the city managers that Nouveau Riche has had in recent years.

A second reason for the developments within the city seems to be a result of emulation. Nouveau Riche equipment service personnel seem to look to their neighbor for advice and guidance. Nouveau Riche did not use the PTI system after Sun City expressed dissatisfaction. Nouveau Riche copied the Sun City system. In fact, if Sun City used Mainstem, it is likely that Nouveau Riche would have adopted Mainstem.

Thus it appears that the above two factors may explain failure to adopt Mainstem. Emulation of the equipment management policies of Sun City and slow development of professionalism appear to explain nonadoption. Nouveau Riche has, however, made remarkable progress in recent years. While it is unquestionably a "retarded" city, at least in the area of fleet management, when one recognizes its position of two years ago, in comparison, they have made dynamic progress in a very short time period and under difficult conditions.

Summary

Mainstem adoption again exemplifies a demand-based, predictable, innovation adoption. The quantitative analysis indicates that cost consciousness is independently related to Mainstem use and that high per capita costs are related to city wealth. The fact that Mainstem adoption was found to be positively related to the city ADP score suggests that city administrators familiar with computer outputs might be those most likely to welcome the Mainstem service. Of some surprise in the quantitative analysis was the negative relationship between public works performs vehicle maintenance and Mainstem use. The case studies, however, seem to offer some explanation for this relationship.

Of the six cities studied, only Convention City and Nouveau Riche did not have vehicle fleet-management programs operated by "professional public works types." In Convention City, however, fleet management was the responsibility of the director of purchasing and central supply. While in every sense a professional (but a CPO), the director was not familiar with PTI or the APWA program. It thus appears that in fleet management, professional "public works types" are aware of, and tend to rely on, APWA and other related professional sources. They appear to have more alternatives available than do the non-PW managers. Several of these cities, for example, tailored Mainstem-type programs to conform to their own specific requirements.

Rocky Mountain, a city that dropped Mainstem, and Nouveau Riche, a city that never used the program, had one characteristic in common. In both cases the DPW was billed for computer services whether they used the services or not. This, in effect, caused Rocky Mountain to abandon Mainstem and probably (although no one would admit it) acted as a constraint on Nouveau Riche.

Conclusions

Police computer use showed little relationship with Mainstem adoption.

When computer use was correlated with the Mainstem dichotomous variable, the resulting coefficient was only .01. In the area of the common functions of city government, then, there was again little direct connection between the adoption of process and product innovations.

While police computer use and the use of Mainstem services were not highly correlated, there nevertheless was some similarity in the patterns of adoption of both innovations. First, both innovations showed a positive independent relationship with the city ADP score. A high level of computer use by all city functions stimulates police computer use and the use of Mainstem services. Thus slack or available resources (or knowledge) is instrumental in the adoption of these two innovations.

In both cases, city SES was a major determinant of the city data-processing capability. This was also found to be the case in the housing and library process models.

In both cases, need or demand was positively and independently related to innovation adoption. This fact suggests that need is accurately perceived (in relation to other cities) and acted on.

And finally, in both cases, city characteristics provided the basis for the operation of the system. In the adoption of computer assistance by police departments, however, the city characteristics were much more important than in Mainstem use.

The study of the adoption of technological innovations by city government apparently broke the pattern or distinction between process and product innovations as shown in the preceding three chapters. In studying the adoption of Mainstem services by city government, Mainstem adoption largely followed the hypothesized model of innovation adoption suggested in Chapter 1. This behavior thus suggests a breakdown of the distinction between process and product innovations and adds credence to the operating versus nonoperating distinction between innovations. But does it?

Is Mainstem use truly a product innovation adoption? Chapter 1 recognized that Mainstem use was not a true "product" in the strict sense of the term but the adoption of a service. After a detailed investigation into Mainstem operation, we no longer believe that it adequately fits the definition of a product innovation. It does not appear to be ". . . physical. That is, the product innovations under study all involve the adoption of a new physical product—a product produced by another organization." Is Mainstem use, then, a process innovation? Does it "require a change in process, or in the way things are done in the organization?" Mainstem use does not fit either definition very well. A purchase has been made from a private vendor—albeit a one-year contract for a service. At the same time, Mainstem use indicates a new way of doing things—managing vehicle fleets.

After the detailed investigation of Mainstem, it appears that Mainstem adoption more closely fits the definition of process innovation than product innovation. Clearly, if the city were to produce Mainstem-type management information itself, a process innovation would have occurred. And yet the Mainstem model suggests that more is involved. The negative relationship between one of the organizational characteristics, PW department does vehicle maintenance, and Mainstem use does not suggest a new process. If a process innovation were involved, it is likely that this relationship would be positive. The Mainstem findings, then, really suggest a new category of innovation adoption—the adoption of a service innovation. Service innovations appear to be closely related to process innovations, but they are done by an outside organization. Such innovations differ from both product and process innovations in that they do not require the level of commitment that new processes and products require. They can be temporary innovations—and, in fact, Mainstem was used in just that way in Indian Head and Rocky Mountain.

The findings concerning innovation adoption by city government thus suggest a new classification for innovations—the service innovation. The service innovation appears to be similar in behavior to the process innovation but adoption is on a temporary basis. The next chapter will deal in some detail with the potential uses of such a classification.

6 Toward a Policy Perspective

This chapter attempts to cover a great deal of ground, much of which has been untouched in previous chapters. There are five sections that will draw on the results of the study and on other literature to contribute to the present understanding of technological innovation in local government. The first section of the chapter covers the diffusion, or spread, of innovations—both geographically and over time. The second section briefly summarizes the findings by functional area and presents the results of the hypothesis testing. This section is followed by the presentation of a model that distinguishes between political and bureaucratic innovations and seeks to explain the influences leading to technological innovation in the bureaucracy. The fourth section, "policy-related questions," attempts to draw the findings of the research together in a policy framework. Finally, the chapter concludes with some suggested policy alternatives.

Innovation Diffusion

The definition of innovation specified in Chapter 1—the Becker and Whisler definition of innovation as "the first or early use of an idea by one of a set of organizations with similar goals"[1] —necessitates some discourse on the S-shaped innovation curve. A variety of social science studies in the past have indicated that over time new innovations are adopted in accordance with a curve resembling an S.[2] These findings have recently been found applicable to the adoption of political policy[3] and the adoption of technological innovations by local government.[4] Roughly, new innovations are adopted slowly over the early period of innovation. This period is followed by a second period of rapid adoption while the innovation is "hot" or popular, and is followed in turn by a slowing in the rate of adoption and waning public interest—thus the S-shaped curve. This process often covers a period of years—twenty to thirty or more.

By adopting the Becker and Whisler definition, however, the eight innovations examined were studied during the early phases of adoption—on the lower half of the S-curve. The conclusions presented in this chapter are thus conclusions concerning leaders or early adopters. The authors of this study consider risk to be an important part of innovation—thus the emphasis on current innovations and early innovators. Therefore, the conclusions presented in this chapter deal specifically with early adopters—those on the lower portion of the S-curve.

The Innovative City

The first question to be examined in considering the diffusion of innovations involves the search for the innovative city. If cities, or more correctly governments within cities, tend to be innovative or noninnovative, as the case may be, there should be some correlation between innovations across governmental units. To test this possibility, each innovation was correlated with the remaining innovations. The results are shown in Table 6-1. Only four of the thirty-six substantive coefficients are significant at the .01 level with the highest correlation being the $r = .29$ between housing computer use and police computer use. Library computer use was also significantly related to both housing and police computer-use scores, suggesting that these relationships are dependent on general city computer capabilities and emphasis. The only other substantial relationship noted was the $r = .21$ between housing prefab and Mainstem use.

Table 6-1 appears to substantiate the independence of innovation adoption across cities. With the exception of computer use, cities that are innovative in one area are not particularly innovative in others. This is true of innovations in all categories. Is this then true of all cities or only cities in general? This study identified only one city that apparently could serve as a model for innovation— River City. River City was in an advanced state concerning most of the innovations covered: public housing, public works, and police. In public libraries and schools they had also adopted the innovations under study but were not at an exceptional level. The only exception was in individualized instruction. In this case River City had only one IPI school—rather low for a large city.

There thus does not appear to be any substantial number of innovative cities. River City was the only exception, and even here, unexpectedly high levels of innovation were not noted across all organizations.

This finding, however, is obviously qualified. It is possible to conclude that there are, in general, no innovative cities only over the eight innovations studied. In a strict sense then, it is not possible to generalize very far beyond these eight innovations—the study can only suggest rather than conclude with certainty.

A second reason for qualification concerns the methodology. Although Gray, in studying a handful of policy innovations in the states, found that her most innovative states corresponded closely with Jack L. Walker's;[5] nevertheless, there is some danger that the study of specific innovations may miss some truly innovative cities.

On the other hand, the preliminary results of a study still in progress substantiate our original conclusions.[6] Feller and Menzel also find that there are no innovative cities. Innovation seldom stretches beyond a particular agency. Their finding, then, seems to substantiate the findings here.

Geographic Diffusion

A second important consideration in innovation diffusion is the location of

Table 6-1
Zero Order Relationships Between All Innovations Studied

	Housing Computer	Housing Modular	Housing Prefab	Individual-ized Instruction	VTRs	Library Computer	Library Theft-detection Systems	Police Computer	Mainstem
Housing Computer	1.000								
Housing Modular	.088	1.000							
Housing Prefab	-.043	.192*	1.000						
Individualized Instruction	-.083	-.038	.011	1.000					
VTRs	-.035	.049	-.043	-.023	1.000				
Library Computer	.205**	-.046	.102	-.045	-.034	1.000			
Library Theft-detection	.141*	.075	.034	.052	-.009	.081	1.000		
Police Computer	.286**	.019	.010	.026	-.056	.258**	.014	1.000	
Mainstem	.110*	-.101	.205**	.015	-.013	.070	.062	.009	1.000

*Significant at the .05 level.
**Significant at the .01 level.

innovating governmental units in relation to noninnovating units. One of the hypotheses of this study suggested that "cities adopting innovations are located in close physical proximity to other innovation adopting cities." To test this possibility, a mean innovation score for each state was computed for each innovation studied and was plotted on the maps in the Appendix. Innovation scores were determined simply by adding the specific innovation scores (e.g., housing computer-use scores) for all the cities with populations over 50,000 in a given state and dividing by the number of cities in that state. Although the measure is obviously biased against the more populous states, it does provide a crude measure of diffusion. Figure 6-1, for example, reproduces the mean housing percent modular from the Appendix. The map clearly shows the regional nature of the innovation. With the exceptions of California, Florida, Georgia, and North Carolina, the innovation is largely restricted to a Northeast-Northcentral belt running from Massachusetts to Illinois. Most of the innovations studied have similar regional concentrations; nor is there significant overlap. Library computer use, for example, is stronger in the West and South than in the Northeast-Northcentral belt.

A number of the case studies illustrated the dependence on physical proximity in the diffusion process. Nouveau Riche, for example, relied heavily on Sun City for guidance in vehicle management. Free Too officials visited Indian Head to learn about Mainstem. The River City Police Department handles a constant stream of visitors concerned with police computer applications. Such experiences point up the importance of interorganizational ties in the spread of innovation. It thus appears that there is some basis to contentions that there is a geographic basis for the spread of innovation.

In-state Diffusion

A third consideration in the diffusion of innovation in local government is the impact of the state. Are large cities in certain states more innovative than cities in other states? To test this possibility each of the state-innovation scores was correlated with the other state-innovation scores. The results of this computation are found in Table 6-2. It does not appear that cities in certain states are more innovative than cities in other states. Only one of the coefficients produced was significant at the .01 level. States in which city governments were likely to be Mainstem users were also likely to have libraries adopting theft-detection systems. These two innovations were the only innovations showing a substantial relationship on a state-by-state basis.

Do policy-innovative states tend to have the most innovative cities? Jack Walker developed composite innovation scores for the American states based on their adoption of new programs or policies.[7] To examine the relationship between innovativeness in cities within each state and Walker's score, an average innovation score for cities within each state was computed. This index was

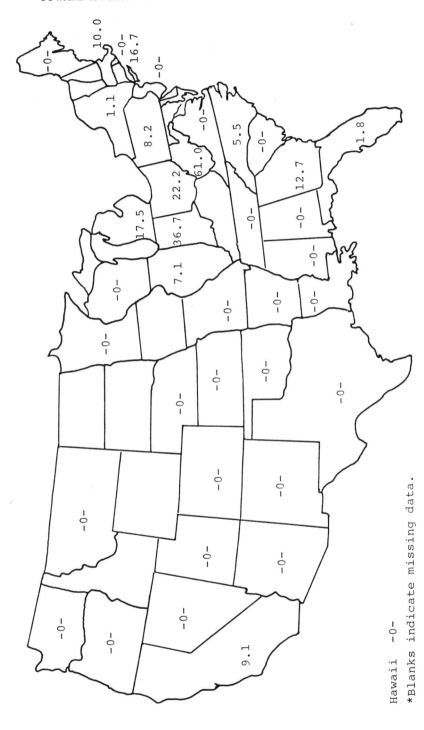

Hawaii -0-

*Blanks indicate missing data.

Figure 6-1. Mean Housing Percentage Modular, by State*

Table 6-2
Zero Order Relationships Between State-Innovation Scores for All Innovations Studied

	Housing Computer	Housing Modular	Housing Prefab	Mainstem	Library Theft-detection Systems	Police Computer	Library Computer	VTRs	Individualized Instruction
Housing Computer	1.000								
Housing Modular	.046	1.000							
Housing Prefab	-.097	.204	1.000						
Mainstem	-.170	-.173	.135	1.000					
Library Theft-detection	-.029	.003	.188	.366**	1.000				
Police Computer	-.106	-.111	-.098	-.202	-.159	1.000			
Library Computer	.116	-.221	.277*	.285*	.279*	.009	1.000		
VTRs	-.174	.205	-.047	-.085	.100	.006	-.055	1.000	
Individualized Instruction	.072	-.109	.077	-.085	-.141	-.057	-.028	-.026	1.000

*Significant at the .05 level.
**Significant at the .01 level.

then correlated with Walker's score to test the relationship between city innovativeness and state policy innovation. A coefficient of $r = -.12$ was produced (not significant at the .05 level). There thus appears to be no substantive relationship between state policy innovation and city bureaucratic innovativeness.

In summary, then, it can reasonably be concluded that there are no national diffusion patterns of innovation in local government. Diffusion patterns and cue-taking appear to exist, but these patterns are determined largely by the specific innovation. In addition, we found little evidence that there are particularly innovative or noninnovative cities (River City being the possible exception). Nor are cities in certain states more innovative than cities in other states.

While the measure was admittedly rough, there was also no relationship between mean innovation scores for each state and Walker's measure of state policy innovation. It thus appears that policy-innovative states do not necessarily contain cities that rapidly adopt new technologies. One important fact did emerge from this exercise, however. While Walker noted that southern states tended to lag behind in terms of policy innovation, we found no such pattern. Cities in southern states are as innovative (or noninnovative) as their counterparts in other parts of the country.

Hypothesis Testing

Before testing the individual hypotheses posed in Chapter 1, it might be a good idea to briefly review the findings in each of the specific governmental units examined.

Summary

Public Housing Authorities. Certain factors emerge from the study of computer-based management information in public housing. First, the data, both quantitative and qualitative, suggest that adoption is based on predictable considerations—considerations influenced by demand, efficiency, and resource availability. Community characteristics are obviously the first step in the process. The quantitative model showed clearly that community characteristics largely determine the management problem (number of units in management). They also determine some of the attributes of the organizational environment that lead to LHA computer use—attributes such as city per capita revenue or city emphasis on ADP use.

The number of units in management was related to the number of authority employees. There was, however, a negative relationship between number of employees and computer use. Both sets of data, quantitative and qualitative, suggest that computers and sophisticated management information systems are adopted in an effort to keep down manpower levels. That is, as authorities grow in size (number of units to be managed), authority decision-makers turn to the computer for assistance rather than to increased personnel levels.

The case studies also indicate that within the organization, the comptroller is perhaps the key decision-maker in computer-use decisions.

The organizational environment was the most important direct determinant of computer use. A high city ADP score (partially based on reformism) and a high city per capita revenue apparently provide the resources necessary for system development. MIP participation was, of course, the most important single variable. The intergovernmental influence took shape in two ways. First, the PHMIP proposal competition allowed federal officials to influence the provision of computer management information by providing them with discretion in selecting program participants. PHMIP also provided the selected LHAs with adequate funding for the development of computer-based systems.

The influence of the consultants in obtaining federal assistance is strongly suggested by the case studies. Two cities, Free City and Easton, were MIP participants. In both cases the applications to HUD for participation in the program were largely the product of outside consultants.

As in the case of the housing process innovation, the product innovation case studies substantiate the quantitative findings. The case studies emphasized the importance of turnkey as a vehicle for product innovations in public housing. In every instance of innovative behavior, in terms of modular or prefab use, turnkey provided the vehicle for innovation.

A second factor was brought out by several of the case studies. The political trend away from large-scale housing projects and their built-in economies, is a trend that favors modular use. Thus the smaller developments in keeping with the scattered-site concept are amenable to factory-built housing.

In one community, restrictive building codes prevented modular and prefab use in public housing as well as in private sector homes and apartments. It is quite likely that similar restrictive codes are in force in many other heavily industrialized (and unionized) areas.

Public School Districts. Quantitative and qualitative analysis of the adoption of individualized instruction indicates that such programs are clearly amenity adoptions with teacher resources being the primary key. All things being equal, school districts with larger staffs are more inclined to adopt individualized instruction programs. These communities generally have a high percentage of college-bound graduates and a low dropout rate. They also muster the financial resources necessary to provide a relatively large staff. City size and socioeconomic characteristics are also important indirect contributors.

While educators around the country were generally in agreement that videotape equipment constituted an important technological innovation in education, little of a positive nature can be said about the adoption pattern of the innovation. Both the quantitative and qualitative studies suggest, however, that the videotape recorders, like programs of individualized instruction, are amenity innovations. While the case studies suggest that levels of adoption may in part be based on the value placed on the innovation by local directors of instructional materials, it is probable that the innovation has been "held in abeyance" pending the resolution of the copyright problems.

Public Libraries. The library process model points up the conflicting nature of innovation adoption. The model appears to indicate that adoption is based both on need and amenity value. The positive independent relationship between staff size and computer use indicates adoption for amenity reasons. As the Aqueduct City Librarian noted: "A primary reason for computerization is not to cut staff but to release the staff for personal services." On the other hand, the positive independent relationship between library organization and computer use suggests a need-based innovation.

The case studies, while interesting, do not add much to the model. In Free City the move toward a regional library system obviously accounted for increased automation, but so did the lucky availability of expert help.

In Aqueduct, automation was obviously the result of the new independence of the Aqueduct Public Library and the immense cataloging task it brought; while in Nouveau County, the strange nature of the library organization accounts for the lack of automation in the library system.

Like the other product innovations studied, professionals in the library field were in general agreement that theft-detection systems constitute an important technological innovation for libraries. Little can be said concerning the reasons for adoption, however. The quantitative analysis was completely unsuccessful in terms of presenting a valid model of theft-detection systems adoption.

Nor was there any underlying motive common to the case studies to suggest reasons for adoption. One factor, however, was common to both the quantitative analysis and the case studies—the difficulty libraries have in determining an accurate theft rate. About the only way to accurately determine losses is through an inventory (either random sample or full inventory)—and such inventories are very expensive.

The Common Functions of City Government. Police computer use is unquestionably based on demand and operationalized by high levels of available resources, although the resources were not necessarily financial. The quantitative model clearly illustrates the demand basis of the system. Two of the community characteristics, ethnic/ghetto and size, were clearly important determinants of the crime rate and the police computer-use score. The crime indices, in turn, were both positively related to the computer-use score and the variables of the organizational environment. Within the organizational environment, the city ADP score proved to be the major determinant of the police computer-use score. This relationship was again emphasized in the case studies. Police computer use was closely related to the city computer capability.

Mainstem adoption again exemplifies a demand-based, predictable innovation adoption. The quantitative analysis indicates that cost consciousness is independently related to Mainstem use and that high per capita costs are related to city wealth. The fact that Mainstem adoption was found to be positively related to the city ADP score suggests that city administrators familiar with computer outputs might be those most likely to welcome the Mainstem service. Of some surprise in the quantitative analysis was the negative relationship between public works performs vehicle maintenance and Mainstem use. The case studies, however, seem to offer some explanation for this relationship.

Testing the Hypotheses

Before moving to a theoretical discussion of innovation adoption in local government, it is necessary to test, one by one, the hypotheses presented in Chapter 1. Table 6-3 presents a summary of the findings of the hypothesis testing over all innovations. In Table 6-3, D indicates a direct relationship while I indicates that the relationship is indirect. City size, for example, indirectly affects the library computer score (though demand) while it affects police computer use both directly and indirectly. The letter P indicates a possible relationship—that is, a relationship suggested by the case studies. Finally, the letter N indicates that the hypothesis was quantitatively tested but that no relationship was found. A subscript "p" (Np) indicates that the relationship was only examined in the case study phase but that no relationship between variables was noted. The subscript w behind one of the indicators (for example, Iw) indicates that the hypothesized relationship between variables does in fact exist, but that the relationship is in the opposite direction from that expected (e.g., city size negatively related to innovation). A case will be made later in this chapter for the process-service-product designations for innovation in local government. While examination within such designations may be premature without a theoretical foundation, nevertheless, in the long run, consideration within these categories should lead to a more complete understanding of innovation adoption.

The hypotheses regarding the relationships between the community environment and demand variables and innovation adoption are largely accepted for process and service innovations. None of the expected relationships, however, materialized for the product innovations. City size was shown to be a major determining factor in innovation adoption although the influence was largely indirect. Size influenced all process and service innovations indirectly while also exhibiting a direct influence on computer use by police departments. These findings, then, are somewhat at odds with earlier policy studies which indicate that size is a direct determinant of output.[8] The findings here are not necessarily conflicting, however, but merely point out differences between policy and technological innovations. It is very likely that size is a direct policy determinant but

Table 6-3
Summary of Findings of Hypothesis Testing Over All Innovations

Hypotheses	Process Innovation				Service Innovation	Product Innovation		
	Housing Computer	School Individual-ized Ed.	Library Computer	Police Computer	Mainstem	Housing Prefab/ Modular	Schools VTRs	Library Theft-detection
Community Environment and Specific Demand Factors								
1. City size is positively related to the adoption of technological innovation.	I	I	I	D, I	I	N	N	N
2. Socioeconomic factors are related to the adoption of technological innovation.	I	I	I	D, I	I	N	N	N
a. Innovation adoption in low-status cities is based on need.	I, P	I	I	N	I	N	N	N
b. Innovation adoption in high-status cities is based on amenity value.	I, P	I	I	N	I	N	N	N
3. The presence of "conservative" political values in a community is negatively related to the adoption of technological innovation.	I	I	N	N	N	N	N	N
Organizational Environment								
1. The adoption of innovation by local government is positively related to federal or state assistance.	D, P	I	P	N		N	N	P
2. Cities adopting innovations are located in close physical proximity to other innovation adopting cities.	yes	yes	yes	yes	yes	yes	no	no
3. "Professionalism" in local government acts to speed up the innovative process.	I	N	N	N, P	I	N	N	N
4. The existence of slack resources in the organizational environment is positively related to the adoption of innovation.	D	I, P	N, P	D, P	D	N	N	N, P

Table 6-3 (cont.)

Hypotheses	Process Innovation				Service Innovation	Product Innovation		
	Housing Computer	School Individual-ized Ed.	Library Computer	Police Computer	Mainstem	Housing Prefab/ Modular	Schools VTRs	Library Theft-detection
5. Vendor activity is positively related to the adoption of innovation.	P	Np	Np	Np	Np	D, P		Np
Organizational Characteristics								
1. The adoption of innovation is positively related to an appointed (vs. elected) decision-making body.	N	N		P	N	N	N	
2. Governmental units directed by elected officials have a high propensity to adopt innovation based on need (versus amenity) value.		N		Pw			N	
3. A formal decision-making structure is negatively related to the adoption of innovation.		Np	Np				N, Np	Np
4. A centralized decision-making structure is negatively related to the adoption of innovation.		Np	Np				N, Np	Np
5. Organizational size is positively related to the adoption of innovation.	Dw, Pw	D	D	N	N	N	N	N
6. The level of organizational funding is positively related to the adoption of innovation.		I	N	N	Iw	N	N	N
7. The presence of a large number of professionally oriented individuals in an organization is positively related to the adoption of innovation.	D, P	N		N	N, P	N	N	Np
8. The presence of a civil service structure and/or employee unions is negatively related to the adoption of innovation.					N	P		

D = Directly   P = Possible   Blank = Not tested
I = Indirectly   N = No relationship   W = Wrong

(from case studies)

only indirectly influences technological innovations. In terms of technological adoptions, however, the influence of city size is largely felt through demand, the organizational environment, and the organizational characteristics.

The same conclusions are basically true concerning the socioeconomic characteristics of the city. Again, for process and service innovations, the influence of socioeconomic variables on innovation adoption is substantial, but indirect. Again no relationship was noted between these variables and the adoption of the technological products studied.

In examining the basis for innovation adoption, the study rather clearly showed a distinction between need and amenity adoptions—a distinction first suggested by Oliver P. Williams and Charles R. Adrian.[9] The need-amenity distinctions could only be made on a post hoc basis, however. Need-amenity distinctions may or may not apply to the innovation itself, but are determined after the fact and are based on adoption patterns. Programs of individualized instruction, for example, do not appear to have been developed explicitly for either low or high expenditure school districts. The innovation itself, then, is not particularly amenity oriented. It is only the post hoc or after-the-fact examination of adoption patterns that suggests this distinction. High levels of use of individualized instruction are found largely in high SES cities with low school dropout rates and a high percentage of college-bound students. These communities also provide high levels of funding for public schools as well as a lower pupil/teacher ratio. The adoption pattern of individualized instruction programs thus conforms to the Williams and Adrian amenity typology.

A word of caution is suggested, however. It is possible that, over the entire time period of the S-curve of adoption, the amenity pattern may disappear. It may be that high SES cities provide the best "laboratories" for trying out new and unproven educational programs. The same may be true of the other apparent amenity adoptions discovered in the preceding chapters.

Regardless of the possible long-term outcomes, however, the post hoc examination of adoption patterns seems to support the idea of a need-amenity continuum. Several innovations appeared to be adopted in an attempt to "upgrade substandard performance or to significantly reduce the governmental unit's operating expenses." On the other hand, other innovation adoption patterns suggest an attempt to "improve already adequate performance." Other innovations showed patterns of adoption suggesting both a need and amenity base.

"Conservative" or "liberal" community attitudes, at least as measured here, have little to do with the adoption of technologies by local bureaucracies. In two cases (again both process innovations), community attitudes appeared to affect funding levels and funding priorities which, in turn, influenced innovation adoption. Community attitudes thus appear to affect adoption only through the provision/withholding of funds or the determination of spending priorities such as emphasizing school expenditures at the expense of other local governments.

Thus the characteristics of the community and the demands they generate

have an extremely important effect upon innovation adoption. While the effect
is largely indirect, it nevertheless provides the basis for a rational demand system
of innovation adoption.

Within the organizational environment, direct or indirect assistance by the
federal or state government was an important determinant of process innovation
adoption (except for LEAA assistance and police computer use). Of equal importance, however, was the intergovernmental assistance provided by city government. The obvious example is the importance of a well-developed city computer
capability in stimulating computer use by other local units. The significant influence of federal programs on innovation adoption was clearly.indicated by the
importance of the HUD MIP program in stimulating computer use.

Did form of government (reformism or professionalism) affect innovation
adoption? Only in a very small way. Other things being equal, reformed cities
were most likely to have highly developed computer capabilities which, in turn,
led to higher levels of adoption in other local units. Overall, however, the effect
of reformism is limited and indirect.

Resource availability, loosely defined as slack resources, was an extremely
important stimulus to innovation adoption. Resources in the form of funds,
equipment, and/or specialized or expert assistance were found to be directly or
indirectly related to process and service innovations in every case. In addition,
in those cases where a number of variables contributed independently to innovation adoption, it was the external resources that carried the greatest weight in
adoption as determined by stepwise multiple regression routines. Resource availability unquestionably provides the major impetus to innovation adoption.

Vendor influence in innovation was quite limited and was largely restricted
to modular/prefab innovations in housing and to computer applications in public
housing. The case studies in the housing area—especially in the development of
computer services—provide an interesting example of the influence of service
vendors on process innovations. Of the twelve (not including San Juan, Puerto
Rico) MIP cities, eight had computer programs developed and/or run by service
innovation firms. The average computer-use score for these eight housing authorities was 9 while the mean computer-use score for all authorities was only 1.7.
In fact, of the six highest computer scores, five were in MIP cities which had service vendors providing computer service by contract or had outside consultants
set up the locally operated system. Thus the service vendor provides an option to
in-house process innovation—an option to be discussed in more detail later in the
chapter.

Within the organizational environment, then, intergovernmental aid and
resource availability, or slack, are the major determinants of innovation. The
influence of vendors and government reformism or professionalism is small and
insignificant although the service vendor appears to offer significant potential for
innovation use and acceptance.

The characteristics of the organization, with the exception of organizational size, do not generally affect adoption levels. With the exception of the trend toward library consolidation and regional organization and its relationship to computer use, it makes little difference in terms of innovation adoption how agencies are organized, whether a governmental unit was reformed or unreformed, or whether it was headed by appointed or elected officials. Such variables were included in the model in all cases except with the common functions of city government and even here the influence of city reformism was tested. These organizational characteristics just do not seem to make very much difference.

The case studies also found no distinction concerning adoption based upon formal decision-making structure or centralization. In fact, these hypotheses were only relevant in the case of the school districts. In libraries, housing authorities, public works departments, and police departments, all decision-making is extremely centralized. There is virtually no chance that more than a handful of employees in any of these organizations will have an input into decisions to innovate. In school districts this was not the case. In school districts, however, formalization and centralization had little bearing on adoption. Some high adopters exhibited extreme centralization in decision-making while others were equally decentralized.

Little independent impact was noted either in terms of organizational funding, union or civil service influence, or professional orientations. Influence of these variables on innovation was indirect or sporadic although organizational funding was an important indirect determinant of individualized education in public schools and professionalsim was important in decisions to use Mainstem and computers in public housing (as suggested by the case studies).

The independent impact of organizational size was striking. In spite of a rather substantial number of size related variables in each model, organizational size was a direct determinant of innovation adoption in three of the four process innovations. Direction of the relationship, however, was dependent on the need-amenity nature of the adoption pattern.

Within local governments, then, the size of the organization is the primary organizational variable determining innovation adoption and level of adoption. While Mohr hypothesized that it was specialization and professionalization that led to the perception of a performance gap in large organizations[10] (and thus innovation), evidence presented here suggests that the independent effect of organizational size is as a resource. The independent relationships between organizational size and innovation in housing authorities, school districts, and public libraries—relationships independent of community size, demand, level of funding, etc.—suggest the resource nature of personnel levels or organizational size. Other things being equal, low personnel levels seem to lead to efficiency or need-based innovations while high personnel levels lead to amenity adoptions.

A number of important conclusions concerning the adoption of innovation by local government are thus suggested by the hypothesis testing. First, of course, is the process-product distinction. The adoption of process innovations is largely determined by those factors included in the model. There is a regularity and predictability to such adoptions. The product innovations studied, on the other hand, are adopted on an irregular or random basis. There is little predictability to such adoptions.

The hypothesis testing also confirmed the existence of, and differing adoption patterns for, need versus amenity innovations. Furthermore, the patterns of adoption of the two types of innovation are based on different community socioeconomic levels. This fact, again suggests a predictable basis for innovation adoption with high-status communities tending to adopt amenity-type innovations while need, or efficiency, innovations are adopted by communities with lower SES levels.

The hypothesis testing also confirmed the important base community characteristics form for innovation adoption. Most community characteristics showed an indirect relationship with adoption. Community characteristics thus determine need or demand and also influence certain characteristics in the organizational environment as well as characteristics of the organization. While previous studies have emphasized the direct relationship between community characteristics and policy innovation, community characteristics influence the adoption of technological innovations largely in an indirect manner.

Two classes of variables in the organizational environment form the major direct determinants of innovation. Intergovernmental assistance, fiscal and otherwise, and resource levels are the most important direct contributors to innovation commitment. Resource availability in one form or another was found to be directly or indirectly related to all process and service innovations. In those cases where intergovernmental aid was specifically available, this assistance also proved to be an important contributor.

And finally, the hypothesis testing suggests that personnel levels, when considered independently of other model variables, serve as a resource rather than sources of professional behavior or other decision-making considerations. Organizational size, then, is an economic resource when controls are introduced.

A Model of Innovation Adoption

While the foregoing material presents a summary of the hypothesis testing, little has been said thus far about the process of innovation or why innovations are adopted. It is suggested that a model for the adoption of technological innovation by local government might be quite similar to Figure 6-2.

The solid directional arrows shown in Figure 6-2 indicate that significant independent relationships between variables in the categories shown existed for at least three of the specific innovations tested. The number in parentheses indicates the number of models in which the relationships were found to exist. This then substantially modifies the hypothesized model of Figure 1-1.

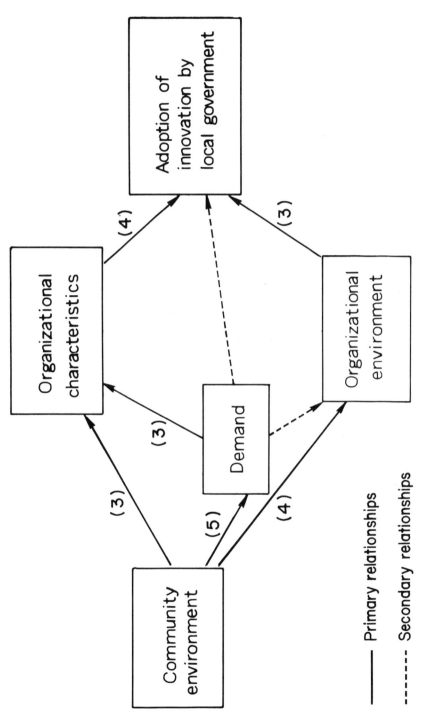

Figure 6-2. A Model for the Adoption of Technological Innovation by Local Government

Community environment affects innovation adoption significantly but only indirectly. The community environment is a significant determinant of all three intervening variables but is not a direct determinant of innovation adoption. The most constant relationship noted was the determining relationship between the community environment and demand. The community environment, however, unquestionably provides the base for innovation. While not directly affecting adoption as hypothesized, the community environment does generate demand variables and works through both organizational factors to affect innovation adoption.

Demand, on the other hand, appears to affect only organizational characteristics with any regularity. Demand, however, was an important variable area in all five process-service innovation models. The dashed lines on Figure 6-2 indicate secondary relationships—that is, relationships existing in two of the models tested. Thus the impact of demand, while scattered, is also shown to be an indirect determinant of innovation.

The organizational characteristics and the organizational environment, as both are influenced by the community environment and demand, are the major direct determinants of innovation adoption and thus offer the policy-maker the best areas for intervention. One organizational characteristic, size, was most consistently related to innovation adoption, however.

In those cases where environmental factors were related (e.g. federal aid), the organizational environment was the most influential. Strangely, the characteristics of the organization are not substantially influenced by the organizational environment. It is the community environment and demand that influence the characteristics of the organization.

Innovation adoption is thus largely influenced through the system hypothesized in Chapter 1—but with some significant modifications. Of major importance is the indirect influence of the community environment and demand upon innovation. Only two of the four independent variable clusters were directly related to adoption with the organizational environment serving as the area most amenable to intervention.

Political versus Bureaucratic Innovations

A second question that must be dealt with is the relationship between the adoption of, or use of, public policies by the political sector and the adoption of technological innovations by local government. While definitional problems have plagued innovation researchers, so has the tendency to lump together all kinds of innovation—from major policy adoptions to new fire hose nozzles. In fact, these two adoptions represent very different kinds of innovation. One way of classifying innovations, then, is by adopting unit. It is therefore helpful to think of innovation in local government in two categories—political and bureaucratic innovations.

Political innovation is public policy. In local government this policy may originate from the executive section (mayor or manager), the legislative (the city council), or through a combination of both. Under this definition, then, political innovation is a first, or early, adoption of a new government policy by one of a set of local governments with similar goals. Bureaucratic innovation, on the other hand, is in response to political innovation or new policy, or is adopted in response to the feedback to public service. Bureaucratic innovation may encompass a change in process, a change in organizational structure, and/or a new product or service. If the board of directors of a local housing authority, for example, adopts a policy of constructing or leasing housing for low-income families on a scattered-site basis only, and if it were one of the first authorities in the country to do so, it has accomplished a political innovation. If the authority bureaucracy then responds by reorganizing the maintenance section to provide mobile and rapid maintenance response to these scattered housing units, a bureaucratic innovation had been adopted. The adoption of techno-logical innovation, in this sense, is merely a specific kind of bureaucratic innova-tion.

Figure 6-3 presents a general model for the adoption of innovations by local government. The model shows the relationship between political and bureaucratic innovations. It suggests that demands for political innovation are created by the environment and are transformed into policy by the political system. This new policy then serves as a demand for change in the bureaucracy, a change that leads to bureaucratic innovation. The output of the bureaucratic innovation is public service. A new or changed public service then acts to alter the environment and public attitudes which, in turn, lead to other innovative policies. The bureaucracy itself may also see a need for a change in the public service it provides without a change in policy. In this case bureaucratic innova-tion may be internally generated. Demand for bureaucratic change may also be generated without a change in policy. Availability of resources such as grants or intergovernmental cooperation also generates an opportunity for bureau-cratic innovation without a change in policy.

The importance of the characteristics of the community environment as a base for innovation cannot be questioned. A multitude of urban policy studies has established the importance of the community environment in the develop-ment of public policy.[11] Socioeconomic variables appear to be good predictors of public policy regardless of whether the policy adoption is innovative or mature. In addition to the standard socioeconomic factors, the community power structure and local political culture also have a direct impact on the adoption of political innovations.

Environmental attitudes are operationalized through the attitudes and behavior of the political leaders.[12] The leaders operating through the executive, legislative, and judicial branches of the political system at all levels of govern-ment produce urban policy outputs. In many cases it takes action by federal, state, and local governments to produce the political innovations of local

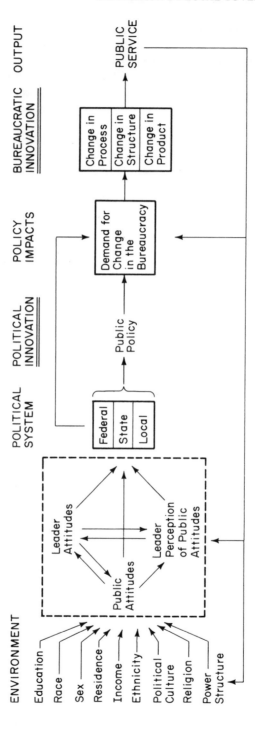

Figure 6-3. A Model for the Adoption of Innovation by Local Government

government. Recall that Hawley studied the adoption of urban renewal by local government when it was a political innovation—that is, before the "fragile" issue had matured. This political innovation, like many others, required action by all three levels of government. The federal government passed the Housing Act of 1949 providing assistance to local government for slum clearance and redevelopment. State governments then had to pass the appropriate enabling legislation, and local government had to adopt the program. Thus local political innovation often requires affirmative action by all three levels of government.

Innovative public policy demands a bureaucratic response—a response leading to bureaucratic innovation, an innovation defined as a change in process, in organizational structure, or in a product used by the agency. Bureaucratic innovation produces a change in public service, in the way a service is delivered, or in the costs involved in providing that service.

Political innovation, however, is not the only determinant of a demand for change in the bureaucracy. Two other areas also produce demand for change. The political system can demand bureaucratic innovation without a change in public policy. Such system induced change is, in fact, very common. Those portions of this study concerned with the adoption of computer technology by local public housing authorities, police departments, and public libraries found that the adoption of these process innovations was independently influenced by intergovernmental cooperation. City governments with well-developed computer capabilities often made these capabilities available to other local government agencies. This "extra resource" provided by the city administration then allowed (and sometimes forced) other local agencies to adopt sophisticated computer-based management information systems.

The availability of financial resources from federal and state governments is also an independent contributor to bureaucratic innovation. This form of resource availability, whether provided annually or on a one-time basis, was directly related to bureaucratic innovation in public housing, police departments, and public schools.

Demand for bureaucratic innovation is also stimulated by the output of the bureaucracy—through the feedback loop. Utilizing the dropout rate and the percentage of high school students going on to college as measures of the output of the public school systems in major American cities, it was found that the most successful school systems in terms of output were the most likely to adopt new and innovative programs (as measured by the adoption of individualized instruction). In this example it is apparent that feedback is a third independent contributor to bureaucratic innovation.

An important distinction must be made concerning the influence of the community environment on the adoption of political and bureaucratic innovations. Public policy, and that class of public policy called *political innovation,* is directly influenced by the conditions of the community environment. Many studies of different public policies confirm this direct relationship. The

community environment is directly related to policy adoptions in local government. The community environment is generally not directly related to
bureaucratic innovation, however. The independent contributors to bureaucratic innovation beyond certain characteristics of the organization itself (e.g.,
size of the organization) are limited to responses to direct feedback from the
public service provided, changes in public policy, and excess resources made
available to the bureaucratic organization by the political system. The characteristics of the local community have an impact on bureaucratic innovation
only indirectly—through the political system. The community environment,
then, is directly related to political innovation but is only indirectly related to
bureaucratic innovation and the adoption of technological innovations by
bureaucracies.

Policy-related Questions

The findings of Chapters 2 through 5 coupled with the summaries presented
thus far in this chapter suggest that certain generalizations may be made concerning the adoption of technological innovation by local government. Obviously
a study of only eight innovations across only four governmental units is a tenuous
base for theory building, and yet striking similarities exist—similarities that suggest logical explanation.

Differences by Governmental Unit. Do technological innovation processes
differ by type of local governmental jurisdiction? Not very much. The reasons
for innovation and the method of innovation (the why and how) are not very
different from one governmental agency to the next.

In terms of the first major research question—why innovation is adopted—the
study turned up no significant difference in reasons for adoption that can be
attributed to differences in governmental jurisdiction. All agencies tend to adopt
or not adopt for pretty much the same reasons. The need-amenity typology,
presented in earlier chapters and elaborated on in the preceding section of this
chapter, tends to form the basis for predictable adoption. Demand also provides
some of the resources necessary for adoption. Again, however, there were no
significant differences in reasons for innovation adoption among the common
functions of local government, public libraries, housing authorities, and school
districts. Furthermore, the way the agency or governmental unit was organized
also made little difference in adoption patterns. As mentioned earlier, with the
exception of the relationship between library regional organization and computer use, it makes little difference in terms of innovation adoption how agencies
are organized, whether a unit was reformed or unreformed, or whether the unit
was headed by an appointed or an elected official.

In terms of the second major research question—how innovation is adopted—

there does seem to be a difference in adoption based on type of jurisdiction. The method of adoption exhibited by school districts was, in some cases, much different than for the other governmental units. While the process differed, the adoption outcome was not related to differences in process.

Decisions to adopt new innovations in the common functions, public libraries, and housing authorities were highly centralized. Only a handful of employees in any of these organizations had any significant input into decisions to innovate. School districts, on the other hand, were not always so centralized. In many cases the decision to adopt individualized programs was made at the local schools. In other districts, however, the central administration made these decisions. In any case, school district decisions to innovate were not necessarily centralized as was the case with the other units. Unfortunately, this characteristic in the case of schools was unrelated to innovation.

Product Distinctions. There were peculiar differences in the successes achieved in model testing based upon process-product distinctions. It is important to recognize at the outset that the product innovations studied are not merely inexpensive devices but represent rather significant financial commitments on the part of adopting units—financial commitments that, in some cases, rival the commitments necessary for the adoption of some of the process innovations examined. This fact thus negates any suggestion that product innovations are merely devices and thus might well be expected to have random adoption patterns.

It seems to us that the distinction between operating and nonoperating innovations made in Chapter 2 is a good one and can be justified. Furthermore, it is logical to suggest that product innovations would be more likely than process innovations to be nonoperating. Certain characteristics were common to the three products that might contribute to an understanding of the random adoption patterns. In the first place, none of the three innovations were developed specifically for use by public agencies. Modular/prefab was not developed for public housing, VTRs were not developed for adoption by public schools, and theft-detection systems were not developed for public libraries. Thus the manufacturers of the product innovations were not specifically oriented to the public market.

There is also a very strong probability that the product innovation vendors in the areas examined in this study do not devote substantial effort to the development of public markets. The 3M ads in *American Libraries* for theft-detection systems were, without exception, directed at college libraries. There are, unfortunately, valid reasons for ignoring the public market. In the first place, public consumption is often limited. After all, how many public libraries are actually large enough to justify the expenditure necessary for a theft-detection system? Another factor limiting product promotion in the public sphere is the difficulty in market aggregation.[13] Technological innovations such as modular or factory-built housing depend on volume production. An inability to aggregate the public market for low-income housing forced modular firms to look to private developers.

The question that must be asked, then, is: Is there something about the nature of local public agencies that makes product innovations irrelevant, or at least unpredictable? In an informal review of this study, one scholar suggested that perhaps product adoptions were not predictable because products are much more visible to the public and therefore possible benefits in relation to costs are more easily weighed in the public's mind.[14] A second scholar agreed—suggesting that visibility may be the best test and suggested that a continuum of visibility or a ranking of innovation visibility might be in order.[15]

Based on the experience gained in this study, the two investigators each independently ranked the eight innovations based on their estimates of the public visibility of the innovations. Results are shown in Table 6-4. While there were some differences in ranking, there was still substantial agreement concerning high or low visibility innovations. Individualized instruction was apparently the most visible innovation followed closely by prefab/modular housing and library theft-detection systems. VTRs and police computer systems apparently are midrange while housing and library computer applications, along with Mainstem, have low visibility. Thus, in terms of the eight innovations studied here, it is difficult to conclude very much concerning public visibility and innovation adoption. In general, the product innovations tended to be more visible than the process innovations, and yet a process variable—individualized instruction—was considered most visible.

The question still remains: Why are product innovations (at least those studied here) unpredictable or nonoperating? It is most likely because the product innovations considered in this study seem to offer the decision-maker in public agencies little incentive to adopt. Decision-makers in bureaucracies seem to seek out and adopt only those innovations that will help them solve real or perceived problems or, in the case of the amenity adoptions, those innovations that will help them maintain an important advantage (or status)

Table 6-4
Public Visibility Rankings of Technological Innovations

Innovation	Investigator 1	Investigator 2	Average
Housing Computer Use	7	6	6.5
Housing Construction	2	3	2.5
Individualized Instruction	1	2	1.5
VTRs	4	4	4.0
Library Computer	7	5	6.0
Library Theft-Detection	4	1	2.5
Police Computer Use	4	7	5.5
Mainstem	7	8	7.5

over similar agencies. In the public sector, products do not always do this.
Since the "product" of a bureaucracy is service, bureaucrats tend to adopt
those kinds of innovations that allow a given service to be provided at a lower
cost (or more accurately at a lower rate of cost increase) or to provide a higher
level of service output (may include patron satisfaction, for example, in the
case of individualized instruction). Process innovations, in general, seem to
provide these kinds of benefits. The process innovations may or may not require the purchase of a new product. In the case of computer assistance in
public-housing management, for example, little in the way of new equipment
was needed by most authorities. On the other hand, a change in a city's
process of solid-waste disposal may require the adoption of transfer stations,
shredders, or other technologies.

A major conclusion of this study, then, is that bureaucrats are not particularly noninnovative, nor are local governments particularly slow to adopt
innovations as sometimes is suggested.[16] The problem appears to be one of
incentive. If incentive is provided, be it need or amenity, local government
will probably respond and, surprisingly, will respond within a very short time
period. The difficulty appears to be in providing incentives. Under our present
system, process innovations (and service innovations, as will be shown later)
are most likely to provide the incentives consistent with the provision of public
services. This, of course, poses special problems for those interested in assuring
that local governments adopt specific products. In the case of nonoperating
product innovations, an incentive must be presented to stimulate adoption.

In summary, then, we find the operating versus nonoperating distinction
concerning innovation adoption to be useful. We also find that process innovations tend to be predictable operating innovations while product innovations
tend to be nonoperating. We suggest that nonoperating innovations are in that
category due to the service-providing nature of local agencies and a lack of
incentive to adopt.

A second significant distinction concerning innovation adoption in local
governments suggest an alternative schema for the consideration of adoption
patterns. This concerns the distinction and potential of a process-service
differential. There actually appear to be three types of innovations adopted by
local government: product innovations, process innovations, and service innovations. Pictorially they might be represented in the following manner:

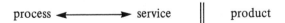

process ◄———————► service   ‖   product

Process and service innovation can be seen as closely related and are, in fact,
often interchangeable. In this study of eight innovations, we ran across a
significant number of service innovations—Mainstem, PTI, MDS, Boeing, OCLC,
IDEA, and Touche Ross, to name a few. Service innovators are public, private,
and private nonprofit. They thus cover the spectrum in terms of organization.

Basically, they provide three process-related functions. First, they may provide a public agency with the materials and training to accomplish a process innovation. This is largely what was done in the area of individualized instruction. Service innovation firms provided material and training for local school personnel to implement IGE, IPI, or PLAN.

Service innovators are also hired to set up new processes for public agencies. In many cases, this exemplifies what was done in the area of public-housing computer use. In this instance, a local housing authority either purchases a computer "package" from a service innovator or hires the service firm to develop and set up the software system. In some cases where a federal grant was involved, the service innovator even wrote the grant proposal.

Service innovators are also hired as a substitute for process innovation. Mainstem and OCLC provide two excellent examples of service innovation in lieu of a process innovation. Mainstem provides management information to local officials—providing the same kinds of information that management could produce itself if it wished to adopt a new process. OCLC does basically the same thing for libraries. It provides computer services and standardized information that the library could produce (to some degree) itself if it adopted a new process.

Thus service innovators often provide local government with "instant expertise." They allow local governments to develop and use processes they normally would not utilize. They also provide local government with a "trial process innovation." Government can contract with a service innovator (e.g., Mainstem) for a certain process output (e.g., vehicle reports) for a given period (one or two years). If government then finds the output useful, it can either continue with the service firm or develop a process of its own. This is exactly what was done by two Mainstem adopters. Both cities had very favorable comments about Mainstem but dropped the service firm to develop and implement a new process on their own. Service innovation thus appears to present policy decision-makers with a significant potential—a potential we suggest should be developed.

Mutable and Nonmutable Variables

Can innovation adoption be stimulated? The findings presented here suggest that this is possible—that certain variables that stimulate innovation adoption may be manipulated. On the other hand, other variables do not lend themselves to intervention. The community environment is nonmutable, at least in the short run. The characteristics of the community are rather inflexible and not subject to immediate change.

The same is true of community attitudes. While community attitudes, at least in two cases, were related to expenditures and expenditure priorities, such attitudes are seldom subject to immediate change. In the short run, then, community attitudes are nonmutable.

Nor were the demand variables mutable. Most were the products of policy adoptions and cannot be altered significantly in the short run.

Certain organizational characteristics are mutable however. The structure of the organization can be changed, elected/appointed leadership patterns can be altered, the size of the organization can be increased or decreased, etc. Unfortunately, manipulation of most of these characteristics will not change the probability of innovation adoption very much. There is one important exception, however. Personnel levels are mutable and do have an effect on innovation adoption. Personnel levels in public housing authorities are directly manipulable by HUD through the budget-approval process. A "squeeze" on personnel levels by HUD should thus stimulate the adoption of efficiency-type innovations (e.g., housing computer use). Similarly, the provision of higher levels of personnel resources may lead to amenity adoptions or experimentation as with individualized instruction in local schools. Within the organization, then, personnel levels provide the policy-maker with the most effective mutable resource.

It is the organizational environment, however, that contains most of the mutable variables. This is largely due to the fact that the external environment provides the resources and external influences in innovation adoption. In the cases of the innovations studied here, there were two classes of mutable variables that seemed to produce the most in the way of innovation adoption and one that was largely disappointing.

Total Resources. Total financial resources is, of course, the first mutable variable concentration. Total resources is mutable through both state and federal aid of the revenue-sharing type. Economic resources, effectively measured on a per capita basis, show a substantial relationship to innovation. Fiscal resources were important contributors to innovation in schools and in the common functions of city government. While high economic resource levels may be important, bloc grants seem to be of limited value. Police departments, for example, did not particularly depend on LEAA assistance for computer funds (although total resources were important). The evidence is obviously sketchy with only one agency receiving bloc grant support (police) and only one receiving revenue-sharing support (schools). Nevertheless, based on the innovations studied here, it is difficult to suggest that either type of grant stimulates innovation.

Spillover Resources. The rather dramatic influence of another mutable variable area, that of externally supplied extra resources or slack, seemed to be extremely important in innovation adoption. The obvious example is the influence of the city computer capability in influencing computer use in public housing, police departments, libraries (case studied), and even in Mainstem adoption. This variable area might be called spillover resources because the resources developed by one local government spillover, or are utilized, by other local agencies—agencies that may or may not be directly connected to the city.

Thus specific aid to local government (e.g., aid for computer development) may have a significant "down the road" impact never imagined in the original aid. Grants of this type may have very favorable effects upon innovation in other agencies over the long run.

Categorical Programs. It is programs such as the HUD MIP program that are the most promising mutable variables, however. HUD seed money, money provided to housing authorities competing with each other to innovate, was extremely influential in the diffusion of computer applications in public housing. There were unquestionably failures—certain MIP participants were never able to accomplish what they set out to do—but that is to be expected with most new programs. Some seemingly good ideas just do not work, or are too complicated, or in the end are too expensive. Programs similar to MIP, however, are obviously mutable and seem to stimulate innovation in a very short period of time. In some part, this is certainly due to the activities of the service innovators.

Other than the manipulation of personnel levels, it appears that the organizational environment contains most of the mutable variables. Bloc grants and revenue-sharing funding, while mutable variables, do not appear to have much effect on innovation adoption. Intergovernmental cooperation in process and equipment use does provide some potential for stimulation of innovation. It is the competitive program like HUD's MIP, however, that appears to offer the policy-maker the largest payoff in terms of rapid and specific innovation adoption.

Other Categories. Other classifications of factors thought to have an impact on innovation adoption have been discussed indirectly in prior sections of this chapter. Conclusions regarding the impact of these distinctions on innovation are by now quite clear. If factors considered in this study were classified as environmental or internal, it is clear that the environment harbors the major innovation determinants. It is the indirect effect of the community environment coupled with the direct influence of the organizational environment that leads to innovation.

Structural characteristics, however, do not influence innovation adoption very much. It is the dynamic variables of the environment, variables often subject to manipulation, that tend to provide the greatest influence.

Policy Alternatives

The research presented here suggests a number of policy alternatives for those interested in stimulating innovation adoption in local government. Some of the suggestions made have already been attempted on a limited scale. Some have failed in the past, and some will be politically difficult to implement.

Nevertheless, the alternatives are presented because we believe that they present effective stimuli to innovation in local government—stimuli that we believe can be provided at a reasonable cost.

Emphasize Process Innovations

Initially, we suggest that there should be a decreased emphasis on the adoption of product innovations. Those concerned with technology transfer or innovation adoption should be concerned largely with process innovations or new and better ways of improving the outputs or services of local government. Concern, then, with specific product adoptions should be limited. Technology transfer agents should concern themselves with general process improvements and only incidentally with specific products. If the city of Milwaukee adopts a solid-waste recycling plant (which it has done), the important measure of output of that decision is an ecologically sound solid waste disposal method rather than the adoption of a specific technological product.

Thus our first recommendation is that product innovations be deemphasized. If officials determine that a product innovation should be emphasized, however, we suggest that the local agency must be presented with an incentive to adopt (recall that most product innovations are nonoperating). The most logical incentive is the categorical matching grant with matching requirement based on anticipated difficulty in persuading local governments to adopt the specific product. Product cost and benefits to be accrued by the local unit are obvious criteria for setting up the matching requirements.

We strongly recommend, however, that those interested in technology transfer emphasize process innovations. By stimulating process innovations, the products will take care of themselves. The old saying, "build a better mousetrap and the world will beat a path to your door" applies to public agencies as well as private—but only to those public agencies that need to catch mice. The emphasis on innovation, then, should be on stimulating mouse catching rather than on the purchase of a specific mousetrap. Emphasize the process goal, and product adoption will take care of itself.

The Potential of the Service Innovator

We suggest that service innovators offer a promising alternative for city governments of all types. Two distinct advantages are offered to local decisionmakers. First, service innovators offer local government "instant expertise" or expert assistance at a price it can afford to pay. And second, service innovators give local government the option of a trial process innovation without the organizational and procedural changes that accompany product innovations. Local government, then, can "try out" the output of a process innovation without going through the headaches of actually adopting.

Although service innovation firms provide promise, there is still a significant element of risk involved in adoption. It is in this "risk" area that the federal government can stimulate adoption. In an earlier study of technological innovation at the state level, Feller, et al, noted that state air-pollution control officials tended to wait until a new technique or innovation had received Environmental Protection Agency approval before they adopted it.[17] Similarly, we suggest a program designed to certify service innovations—those provided by both public and private firms or agencies. We suggest, for example, that HUD certify standardized computer software packages for housing authorities. Such a program would offer local housing officials interested in computer-produced management information a low-risk alternative. The HUD certified firm would obviously be producing an output satisfactory for the annual HUD reports that every authority must prepare. In addition, the cost of the innovation could be spread across all adopters. A certain standardization would also result. And, most importantly, the local official would have an added tool for bargaining with the vendor—if he found service of poor quality, he could made complaints to HUD, perhaps having the vendor's product removed from the certified list. Vendors, since they are interested in selling services, would obviously be aware of the special advantages they accrued by virtue of the fact that their products were certified. Hopefully, then, vendors would be interested in ironing out the problems local units might be having with their outputs.

Concerning the one service innovation we examined, it was interesting to note that we did not hear one adverse remark about Mainstem during the study. Mainstem apparently provided the exact output the firm promised in a timely manner and at a reasonable cost. Even the officials in the two cities having used Mainstem until they developed a process capability of their own had nothing but praise for the firm. Service innovation, then, can be an effective alternative.

Informal Certification

Should a federal (or state) certification program be politically infeasible or undesirable, we suggest, as an alternative, certification by professional associations. Mainstem was, in effect, an informally certified service. APWA approval of the service actually gave Mainstem an informal certification. While obviously not quite the same as a federal certification, APWA approval gave Mainstem a vendor "respectability" not often attributed to firms in the private sector.

Professional associations provide an ideal vehicle for such a program. They are usually governed by the top professionals—men and women capable of passing judgment on the product of a service firm. A good association often provides leadership in innovation through convention papers, workshops, etc.

Professional association journals might also be useful in passing on information about certified firms or processes.

Process Grants

The fourth policy alternative we suggest is the process grant. Patterned after the HUD MIP program, the process grant would provide seed money for process innovations to selected cities or agencies. The awards would be made on a competitive basis like MIP or Model Cities but would be for the development of specific process innovations. Innovations developed with process grant funds would be public property and could be adopted, at cost, by other public agencies. If, for example, the Chicago Housing Authority developed a computer management package under a process grant, this package would be made available at limited cost to other housing authorities. Under the terms of the grant, the software package and documentation would be public property.

Professional Associations

Our final recommendation concerns the use of professional associations. It is our belief that professional associations offer a significant potential for the diffusion of process or service innovations. In some cases, the professional association might provide the service innovation itself, while in other cases it might stimulate the adoption of a new process. We believe that federal funding of process innovation development through professional associations offers the most effective and low-cost method of stimulating the adoption of technological innovation by local government. Such a plan stimulates the professional association to act as a service innovator. It might develop a new process itself and then push for adoption or, as with the APWA fleet-management program, work with private and public firms to develop new programs (APWA worked with Mainstem and PTI).

We believe that this area offers the most potential for technology transfer. The potential influence of the professional associations is enormous and is growing every day. Obviously, more must be learned about diffusion processes in professional organizations as well as the potential for influence association proposals might have.

In conclusion, three policy proposals emerge from the study. First we suggest a deemphasis on hardware and an increasing emphasis on process. Second we suggest a program for the certification of service innovators. And third we suggest federal funding for innovation adoption through professional associations. We suggest that the combination of the three proposals into a coherent policy of technology transfer will assist in the rapid adoption of technology by all types of local government.

Appendix: Geographic Diffusion of Innovations

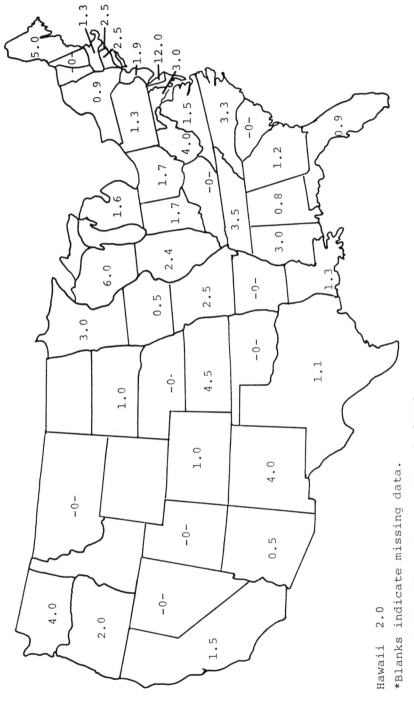

Hawaii 2.0

*Blanks indicate missing data.

Figure A-1. Mean Housing Computer Score, by State*

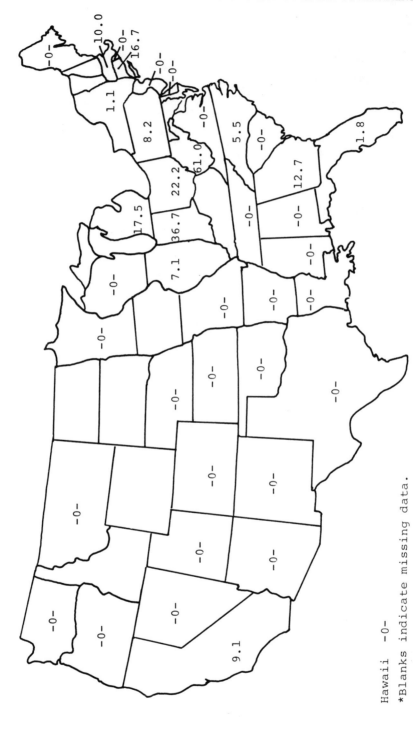

Hawaii   -0-

*Blanks indicate missing data.

Figure A-2. Mean Housing Percentage Modular, by State*

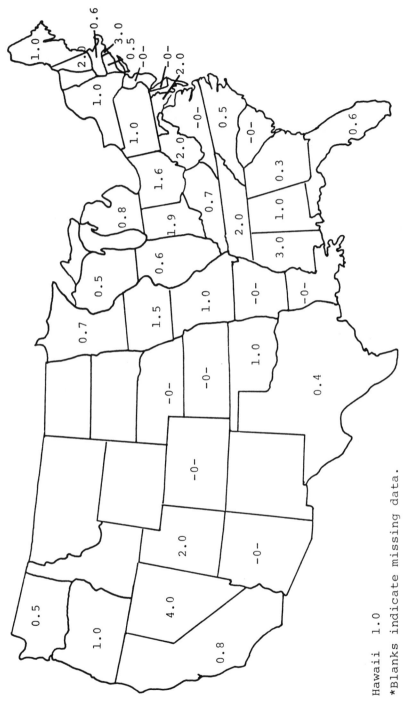

Hawaii 1.0

*Blanks indicate missing data.

Figure A-3. Mean Housing Prefab Score, by State*

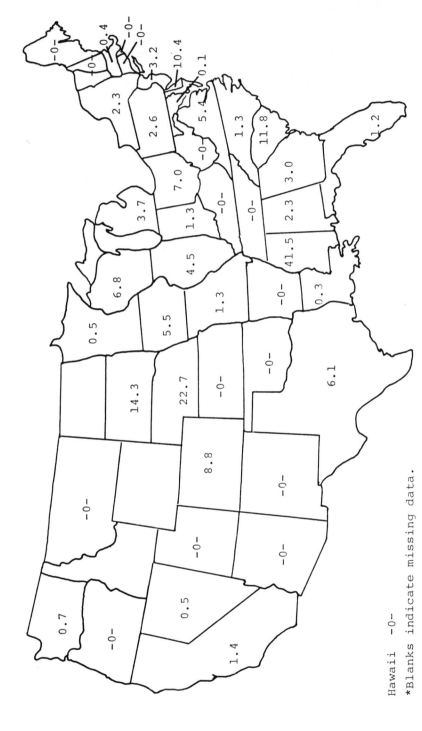

Hawaii -0-

*Blanks indicate missing data.

Figure A-4. Mean Percentage Teachers Using Individualized Instruction, by State*

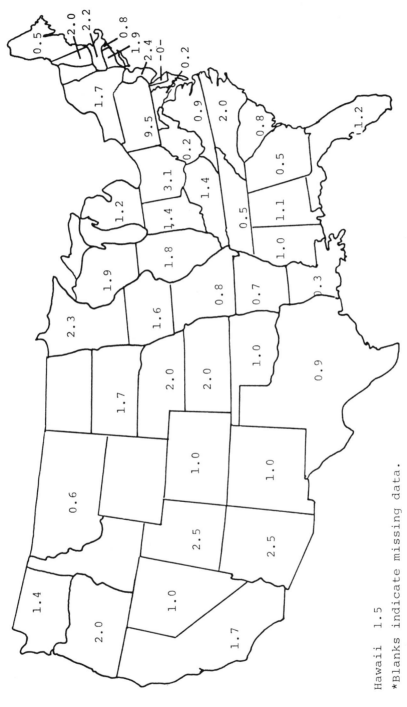

Hawaii 1.5

*Blanks indicate missing data.

Figure A-5. Mean VTRs per Secondary School, by State*

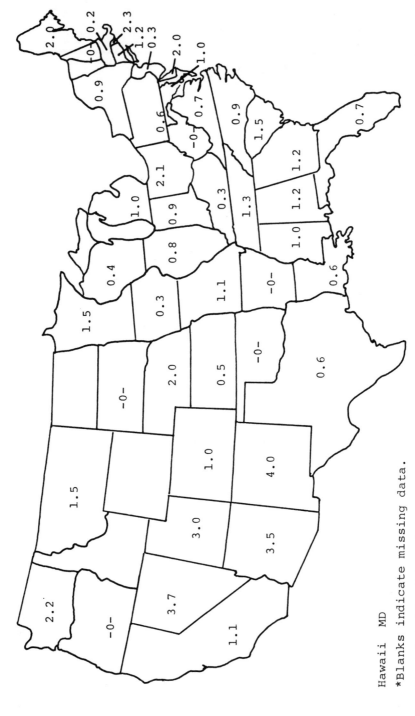

Hawaii MD

*Blanks indicate missing data.

Figure A-6. Mean Library Computer-use Score, by State*

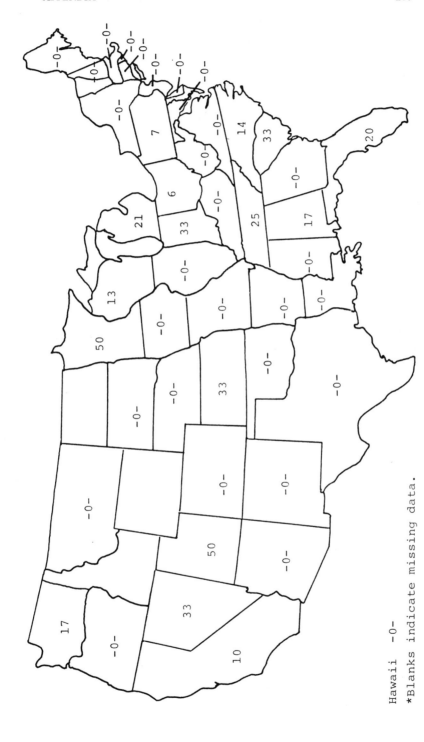

Hawaii -0-

*Blanks indicate missing data.

Figure A-7. Mean Theft-detection System Use, by State* (Percentage of Libraries with Theft-detection Systems)

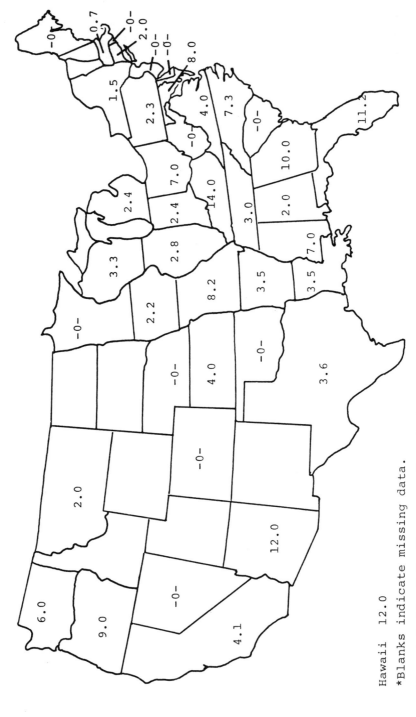

Hawaii 12.0

*Blanks indicate missing data.

Figure A-8.   Mean Police Computer-use Score, by State*

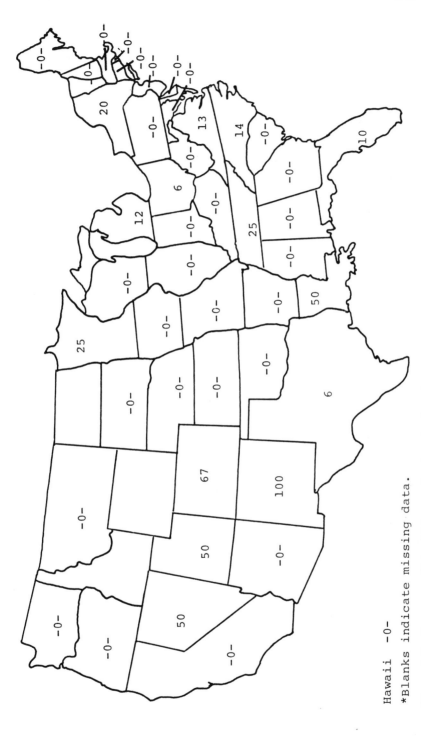

Hawaii   -0-

*Blanks indicate missing data.

Figure A-9. Percentage Using Mainstem Services, by State*

Notes

Chapter 1
Innovation in the Public Sector

1. See, for example, Everett M. Rogers and F. Floyd Shoemaker, *Communication of Innovations: A Cross-Cultural Approach*, 2nd ed. (New York: Free Press, 1971); and Gerald Zaltman, Robert Duncan, and Jonny Holbek, *Innovations and Organizations* (New York: Wiley, 1973).
2. Frederick O'R. Hayes and John E. Rasmussen, eds., *Centers for Innovation in the States and Cities* (San Francisco: San Francisco Press, 1972).
3. Robert Crawford, "The Application of Science and Technology in Local Governments in the United States," *Studies in Comparative Local Government* 7 (Winter, 1973): 11.
4. Neal Lansing, *A Strategy for Application of Science and Technology to Local Government Problem Areas* (Redondo Beach, Calif.: Thompson, Ramo, Woolridge, (1972), summarized in Crawford, "Application of Science," 6.
5. Jerald Hage and Michael Aiken, *Social Change in Complex Organizations* (New York: Random House, 1970), pp. 13-14.
6. Lawrence B. Mohr, "Determinants of Innovation in Organizations," *American Political Science Review* 63 (1969): 112.
7. Terry N. Clark, "Community Structure, Decision-Making, Budget Expenditures, and Urban Renewal in 57 American Communities," *American Sociological Review* 33 (1968): 576-593.
8. Amos H. Hawley, "Community Power and Urban Renewal Successes," in *Community Structure and Decision-Making: Comparative Analyses*, ed. by Terry N. Clark (San Francisco: Chandler, 1968), pp. 393-405.
9. Selwyn W. Becker and Thomas L. Whisler, "The Innovative Organization: A Selective View of Current Theory and Research," *Journal of Business* 40 (1969): 463.
10. Rogers, *Diffusion*, p. 13.
11. Homer G. Barnett, *Innovation: The Basis of Culture Change* (New York: McGraw-Hill, 1953), p. 7.
12. Kenneth E. Knight, "A Descriptive Model of the Intra-firm Innovation Process," *Journal of Business* 40 (1967): 478.
13. David Easton, *A Framework for Political Analysis* (Englewood Cliffs:

Prentice-Hall, 1965); and David Easton, *A Systems Analysis of Political Life* (New York: Wiley, 1965).

14. See, for example, Thomas R. Dye, *Politics, Economics, and the Public: Policy Outcomes in the American States* (Chicago: Rand McNally, 1966).

15. Michael Aiken and Robert R. Alford, "Community Structure and Innovation: The Case of Urban Renewal," *American Sociological Review* 35 (August, 1970): 650–665; Michael Aiken and Robert R. Alford "Community Structure and Innovation: The Case of Public Housing," *American Political Science Review* 64 (September, 1970): 843–864.

16. Richard D. Bingham, *Public Housing and Urban Renewal: An Analysis of Federal-Local Relations* (New York: Praeger, 1975).

17. Oliver P. Williams and Charles R. Adrian, "Community Types and Policy Differences," in *City Politics and Public Policy,* ed. by James Q. Wilson (New York: Wiley, 1968), pp. 17–36.

18. Aiken and Alford, "Urban Renewal," 653.

19. Bingham, *Public Housing and Urban Renewal.*

20. Robert D. Wrinkle and Jerry L. Polinard, "Populism and Dissent: The Wallace Vote in Texas," *Social Science Quarterly* 54 (September, 1973): 306–320.

21. Daniel J. Elazar, *American Federalism: A View from the States,* 2nd ed. (New York: Crowell, 1972), pp. 93–139.

22. Alan K. Campbell and Seymour Sacks, *Metropolitan American* (New York: Free Press, 1967), pp. 53–66.

23. See, for example, Roy W. Bahl, Jr., and Robert J. Saunders, "Determinants of Changes in State and Local Expenditures," *National Tax Journal* 18 (March, 1965): 50–57; Jack W. Osman, "The Dual Impact of Federal Aid on State and Local Government Expenditures," *National Tax Journal* 19 (December, 1966): 362–373; Edward M. Gramlich, "Alternative Federal Policies for Stimulating State and Local Expenditures: A Comparison of Their Effects," *National Tax Journal* 21 (June, 1968): 119–129; David L. Smith, "The Response of State and Local Governments to Federal Grants," *National Tax Journal* 21 (September, 1968): 349–357; Thomas O'Brien, "Grants-In-Aid: Some Further Answers," *National Tax Journal* 24 (March, 1971): 65–77.

24. Jack L. Walker, "The Diffusion of Innovations Among the American States," *American Political Science Review,* 63 (1969): 898.

25. Rogers and Shoemaker, *Communication,* pp. 354–356.

26. Maw Lin Lee, "A Conspicuous Production Theory of Hospital Behavior," *Southern Economic Journal* 38 (July, 1971): 48–58.

27. Williams and Adrian, "Community Types."

28. Bernard H. Booms, "City Governmental Form and Public Expenditure Levels," *National Tax Journal* 19 (June, 1966): 187–199.

29. Becker and Whisler, "The Innovative Organization," 465.

30. Victor A. Thompson, *Bureaucracy and Innovation* (Tuscaloosa: University of Alabama Press, 1969).

31. J. David Roessner, "Innovation in Public Organizations," a paper presented at the National Conference on Public Administration, Syracuse, N.Y., May 5-8, 1974, p. 3.

32. Heinz Eulau and Robert Eyestone, "Policy Maps of City Councils and Policy Outcomes: A Developmental Analysis," *American Political Science Review* 62 (March, 1968): 124-143; and Robert Eyestone and Heinz Eulau, "City Councils and Policy Outcomes: Developmental Profiles" in *City Politics and Public Policy*, ed. by James Q. Wilson (New York: Wiley, 1968), pp. 17-36.

33. Irwin Feller, Donald C. Menzel, and Alfred Engel, *Diffusion of Technology in State Mission-Oriented Agencies*, Report to the National Science Foundation, DA-39596 (State College: Center for the Study of Science Policy, The Pennsylvania State University, 1974), pp. 168-169.

34. *Ibid.*, p. 199.

35. Edward C. Banfield and James Q. Wilson, *City Politics* (New York: Random House, 1963).

36. Zaltman, Duncan, and Holbek, *Innovations,* p. 55.

37. Feller, Menzel, and Engel, *Diffusion,* pp. 208-210.

38. Zaltman, Duncan, and Holbek, *Innovations,* pp. 138-143.

39. Mohr, "Determinants," 126.

40. Rogers and Shoemaker, *Communication,* pp. 347-385.

41. Feller, Menzel, and Engel, *Diffusion,* p. 199.

42. Harvey P. Utech and Ingrid D. Utech, *The Communication of Innovations Between Local Government Departments*, A pilot study for the National Science Foundation (mimeograph, nd.), p. 2.

43. Michael J. Robinson, "Please, Let's Not Start All That Nonsense About Industrialized Housing Again," *House and Home* (May, 1974), pp. 64-65.

44. Richard L. Worsnop, "Low-Income Housing," *Editorial Research Reports* 2 (October, 1970): 806.

45. "The Decline and Fall of Stirling Homex," *Business Week* (28 October 1972), pp. 90-95.

46. "HUD Tests New Strategies For Mass Housing Systems," *Savings and Loan News* (January, 1971), p. 44.

47. Worsnop, "Low-Income Housing," p. 809.

48. *Ibid.*

49. "Special Report: Third Annual Modular Survey, Year of the Shakeout," *House and Home* (March, 1973), p. 76.

50. U.S. Congress, House of Representatives, Subcommittee on Urban Affairs, *Industrialized Housing*, by R.F. Kaufman (Washington, D.C.: Government Printing Office, 1969), p. 192.

51. "Production: Prefab Housing Looks For a Home in U.S.," *Business Week*

(1 March 1969), p. 45.

52. Alvin Toffler, *Future Shock* (New York: Bantam Books, 1970).

53. Paul L. St. Pierre, "Systems Study as Related to Library Operations," in *Library Automation: A State of the Art Review*, ed. by Stephen R. Salmon (Chicago: American Library Association, 1969), pp. 13-29.

54. Barbara Evans Markuson, et al, *Guidelines for Library Automation: A Handbook for Federal and Other Libraries* (Santa Monica, Calif.: System Development Corporation, 1972), p. 92.

55. *Ibid,* p. 109.

56. *Ibid,* p. 126.

57. "Protection of Resources: Theft Detection Systems for Libraries," *Library Technology Reports* (Chicago: American Library Association, May, 1974), pp. 1, 4.

58. Defense Supply Agency, "Analysis of Construction/Engineer Equipment Maintenance," *Construction/Engineer Equipment Maintenance Study* (CEEMS) 1 (October, 1973): 202-206.

59. Kent W. Colton, "Police and Computers: Use, Acceptance, and the Impact of Automation," *Municipal Yearbook 1972* (Washington, D.C.: International City Management Association, 1972), pp. 119-136.

60. *Ibid,* p. 119.

61. Bingham, *Public Housing and Urban Renewal.*

62. R.J. Rummel, *Applied Factor Analysis* (Evanston, Ill.: Northwestern University Press, 1970).

63. Jeffrey K. Hadden and Edgar F. Borgatta, *American Cities: Their Social Characteristics* (Chicago: Rand McNally, 1965); Richard L. Forstall, "A New Social and Economic Grouping of Cities," *Municipal Year Book 1970* (Washington, D.C.: International City Management Association, 1970), pp. 102-159. A fine review of this literature is found in Desmond S. Cartwright, "Ecological Variables," in *Sociological Methodology 1969*, ed. by Edgar F. Borgatta (San Francisco: Jossey-Bass, 1969), pp. 155-218.

64. Rummel, *Applied Factor Analysis,* pp. 384-389.

65. Bruce M. Russett, "Discovering Voting Groups in the United Nations," in *Quantitative Analysis of Political Data,* ed. by Samuel A. Kirkpatrick (Columbus, Oh.: Merrill, 1974), p. 303.

66. Norman H. Nie, Dale H. Bent, and C. Hadlai Hull, *SPSS: Statistical Package for the Social Sciences* (New York: McGraw-Hill, 1970), pp. 226-227.

67. Richard M. Scammon, ed., *America Votes 7* (Washington, D.C.: Governmental Affairs Institute, 1968); and Richard M. Scammon, ed. *America Votes 8* (Washington, D.C.: Governmental Affairs Institute, 1970).

68. Elazar, *American Federalism.*

69. Hubert M. Blalock, Jr., *Causal Inferences in Nonexperimental Research* (Chapel Hill: University of North Carolina Press, 1964). See also Samuel A. Kirkpatrick, *Quantitative Analysis of Political Data* (Columbus, Oh.: Merrill, 1974), Chapter 3.

70. Arthur S. Goldberg, "Discerning a Causal Pattern Among Data on Voting Behavior," *American Political Science Review* 60 (1966): pp. 913-922.

71. See Denton E. Morrison and Ramon E. Henkel, eds., *The Significance Test Controversy: A Reader* (Chicago: Aldine, 1970) for a discussion of the significance test issue.

72. See Peter Bachrach and Morton S. Baratz, "Decisions: An Analytical Framework," *American Political Science Review* 62 (1963): 632-642; Peter Bachrach and Morton S. Baratz, "The Two Faces of Power," *American Political Science Review* 61 (1962): 947-952; David Ricci, *Community Power and Democratic Theory: The Logic of Political Analysis* (New York: Random House, 1971).

73. Richard D. Bingham, Thomas P. McNaught, and Thomas J. Westerheide, *Codebook for the Adoption of Innovation by Local Government* (Milwaukee: Office of Urban Research/Marquette University, 1975).

Chapter 2
Adoption of Innovation by Public Housing Authorities

1. U.S. Department of Commerce, Bureau of the Census, *City Government Finances in 1969-70* (Washington, D.C.: Government Printing Office, 1971).

2. Survey ADP/70, "Survey of Automated Data Processing (ADP) in Local Government," and "ADP Organization and Applications in Local Government," by the Urban Data Services of the International City Management Association, 1970.

3. *Municipal Year Book 1965* (Washington, D.C.: International City Management Association, 1965), pp. 120-128; and *Municipal Year Book 1968* (Washington, D.C.: International City Management Association, 1968), pp. 64-79.

4. National Association of Housing and Redevelopment Officials, *NAHRO Housing Directory* (Washington, D.C.: NAHRO, 1968).

5. National Association of Housing and Redevelopment Officials, *NAHRO Roster: 1971,* NAHRO Publication No. N549 (Washington, D.C.: National Association of Housing and Redevelopment Officials, 1971).

6. Richard D. Bingham, *Public Housing and Urban Renewal: An Analysis of Federal-Local Relations* (New York: Praeger, 1975).

7. Jack L. Walker, "The Diffusion of Knowledge and Policy Change: Toward a Theory of Agenda Setting," a paper presented at the 1974 Annual Meeting of the American Political Science Association, Chicago, Ill.; Aug. 29-Sept. 2, 1974, p. 9.

8. U.S. Department of Housing and Urban Development, *1972 HUD Statistical Yearbook* (Washington: Government Printing Office, 1974), p. 149.

9.　"The Decline and Fall of Stirling Homex," *Business Week* (28 October 1972), pp. 90-95.

10.　Frederick O'R. Hayes and John E. Rasmussen, eds., *Centers for Innovation in the States and Cities* (San Francisco: San Francisco Press, 1972).

Chapter 3
Innovation Adoption in Public Schools

1.　Data on IGE utilization were obtained from Wisconsin Research and Development Center for Cognitive Learning, *1973-74 Multiunit School Directory* (Madison, Wisc.: WRDCCL, 1974), pp. 15-233, and the Institute for Development of Educational Activities (IDEA), "Computer Printout of IGE Schools Associated with IDEA of the Kettering Foundation, Unpublished, 1974. IPI data from Research for Better Schools, *RBS Schools Directory* (Philadelphia: Research for Better Schools, 1973), pp. 1-163. City listing of PLAN provided by the Westinghouse Learning Corporation.

2.　U.S. Department of Commerce, Bureau of the Census, *1972 Census of Governments: Government Finances*, vol. 4, *Finances of School Districts*, No. 1 (Washington, D.C.: Government Printing Office, 1972), pp. 44-91.

3.　U.S. Department of Commerce, Bureau of the Census, *City Government Finances in 1968* (Washington, D.C.: Government Printing Office, 1969), pp. 9-48.

4.　Bureau of the Census, *1972 Census of Governments,* pp. 44-91.

5.　U.S. Department of Health, Education, and Welfare, National Center for Educational Statistics, *Statistics of Local Public School Systems; Fall, 1970* (Washington, D.C.: Government Printing Office, 1973), pp. 18-141.

6.　Herbert J. Klausmeier, et al, *Individually Guided Education and the Multiunit Elementary School: Guidelines for Implementation* (Madison, Wisc.: Wisconsin Research and Development Center for Cognitive Learning/University of Wisconsin, 1971), p. 13.

7.　Oliver P. Williams and Charles R. Adrian, "Community Types and Policy Differences," in *City Politics and Public Policy*, ed. by James Q. Wilson (New York: Wiley, 1968), pp. 17-36.

8.　William Glasser, *Schools Without Failure* (New York: Harper and Row, 1969).

9.　HEW, *Statistics of School Systems.*

10.　Computed from U.S. Department of Commerce Bureau of the Census, *1972 Census of Governments,* Vol. 4, *Government Finances, No. 1, Finances of School Districts* (Washington, D.C.: Government Printing Office, 1974), p. 3.

Chapter 4
Innovation Adoption in Public Libraries

1. Selection of specific computer uses were drawn largely from Barbara Evans Markuson, et al. *Guidelines for Library Automation* (Santa Monica, Calif.: System Development Corporation, 1972).

2. Eleanor F. Steriner-Prag, ed., *1968-1969 American Library Directory*, 26th ed. (New York: R.R. Bowker, 1968), pp. 1-908.

3. *Ibid.*

4. Pamphlet, "Ohio College Library Center," (Columbus, Oh.: OCLC, Summer, 1973).

5. Obtained from the Director, Ohio College Library Center, Ohio State University, Columbus, Ohio.

6. Steiner-Prag, *American Library Directory.*

7. Markuson, et al, *Guidelines for Library Automation.*

8. *Ibid,* p. 8.

9. Roberta Bowler, ed., *Local Public Library Administration* (Chicago: International City Managers' Association, 1964), p. 30.

10. List of manufacturers was obtained from Library Technology Reports, *Theft Detection Systems for Libraries: A Survey* (Chicago: American Library Association, 1974).

Chapter 5
Adoption of Innovation in the Common Functions
of City Government

1. Kent W. Colton, "Police and Computers: Use, Acceptance, and Impact of Automation," *The Municipal Yearbook 1975* (Washington, D.C.: International City Management Association, 1972), p. 119.

2. U.S. Department of Justice, *Crime in the United States: Uniform Crime Reports-1969* (Washington, D.C.: Government Printing Office, 1970), pp. 169-185; U.S. Department of Justice, *Crime in the United States: Uniform Crime Reports-1964* (Washington, D.C.: Government Printing Office, 1965), pp. 171-186.

3. Unpublished data obtained from Preston L. Horstman, Executive Director, National Association of State Directors of Law Enforcement Training, August 12, 1974.

4. Survey ADP/71, "Application of Automated Data Processing in Police Departments-1971," (2 parts), by the Urban Data Service of the International City Management Association, 1971.

5. U.S. Bureau of the Census, *City Government Finances in 1968,* pp. 9-48.

6. U.S. Department of Justice, *Crime Reports-1969*, pp. 152-156.

7. *The Municipal Year Book 1968* (Washington, D.C.: International City Management Association, 1968), pp. 357-374.

8. *The Municipal Year Book 1969* (Washington, D.C.: International City Management Association, 1969).

9. Colton, "Police and Computers," p. 199.

10. *Ibid,* p. 120.

11. President's Commission on Law Enforcement and Administration of Justice, *Task Force Report: Crime and Its Impact—An Assessment* (Washington: Government Printing Office, 1967), pp. 17-19.

12. Wesley G. Skogan, "The Validity of Official Crime Statistics: An Empirical Investigation," *Social Science Quarterly* 55 (June, 1974): 25-38.

13. *Ibid,* 31.

14. Neal A. Miner, *The Court and Local Law Enforcement: The Impact of Miranda* (Beverly Hills: Sage, 1971), pp. 249-252.

15. International City Management Association, *The Municipal Yearbook 1975* (Washington, D.C.: International City Management Association, 1975), p. 229.

16. Survey APWKS/69, "Study on Public Works Organization and Administration," by the Urban Data Service of International City Management Association, 1969.

17. *Ibid.*

18. *Ibid.*

19. American Public Works Association, *1973-74 Directory* (Chicago: American Public Works Association, 1974), pp. D275-D340.

20. For example: "APWA Initiates Equipment Service Program and Data Bank," *APWA Reporter* (March, 1972), p. 4; "APWA Data Bank Project Moves Ahead," *APWA Reporter* (March, 1973), p. 4.

Chapter 6
Toward a Policy Perspective

1. Selwyn W. Becker and Thomas L. Whisler, "The Innovative Organization: A Selective View of Current Theory and Research," *Journal of Business* 40 (1969): 463.

2. For example, James S. Coleman, Elihu Katz, and Herbert Menzel, *Medical Innovations: A Diffusion Study* (Indianapolis: Bobbs-Merrill, 1966).

3. Virginia Gray, "Innovation in the States: A Diffusion Study," *American Political Science Review* 67 (December, 1963): 1174-1185.

4. Irwin Feller and Donald Menzel, "Diffusion of Technology in Municipal Governments" (University Park, Penn.: Center for the Study of Science Policy, The Pennsylvania State University, forthcoming).

5.   Gray, "Innovation in the States," 1183.

6.   Feller and Menzel, "Diffusion of Technology."

7.   Jack L. Walker, "The Diffusion of Innovations Among the American States," *American Political Science Review* 62 (1969): 880-899.

8.   For example, Michael Aiken and Robert R. Alford, "Community Structure and Innovation: The Case of Urban Renewal," *American Sociological Review* 35 (August, 1970): 650-665; Richard D. Bingham, *Public Housing and Urban Renewal: An Analysis of Federal-Local Relations* (New York: Praeger, 1975).

9.   Oliver P. Williams and Charles R. Adrian, "Community Types and Policy Differences, in *City Politics and Public Policy,* ed. by James Q. Wilson (New York: Wiley, 1968), pp. 17-36.

10.   Lawrence B. Mohr, "Determinants of Innovation in Organizations," *American Political Science Review* 63 (1969): 112.

11.   See Brett W. Hawkins, *Politics and Urban Policies* (Indianapolis: Bobbs-Merrill, 1971) for a discussion of these studies.

12.   This portion of the model was suggested by Warren E. Miller and Donald E. Stokes, "Constituency Influence in Congress, *American Political Science Review* 57 (March, 1963): 45-56.

13.   Similar to Robert Crawford, "The Application of Science and Technology in Local Governments in the United States," *Studies in Comparative Local Government* 7 (Winter, 1973): 6.

14.   Suggested by Irwin Feller, The Pennsylvania State University, on July 22, 1975.

15.   Suggested by Robert Yin, Rand Corporation, on July 22, 1975.

16.   Frederick O'R. Hayes and John E. Rasmussen, eds., *Centers for Innovation in States and Cities* (San Francisco: San Francisco Press, 1972).

17.   Irwin Feller, Donald C. Menzel, and Alfred J. Engel, *Diffusion of Technology in State Mission-Oriented Agencies* (University Park, Penn.: Center for the Study of Science Policy, The Pennsylvania State University, October 1974), p. 109.

Selected Bibliography

Books

American Library Association. "Theft Detection Systems for Libraries: A
Survey." *Library Technology Reports.* Chicago: American Library
Association, 1974.

American Public Works Association. *Local Public Works Organizations.*
Special Report No. 35. Chicago: American Public Works Association,
1970.

——— *Motor Vehicle Fleet Management.* Special Report No. 37. Chicago:
American Public Works Association, 1970.

Argyris, Chris. *Intervention Theory and Method.* Reading, Mass.: Addison-
Wesley, 1970.

——— *Organization and Innovation.* Homewood, Ill.: Dorsey Press, 1965.

Banfield, Edward C., and James Q. Wilson. *City Politics.* New York: Random
House, 1963.

Banton, Michael. *The Policeman and the Community.* London: Tavistock,
1964.

Barnett, Homer G. *Innovation: The Basis of Culture Change.* New York:
McGraw-Hill, 1953.

Bennis, Warren. *Changing Organizations.* New York: McGraw-Hill, 1966.

Bingham, Richard D. *Public Housing and Urban Renewal: An Analysis of
Federal-Local Relations.* New York: Praeger, 1975.

Bingham, Richard D.; Thomas P. McNaught; and Thomas J. Westerheide.
Codebook for the Adoption of Innovation by Local Government.
Milwaukee, Wisc.: Office of Urban Research, Marquette University,
1975.

Blalock, Hubert M., Jr. *Causal Inferences in Nonexperimental Research.*
Chapel Hill, N.C.: University of North Carolina Press, 1964.

Blau, Peter, and W. Richard Scott. *Formal Organizations: A Comparative
Approach.* San Francisco: Chandler Publishing, 1962.

Bowler, Roberta, ed. *Local Public Library Administration.* Chicago: International City Managers Association, 1964.

Campbell, Alan K., and Seymour Sacks. *Metropolitan American.* New York:
Free Press, 1967.

Clark, Terry N., ed. *Community Structure and Decision-Making: Comparative
Analyses.* San Francisco: Chandler, 1968.

253

Coleman, James S.; Elihu Katz; and Menzel, Herbert. *Medical Innovation.* New York: Bobbs-Merrill Co., 1966.

Coleman, James S. et al. *Equality of Educational Opportunity.* Washington, D.C.: Government Printing Office, 1966.

Cyert, Richard, and James March. *A Behavioral Theory of the Firm.* Englewood Cliffs, N.J.: Prentice-Hall, 1963.

Dahl, Robert A. *Who Governs?* New Haven, Conn.: Yale University Press, 1961.

Derthick, Martha. *New Towns In-Town: Why a Federal Program Failed.* Washington, D.C.: Urban Institute, 1972.

———— *The Influence of Federal Grants: Public Assistance in Massachusetts.* Cambridge, Mass.: Harvard University Press, 1970.

DeProspo, Ernest R.; Ellen Altman; and Kenneth E. Beasley. *Performance Measures For Public Libraries.* Chicago: American Library Association, 1973.

Downs, Anthony. *Inside Bureaucracy.* Boston: Little, Brown, 1966.

Dye, Thomas R. *Politics, Economics and the Public: Policy Outcomes in the American States.* Chicago: Rand McNally, 1966.

Easton, David. *A Framework for Political Analysis.* Englewood Cliffs, N.J.: Prentice-Hall, 1965.

———— *A Systems Analysis of Political Life.* New York: Wiley, 1965.

Editorial Research Reports. "Video Revolution." (March 26, 1971): 229-241.

Elazar, Daniel J. *American Federalism: A View From the States,* 2nd ed. New York: Crowell, 1972.

Fabricant, Solomon. *The Trend of Governmental Activity in the United States Since 1900.* New York: National Bureau of Economic Research, 1952.

Feller, Irwin; Donald C. Menzel; and Alfred Engel. *Diffusion of Technology in State Mission-Oriented Agencies.* Report to the National Science Foundation, DA-39596. State College: Center for the Study of Science Policy, The Pennsylvania State University, 1974.

Gawthrop, Louis C. *Bureaucratic Behavior in the Executive Branch.* New York: Free Press, 1969.

Glasser, William. *Schools Without Failure.* New York: Harper and Row, 1969.

Graves, Jack R. "The APWA Equipment Management Improvement Program and Data Bank." Kansas City, Mo., 1974.

Gross, Neal; Joseph B. Giacquinta; and Marilyn Bernstein. *Implementing Organizational Innovations: A Sociological Analysis of Planned Educational Change.* New York: Basic Books, 1971.

Hadden, Jeffrey K., and Edgar F. Borgatta. *American Cities: Their Social Characteristics.* Chicago: Rand McNally, 1965.

Hage, Jerald, and Michael Aiken. *Social Change in Complex Organizations.* New York: Random House, 1970.

Hahn, Harlan, ed. *Police in Urban Society.* Beverly Hills, Calif.: Sage, 1971.

Hawkins, Brett W. *Politics and Urban Policies.* Indianapolis: Bobbs-Merrill, 1971.

Hayes, Frederick O'R., and John E. Rasmussen, eds. *Centers for Innovation in the States and Cities.* San Francisco Press, 1972.

IDEA. *I/D/E/A/'S Guide to an Improvement Program For Schools.* Dayton, Oh.: IDEA Change Program for Individually Guided Education, Kettering Foundation, 1974.

Katz, Daniel, and Robert Kahn. *The Social Psychology of Organizations.* New York: Wiley, 1966.

Kirkpatrick, Samuel A. *Quantitative Analysis of Political Data.* Columbus, Oh.: Merrill, 1974.

Klausmeier, Herbert J.; Mary R. Quilling; Juanita S. Sorenson; Russel S. Way; and George R. Glasrud. *Individually Guided Education and the Multiunit Elementary School: Guidelines for Implementation.* Madison: Wisconsin Research and Development Center for Cognitive Learning, 1971.

Lineberry, Robert L., and Ira Sharkansky. *Urban Politics and Public Policy.* New York: Harper and Row, 1971.

Management Data Systems, Inc. *Computer Service for Local Housing Authorities.* Madison, Wisc.: Management Data Systems, Inc., 1975.

March, James, and Herbert Simon. *Organizations.* New York: Wiley, 1958.

Markuson, Barbara Evans; Judith Wanger; Sharon Schatz; and Donald V. Black. *Guidelines for Library Automation: A Handbook for Federal and Other Libraries.* Santa Monica, Calif.: System Development Corporation, 1972.

Merewitz, Leonard, and Stephen H. Sosnick. *The Budget's New Clothes.* Chicago: Markham Publishing, 1971.

Merton, Robert K. *The Sociology of Science: Theoretical and Empirical Investigations.* Edited and with an introduction by Norman W. Stover. Chicago: University of Chicago Press, 1973.

Miner, Neal A. *The Court and Local Law Enforcement: The Impact of Miranda.* Beverly Hills, Calif.: Sage, 1971.

Morrison, Denton E., and Ramon E. Henkel, eds. *The Significance Test Controversy: A Reader.* Chicago: Aldine, 1970.

National Association of Housing and Redevelopment Officials. *NAHRO Housing Directory 1968.* Washington, D.C.: National Association of Housing and Redevelopment Officials, 1968.

_____ *NAHRO Roster 1971.* NAHRO Publication No. N549. Washington, D.C.: National Association of Housing and Redevelopment Officials, 1971.

Ohio College Library Center. *Ohio College Library Center* (Pamphlet) Columbus, Oh.: 1973.

The President's Commission on Law Enforcement and Administration of Justice. *Task Force Report: Crime and Its Impact—An Assessment.* Washington, D.C.: Government Printing Office, 1967.

———— *Task Force Report: The Police.* Washington, D.C.: Government Printing Office, 1967.

———— *Task Force Report: Science and Technology.* Washington, D.C.: Government Printing Office, 1967.

Research for Better Schools, Inc. *Individualizing Learning Programs.* Philadelphia: Research for Better Schools, Inc., 1973.

Ricci, David. *Community Power and Democratic Theory: The Logic of Political Analysis.* New York: Random House, 1971.

Rogers, Everett M. *Diffusion of Innovations.* New York: Free Press, 1962.

Rogers, Everett M., and F. Floyd Shoemaker. *Communication of Innovations: A Cross-Cultural Approach,* 2nd ed. New York: Free Press, 1971.

Rosenbloom Richard S., and John R. Russell. *New Tools for Urban Management.* Cambridge, Mass.: Harvard Business School, 1971.

Ruchelman, Leonard. *Who Rules the Police?* New York: New York University Press, 1973.

Rummel, R.J. *Applied Factor Analysis.* Evanston, Ill.: Northwestern University Press, 1970.

Scammon, Richard M., ed. *America Votes 7.* Washington, D.C.: Governmental Affairs Institute, 1968.

———— *America Votes 8.* Washington, D.C.: Governmental Affairs Institute, 1970.

Schoenberger, Robert A., ed. *The American Right Wing: Readings in Political Behavior.* New York: Holt, Rinehart, 1969.

Sindler, Allan P., ed. *Policy and Politics in America.* Boston; Little, Brown, 1973.

Steiner, Gary A., ed. *The Creative Organization.* Chicago: University of Chicago Press, 1965.

Steiner-Prag, Eleanor F., ed. *1968-1969 American Library Directory.* 26th ed. New York: R.R. Bowker, 1968.

Sundquist, James L., and David W. Davis. *Making Federalism Work: A Study of Program Coordination at the Community Level.* Washington, D.C.: Brookings Institution, 1969.

Thompson, Victor A. *Modern Organization.* New York: Alfred Knopf, 1961.

———— *Bureaucracy and Innovation.* Tuscaloosa: University of Alabama Press, 1969.

Tilton, John E. *International Diffusion of Technology: The Case of Semiconductors.* Washington, D.C.: Brookings Institution, 1971.

Toffler, Alvin. *Future Shock.* New York: Bantam Books, 1970.

Touche Ross and Co. *Summary of Capabilities and Experience in Public Housing and Urban Renewal* (Summer, 1973). New York: Touche Ross and Co., 1973.

U.S. Congress, House of Representatives, Subcommittee on Urban Affairs, *Industrialized Housing,* by R.F. Kaufman. Washington, D.C.: Government Printing Office, 1969.

U.S. Department of Housing and Urban Development. *Low-Rent Housing Manual 221.1 September 1967.* Washington, D.C.: U.S. Department of Housing and Urban Development, 1967.

Wendell, French, and Cecil Bell, Jr. *Organization Development: Behavioral Science Interventions for Organization Improvement.* Englewood Cliffs: Prentice-Hall, 1973.

Westin, Alan F., and Michael A. Baker. *Databanks in a Free Society.* New York: Quadrangle, 1974.

Whyte, William F. *Organizational Behavior: Theory and Application.* Homewood, Ill.: Irwin-Dorsey, 1969.

Wilson, James Q. *Varieties of Police Behavior: The Management of Law and Order in Eight Communities.* Cambridge, Mass.: Harvard University Press, 1968.

Wolf, Eleanor Paperno, and Charles N. Lebeaux. *Change and Renewal in an Urban Community.* New York: Praeger, 1969.

Zaltman, Gerald; Robert Duncan; and Jonny Holbek. *Innovations and Organizations.* New York: Wiley, 1973.

Zimet, Melvin. *Decentralization and School Effectiveness.* New York: Teachers College Press, 1973.

Articles

Aiken, Michael, and Robert R. Alford. "Community Structure and Innovation: The Case of Public Housing." *American Political Science Review* 64 (September, 1970): 843-864.

———— "Community Structure and Innovation: The Case of Urban Renewal." *American Sociological Review* 35 (August, 1970): 650-665.

American Libraries (1970-1973).

American Library Association Bulletin (1964-1969).

"APWA Data Bank Project Moves Ahead." *APWA Reporter* (March, 1973).

"APWA Initiates Equipment Service Program and Data Bank." *APWA Reporter* (March, 1972).

The APWA Reporter (1964-1973).

Aveilhe, Heather. "The Public Housing Management Improvement Program." *HUD Challenge* (June, 1974): 4-7.

Bachrach, Peter, and Morton S. Baratz. "Decisions: An Analytical Framework." *American Political Science Review* 57 (1963): 632-642.

———— "The Two Faces of Power." *American Political Science Review* 51 (1962): 947-952.

Bahl, Roy W., Jr., and Robert J. Saunders. "Determinants of Changes in State and Local Expenditures." *National Tax Journal* 18 (March, 1965): 50-57.

Becker, Joseph. "The Future of Library Automation and Information Networks," in *Library Automation: A State of the Art Review,* pp. 1-6. Edited by Stephen R. Salmon. Chicago: American Library Association, 1969.

Becker, Selwyn W., and Thomas L. Whisler. "The Innovative Organization: A Selective View of Current Theory and Research." *Journal of Business* 40 (1969): 462-469.

Bishop, George A. "Stimulative Versus Substitutive Effects of State School Aid in New England." *National Tax Journal* 17 (June, 1964): 133-143.

Bockelman, Melvin F. "Privacy and Security of Computerized Criminal Justice Systems." *Computers and Society* 6 (Spring, 1975): 3-6.

Booms, Bernard H. "City Governmental Form and Public Expenditure Levels." *National Tax Journal* 19 (June, 1966): 187-199.

Booth, David A. "The Growing Professionalization of the Police in Massachusetts." *Police* 16 (January, 1972): 40-44.

Business Week (7 March 1970, 28 Octqber 1972, 6 January 1968, 1 March 1969).

Cartwright, Desmond S. "Ecological Variables." In *Sociological Methodology 1969,* pp. 155-218. Edited by Edgar F. Borgatta. San Francisco: Jossey-Bass, 1969.

Chackerian, Richard. "Police Professionalism and Citizen Evaluations: A Preliminary Look." *Public Administration Review* 34 (March/April, 1974): 141-148.

Clark, Terry N. "Community Structure, Decision-Making, Budget Expenditures, and Urban Renewal in 57 American Communities." *American Sociological Review* 33 (1968): 576-593.

Coe, Rodney M., and Elizabeth A. Barnhill. "Social Dimensions of Failure in Innovation." *Human Organization* 26 (Fall, 1967): 149-156.

Colcord, Frank C., Jr. "Decision-Making and Transportation Policy: A Comparative Analysis." *Southwestern Social Science Quarterly* (December, 1967): 383-397.

Colton, Kent W. "Police and Computers: Use, Acceptance, and the Impact of Automation." *The Municipal Yearbook 1972,* pp. 119-136. Washington, D.C.: International City Management Association, 1972.

Crain, Robert L., and Donald B. Rosenthal. "Community Status as a Dimension of Local Decision-Making." *American Sociological Review* 32 (1967): 970-984.

Crain, Robert L., and James J. Vanecko. "Elite Influence in School Desegregation." In *City Politics and Public Policy,* pp. 127-148. Edited by James Q. Wilson. New York: John Wiley and Sons, 1968.

Crain, Robert L. "Flouridation: The Diffusion of an Innovation Among Cities." *Social Forces* 44 (June, 1966): 467-476.

Crawford, Robert. "The Application of Science and Technology in Local Governments in the United States." *Studies in Comparative Local Government (The Hague)* 7 (Winter, 1973): 5-23.

Dales, Sophie R. "Federal Grants to State and Local Governments, 1967-68." *Social Security Bulletin* 32 (August, 1969): 15-22.

Danish, Steven J., and Nancy Ferguson. "Training Police to Intervene in Human Conflict." In *The Urban Policeman in Transition: A Psychological and Sociological Review,* pp. 486-506. Edited by John R. Snibbe and Homa M. Snibbe. Springfield, Ill.: Charles C. Thomas, 1973.

Dawson, Richard E., and James A. Robinson. "Inter-Party Competition, Economic Variables, and Welfare Policies in the American States." *Journal of Politics* 25 (May, 1963): 265-289.

"The Decline and Fall of Stirling Homex." *Business Week* (October 28, 1972), pp. 90-95.

Dietrich, John. "Sharing Successes of PHMIP." *HUD Challenge* (June, 1974): 18.

Duncan, Robert B. "Organizational Climate and Climate for Change in Three Police Departments: Some Preliminary Findings." *Urban Affairs Quarterly* 8 (1972): 205-246.

Dye, Thomas R. "City-Suburban Social Distance and Public Policy." *Social Forces* 44 (September, 1965): 100-106.

_____ "Government Structure, Urban Environment, and Educational Policy." *Midwest Journal of Political Science.* (August, 1967): 353-380.

Educational Products Information Exchange Institute. "Evaluating Instructional Systems: PLAN*, IGE, IPI." *EPIE Report* 58, New York: EPIE, 1974.

Eicholtz, Gerhard, and Everett M. Rogers. "Resistance to the Adoption of Audiovisual Aids by Elementary School Teachers." In *Innovation in Education,* pp. 299-316. Edited by Matthew Miles. New York: Teachers College Press, Columbia University, 1964.

Eulau, Heinz, and Robert Eyestone. "Policy Maps of City Councils and Policy Outcomes: A Developmental Analysis." *American Political Science Review* 62 (March, 1968): 124-143.

Euston, Andrew F., Jr. "The Role of Design in HUD Programs." *HUD Challenge* (December, 1972): 18-21.

Eyestone, Robert, and Heinz Eulau. "City Councils and Policy Outcomes: Developmental Profiles." In *City Politics and Public Policy,* pp. 17-36. Edited by James Q. Wilson. New York: Wiley, 1968.

Finger, Harold B. "Operation Breakthrough: A Nationwide Effort to Produce Millions of Homes." *HUD Challenge* (November/December, 1969): 6-9.

_____ "Operation Breakthrough: The Scientific Approach." *HUD Challenge* (March, 1971): 12-14.

Fisher, Glenn W. "Determinants of State and Local Government Expenditures: A Preliminary Analysis.:: *National Tax Journal* 14 (December, 1961): 349-355.

Forstall, Richard L. "A New Social and Economic Grouping of Cities." In *Municipal Yearbook 1970,* pp. 102-159. Washington, D.C.: International City Management Association, 1970.

Gabor, Stanley C. "The Video Cassette as an Educational Reality." *Educational Technology* (April, 1972): 35-37.

Gilfert, Dorothy. "Community Support in the PHMIP." *HUD Challenge* (June, 1974): 12-13.

Gold, Ronald B. "Fiscal Capacities and Welfare Expenditures of States." *National Tax Journal* 22 (December, 1969): 496-505.

Goldberg, Arthur S. "Discerning a Causal Pattern Among Data on Voting Behavior." *American Political Science Review* 60 (1966): 913-922.

Gordon, George N., and Irving A. Falk. "Videocassettes, Formalists and Informalists in Education." *Educational Technology* (January, 1972): 61-65.

Gramlich, Edward M. "Alternative Federal Policies for Stimulating State and Local Expenditures: A Comparison of Their Effects." *National Tax Journal* 21 (June, 1968): 119-129.

Gray, Virginia. "Innovation in the States: A Diffusion Study." *American Political Science Review* 67 (December, 1973): 1173-1185.

Hancock, James, and Douglas A. Backus. "User-Oriented Data System." *Journal of Housing* 28 (June, 1971).

Harvey, Edward, and Russell Mills. "Patterns of Organizational Adaptation: A Political Perspective." In *Power in Organizations,* pp. 181-213. Edited by Mayer N. Zald. Nashville: Vanderbilt University Press, 1970.

Hawley, Amos H. "Community Power and Urban Renewal Successes." In *Community Structure and Decision-Making: Comparative Analyses,* pp. 393-405. Edited by Terry N. Clark. San Francisco: Chandler, 1968.

Hebert, F. Ted, and Richard D. Bingham. "The City Manager's Knowledge of Grants-In-Aid: Some Personal and Environmental Influences." *Urban Affairs Quarterly* 7 (March, 1972): 303-306.

Hill, Roger W., Jr. "Instructional Technology: Some Implications For Teachers—Cable TV. *Today's Education* 59 (November, 1970): 37-39.

Hofferbert, Richard I. "The Relation Between Public Policy and Some Structural and Environmental Variables in the American States." *American Political Science Review* 50 (March, 1966): 73-82.

Hotowitz, Ann R. "Simultaneous Equation Approach to the Problem of Explaining Interstate Differences in State and Local Government Expenditures." *Southern Economic Journal* 34 (April, 1968): 459-476.

House and Home (January 1974, July 1973, May 1974, June 1974, February 1974).

Hurwitz, Mark W. "What Works Best: An Elected or an Appointed School Board?" *American School Board Journal* (July, 1972): 21-23.

Journal of Housing (1966-1974).

Klausmeier, Herbert J. "IGE: An Alternative Form of Schooling." Madison, Wisc.: University of Wisconsin, 1974.

Knight, Kenneth E. "A Descriptive Model of the Intrafirm Innovation Process." *Journal of Business* 40 (1967): 478-496.

Lansing, Neal. *A Strategy for Application of Science and Technology to Local Government Problem Areas.* Redondo Beach, Calif.: Thompson, Ramo, Woolridge, 1972.

Lee, Maw Lin. "A Conspicuous Production Theory of Hospital Behavior."
    Southern Economic Journal 38 (July, 1971): 48-58.

Leedham, J.F. "The Video Cassette; Some Experiences and an Estimate of its
    Potential for Education." In *Aspects of Educational Technology* VII:
    187-198. Edited by John Leedham. London: The Pitman Press, 1973.

Lineberry, Robert L. and Edmund P. Fowler. "Reformism and Public Policies
    in American Cities." *American Political Science Review* 61 (September,
    1967): 701-716.

McIntyre, M. Charles. "Determinants of Expenditures for Public Higher
    Education." *National Tax Journal* 22 (June, 1969): 262-272.

Miles, Matthew B. "Educational Innovation: The Nature of the Problem." In
    Innovation in Education, pp. 1-46. Edited by Matthew B. Miles. New York:
    Teachers College, Columbia University, 1964.

Mohr, Lawrence B. "Determinants of Innovation in Organizations." *American
    Political Science Review* 63 (1969): 111-126.

Mossberg, Walter S. "A Blue-Collar Town Fears Urban Renewal Perils its Way
    of Life." *Wall Street Journal* (2 November 1970), p. 1.

Mushkin, Selma J. "PPB in Cities." *Public Administration Review* 29 (March/
    April, 1969): 167-178.

The National Elementary Principal (1964-1973).

Newburg, Arthur S. "Operation Breakthrough: Catalyst for Change." *HUD
    Challenge* (June, 1972): 9-10.

O'Brien, Thomas. "Grants-In-Aid: Some Further Answers." *National Tax
    Journal* 24 (March, 1971): 65-77.

Osman, Jack W. "The Dual Impact of Federal Aid on State and Local Govern-
    ment Expenditures." *National Tax Journal* 19 (December, 1966): 362-
    373.

Pogue, Thomas F., and L.G. Sgontz. "The Effect of Grants-In-Aid on State-
    Local Spending." *National Tax Journal* 17 (March 1964): 75-85.

Police Chief (1964, 1967-1973).

Research for Better Schools. "Individually Prescribed Instruction." In packet
    entitled *Individualizing Learning Programs.* Philadelphia: Research for
    Better Schools, 1972.

Robinson, Michael J. "Please, Let's Not Start All That Nonsense About Indus-
    trialized Housing Again." *House and Home* 44 (May, 1974): 63-71.

Roessner, J. David. "Innovation in Public Organizations." Paper presented at
    the National Conference on Public Administration, Syracuse, N.Y. May
    5-8, 1974.

Romnes, Jon R., and Douglas A. Backus. "Four Local Housing Authorities
    Report on Use of Computer Systems for Accounting, HUD Reporting,
    Tenant Information." *Journal of Housing* 28 (July, 1971).

Romney, George. "Accomplishments of HUD/1969-1972." *HUD Challenge*
    (February, 1972): 4-6.

Rosenthal, Donald B., and Robert L. Crain. "Structure and Values in Local

Political Systems: The Case of Flouridation Decisions." In *City Politics and Public Policy*, pp. 217-242. Edited by James Q. Wilson. New York: Wiley, 1968.

Rowe, Lloyd A., and William B. Boise. "Organizational Innovation: Current Research and Evolving Concepts." *Public Administration Review* 34 (May/June, 1974): 284-293.

Russett, Bruce M. "Discovering Voting Groups in the United Nations." In *Quantitative Analysis of Political Data*, pp. 297-314. Edited by Samuel A. Kirkpatrick. Columbus, Oh.: Merrill, 1974.

Rybeck, Walter. "Measuring Performance in the Public Housing Management Improvement Program." *HUD Challenge* (June, 1974): 20-21.

Sacks, Seymour, and Robert Harris. "The Determinants of State and Local Government Expenditures and Intergovernmental Flow of Funds." *National Tax Journal* 17 (March, 1964): 75-85.

St. Pierre, Paul L. "Systems Study as Related to Library Operations." In *Library Automation: A State of the Art Review*, pp. 13-29. Edited by Stephen R. Salmon. Chicago: American Library Association, 1969.

Salkowitz, Susan M. "Data Systems: Housing Production Monitoring System— Its Origin, Design, Implementation and Operation." *Journal of Housing* (March, 1971): 134-136.

———. "Data Systems: Housing Code Enforcement Data System Not Only Solves Code Records Problems But Becomes Base for General Housing Information System." *Journal of Housing* (February, 1971): 79-81.

———. "Data Systems: How and Why Philadelphia Developed Its Housing Data System." *Journal of Housing* (January, 1971): 28-29.

Saltzstein, Alan L. "City Managers and City Councils: Perceptions of the Division of Authority." *The Western Political Quarterly* 27 (June, 1974): 275-288.

Scott, Thomas M. "The Diffusion of Urban Governmental Forms as a Case of Social Learning." *Journal of Politics* 30 (1968): 1091-1108.

Segal, Morley, and A. Lee Fritschler. "Emerging Patterns of Intergovernmental Relations." In *The Municipal Year Book 1970*. Washington; D.C.: International City Management Association, 1970.

Seymour, Jim. "Videocassettes: A Technology Whose Time Has Come." *Educational Technology* (April, 1973): 14-18.

Shaftel, Timothy L. "How Modular Design Reduces Production Costs." *Arizona Review* 21 (June-July, 1972): 1-5.

Sharkansky, Ira. "The Utility of Elazar's Political Culture." *Polity* 2 (Fall, 1969): 66-83.

———. "Economic and Political Correlates of State Government Expenditures: General Tendencies and Deviant Cases." *Midwest Journal of Political Science* 11 (May, 1967): 173-192.

———. "Regional Patterns in the Expenditures of American States." *Western*

Political Quarterly 20 (December, 1967): 955-971.

Shepard, Herbert A. "Innovation-Resisting and Innovation-Producing Organizations." *Journal of Business* 40 (1967): 470-477.

Simms, Howard H. "Educational Technology: Videotape." *Today's Education* 59 (November, 1970): 39-40.

Skogan, Wesley G. "The Validity of Official Crime Statistics: An Empirical Investigation." *Social Science Quarterly* 55 (June, 1974): 25-38.

Smith, David H., and Erra Stotland. "A New Look at Police Officer Selection." In *The Urban Policeman in Transition: A Psychological and Sociological Review*, pp. 5-24. Edited by John R. Snibbe and Homa M. Snibbe. Springfield: Ill.: Charles C. Thomas, 1973.

Smith, David L. "The Response of State and Local Governments to Federal Grants." *National Tax Journal* 21 (September, 1968): 349-357.

Sourisseau, Leslie D. "The Diffusion of Innovations: A Study of Los Angeles County." *Police Chief* 9 (August, 1972): 20-26.

"Special Report: Third Annual Modular Survey, Year of the Shakeout." *House and Home* 43 (March, 1973): 75-89.

Stephens, G. Ross. "State Centralization and the Erosion of Local Autonomy." *Journal of Politics* 36 (February, 1974): 44-76.

Stephens, G. Ross, and Henry J. Schmandt. "Revenue Patterns of Local Governments." *National Tax Journal* 15 (December, 1962): 432-437.

Tocchio, O.J. "It's Time to Develop a New Caliber of Policeman." *Police* 14 (January/February, 1970): 14-19.

Today's Education (1964-1973).

Walker, Jack L. "The Diffusion of Innovations Among the American States." *American Political Science Review* 63 (1969): 880-899.

_____ "The Diffusion of Knowledge and Policy Change: Toward a Theory of Agenda Setting." A Paper Presented at the 1974 Annual Meeting of the American Political Science Association, Chicago, Ill. August 29-September 2, 1974.

Williams, Oliver P., and Charles R. Adrian. "Community Types and Policy Differences." In *City Politics and Public Policy*, pp. 17-36. Edited by James Q. Wilson. New York: Wiley, 1968.

Wilson, James Q., and Edward C. Banfield. "Public-Regardingness as a Value Premise in Voting Behavior." *American Political Science Review* 58 (December, 1964): 876-887.

Wolfinger, Raymond E., and John Osgood Field. "Political Ethos and the Structure of City Government." *American Political Science Review* 60 (June, 1966): 306-326.

Worsnop, Richard L. "Low-Income Housing." *Editorial Research Reports* 2 (October, 1970): 795-812.

Wright, Deil S. "The States and Intergovernmental Relations." *Publius* 1 (Winter, 1972): 7-68.

Wrinkle, Robert D., and Jerry L. Polinard. "Populism and Dissent: The Wallace Vote in Texas." *Social Science Quarterly* 54 (September, 1973): 306-320

Index

Index

Adrian, Charles R., 7, 9, 211
Aiken, Michael, 5, 7
Alford, Robert, 5, 7
amenity innovation, 148, 207, 211,
    214; defined, 7; individualized
    instruction as, 89, 104, 206;
    videotape recorders as, 82, 109,
    207
American Libraries, 125–126, 140
American Library Association (ALA),
    20; Information Science and
    Automation Division, 20
*American Library Association Bul-
    letin,* 125–126, 140
American Public Works Association
    (APWA), 21–23, 167, 171–172,
    179
American Public Works Association
    Reporter, 171

Banfield, Edward C., 11
Barnett, Homer G., 4
Becker, Selwyn W., 4, 10, 199
Bingham, Richard D., 5, 7
Boeing Computer Services, Inc., 15,
    52–55
Book Mark, 142–144
Booms, Bernard H., 10
bureaucratic innovation, 216–220

Campbell, Alan K., 9
certification. *See* service innovation,
    certification of
Checkpoint, 142
Clark, Terry N., 3, 5
Colton, Kent W., 23, 149
community environment: attitudinal
    characteristics of, 27–28; as a
    determinant of innovation, 5–8,
    214, 216–220; *ethnic/ghetto* as
    a factor of, 25; hypothesis of
    relation to innovation adoption,
    8; *liberalism* as a factor of, 27;
    as nonmutable variable, 224;

physical characteristics of, 24–
    25, 27; related to individualized
    instruction adoption, 82; related
    to Mainstem vehicle manage-
    ment system adoption, 166;
    related to police department
    computer use, 149; related to
    public housing authority com-
    puter use, 33; related to public
    housing authority prefab and
    modular use, 59; related to
    public library computer use,
    121; related to videotape re-
    corder adoption, 106; *size* as a
    factor of, 27; *socioeconomic
    status* (SES) as a factor of, 25;
    suburb as a factor of, 25
computerization. *See* police depart-
    ment computer use; public hous-
    ing authority computer use;
    public library computer use
consulting firm, role in innovation
    adoption, 56–57, 206
contracting. *See* conventional con-
    tracting; turnkey contracting
contractor, influence of, 59
conventional contracting, 58–59, 62,
    71
council-manager form of government,
    related to efficiency, 10, 36
Crawford, Robert, 1

decisional unit, determination of, 31
demand: as a determinant of innova-
    tion, 8, 28, 216, 219; as a non-
    mutable variable, 225; related to
    individualized instruction adop-
    tion, 82; related to Mainstem
    vehicle management system
    adoption, 166, 208; related to
    police computer use, 149, 207;
    related to public housing author-
    ity computer use, 33–34, 46;
    related to public housing author-

ity prefab and modular use, 59; related to public library computer use, 121, 126–128; related to videotape recorder adoption, 106

deviant organizations, defined, 30–31

Easton, David, 5
Education, Office of, of the Department of Health, Education and Welfare, 17
Elazar, Daniel J., 8; concept of political cultures, 27
Equipment Management Information System (EMIS), 23
Erie Data Processing Housing Service Center, 15
ethnic/ghetto. See community environment
Eulau, Heinz, 10
Eyestone, Robert, 10

factor analysis, 24
Federal Bureau of Investigation. *See Uniform Crime Report*
Feller, Irwin, 10–12, 200
fragility, 3
Future Shock. See Toffler, Alvin

Goldwater, Barry, presidential vote, 27
Goodlad, John, 96–97
Goodlad Laboratory School at UCLA, 96–97, 102
Gray, Virginia, 200

Hawley, Amos H., 3, 5, 219
Hayes, Frederick O'R., 1, 78
House and Home, 16
housing, factory-built, 15
housing, modular, 15–16; and building codes, 64, 77, 206; union opposition to, 64. *See also* public housing authority use of modular housing
housing, prefabricated, 15–17; and building codes, 77, 206; union opposition to, 65. *See also* pub-

lic housing authority use of prefabricated housing components
Housing and Urban Development, Department of (HUD), 14, 47–54, 66–73
Hunter, Madeline, 97, 102

incentive, role of in innovation adoption, 79, 222–223
individualized instruction: case studies, 93–104; described, 17–19; model for adoption by elementary schools, 81–87; revised adoption model, 91–93; role of administration in adoption, 103–104; testing of adoption model, 87–91
Individually Guided Education (IGE), 17, 19, 93–102
Individually Prescribed Instruction (IPI), 17–19, 100–101
innovation: defined, 1–4; selection of innovations studied, 13–24; visibility of, 222. *See also* amenity innovation; bureaucratic innovation; need innovation; nonoperating innovation; operating innovation; policy innovation; political innovation; process innovation; product innovation; service innovation; technological innovation
innovation adoption, 208–226; literature of, 1; model for, 5, 214-216
innovation diffusion, 199–205
Institute for Development of Educational Activities, Inc. (IDEA), 18, 93, 97
Institute for Equipment Service (IES), 167, 172
intergovernmental influence, 9; related to individualized instruction adoption, 82; related to police computer use, 149–150; related to public housing innovations, 39, 46–47

International Association of Chiefs of Police (IACP), 23, 154
International City Management Association (ICMA), 23, 36, 149, 151

Journal of Housing, 40, 63

Kettering, Charles F., Foundation, 97–98. *See also* Institute for Development of Educational Activities, Inc.
Knight, Kenneth E., 4

LEAA, 152, 212
Lee, Maw Lin, 9
liberalism. See community environment
libraries, public. *See* public libraries; public library computer use
library book theft rate. *See* theft rate in libraries
library theft-detection systems. *See* theft-detection systems for libraries

Mainstem, Inc. vehicle management system adoption by city government, 21–23, 223–224; case studies, 178, 195; model for, 166–167; related to city government computer use, 175, 208; related to location of vehicle maintenance function, 178, 208; related to socioeconomic characteristics of the community, 175; revised model, 175–178; testing of model, 167–175
Management Data Systems, Inc., 15, 53
Markuson, Barbara Evans, 124–126, 130
Menzel, Donald, 200
Mohr, Lawrence B., 12
Multi-Unit School-Elementary (MUS-E), 97
mutable variable, 224–226

National Association of Housing and Redevelopment Officials (NAHRO), 14–15, 63–64; participation in, 37, 39
National Education Association (NEA), 17, 85–87
National Elementary Principal, The, 85–87
need innovation, 148, 207, 211, 214; defined, 7; individualized instruction hypothesized as, 82
Nixon, Richard, presidential vote in 1968, 27
nonmutable variable, 224–226
nonoperating innovation, 79, 118–119, 147, 221

Ohio College Library Center (OCLC), 122, 124, 125, 130, 138, 223–224
operating innovation, 79, 118, 147, 221
Operation Breakthrough, 16, 60, 67, 69, 71, 75
organizational characteristics: as a determinant of innovation, 11–13, 28, 212, 216; hypotheses of relation to innovation adoption, 12–13; as mutable variable, 225; related to individualized instruction adoption, 82; related to Mainstem vehicle management system adoption, 166; related to police computer use, 151; related to public housing authority computer use, 37; related to public housing authority prefab and modular use, 58; related to public library computer use, 122, 128; related to videotape recorder adoption, 105
organizational environment: as a determinant of innovation, 8–11, 28, 212, 216; hypotheses of relation to innovation adoption, 11; intergovernmental influence as

an aspect of, 9; as mutable
variable, 225–226; professionalism as an aspect of, 9; related to
individualized instruction adoption, 82; related to Mainstem
vehicle management system adoption, 166; related to police computer use, 150–151, 207; related
to public housing authority computer use, 34–37, 46–47, 206;
related to public housing authority prefab and modular use, 58–
59, related to public library
computer use, 122; related to
public library theft-detection
system use, 138; related to
videotape recorder adoption,
105; slack resource availability
as an aspect of, 10
orthogonal rotation, use of, 24

partials, use of, 29
performance gap, 11, 31, 81
Police Chief, 154–155
police department computer use, 23–
24, 149, 165–166; case studies,
159–165; city government computer use related to, 154, 207;
model for adoption, 149–151;
related to community characteristics, 156–157, 207; revised
adoption model, 157, 159,
165–166; testing of adoption
model, 151–157; unionism
related to, 152–153
policy innovation, 208, 216. *See also*
political innovation
Polinard, Jerry L., 8
political innovation, 216–220
process grant, 229
process innovation, 14, 147–148,
208, 211, 213–214, 221–224,
227; in common functions of
city government, 149–166,
195–197; in public housing,
33–57, 77–79; in public libraries, 121–138, 147–148; in

public schools, 81-104, 118-119
product innovation, 1, 4, 147–148,
208, 214, 221–223, 227; in
common functions of city
government, 166–167; in public
housing, 57–79; in public
libraries, 138–148; in public
schoools, 104–119
professional association, role in innovation adoption, 39–40, 87,
228–229
professionalism, 9, 213; related to
individualized instruction, 82,
85; related to public housing,
39, 46
Program for Learning in Accordance
with Needs (PLAN), 17–19,
100–101
public housing authorities, organization of, 13
public housing authority computer
use: advantages of, 14–15; case
studies, 47–57; and manpower
levels, 44, 205; model for
adoption, 33–37; revised adoption model, 44–47; role of
comptroller in, 56; testing of
adoption model, 37–43
public housing authority use of modular housing: case studies, 64–73;
model for, 59; testing of model,
59–61
public housing authority use of prefabricated housing components:
case studies, 73–77; model for,
57–59; testing of model, 61–63
Public Housing Management Improvement Program (PHMIP), 34–35,
49–50, 54–57, 212, 229; as
mutable variable, 226
public libraries, organization of, 13
public library computer use, 20–21;
case studies, 131–138; model
for adoption, 121–122; revised
adoption model, 128–131;
testing of adoption model,
123–128

Public Technology, Inc., (PTI), 23, 181

Rasmussen, John E., 1, 78
regression equation, use of, 30
Roessner, J. David, 10
Rogers, Everett M., 4, 9, 12
Romney, George, 16
Russett, Bruce M., 25

Sacks, Seymour, 9
Saint Louis, Mo., 23, 149
St. Pierre, Paul L., 20
scattered-site public housing, 16, 77
school districts, organization of, 13
service innovation, 197, 208, 211, 223–224, 227–229; certification of, 228–229
Shoemaker, F. Floyd, 9, 12
size: as a determinant of innovation, 12, 208, 213, 216; related to individualized instruction adoption, 85, 87; related to library computer use, 123–125, 130; related to police computer use, 151–153; related to public housing innovation, 37; related to videotape recorder adoption, 105. See also community environment
Skogan, Wesley G., 151
slack resource availability, 10, 212; related to individualized instruction adoption, 82, 88–89, 91; related to police computer use, 154, 207; related to public housing authority computer use, 38–39; related to public library computer use, 124–125, 147
socioeconomic status. See community environment
Sperry Remington, 142–144
S-shaped innovation curve, 199, 211
Stirling Homex Corporation, 15, 67–70
suburb. See community environment

technological innovation, 208, 216, 220. See also bureaucratic innovation
theft-detection system adoption by public libraries: case studies, 140–147; model for, 138–139; testing of model, 139–140
theft-detection systems for libraries, 20; bypass system, 21, 144; full-circulation system, 21, 144
theft rate in libraries, 138–139; difficulty in determining, 147, 207
3M Tattle Tape, 140, 142–144
time lag, in innovation models, 29
Today's Education, 85–87, 106
Toffler, Alvin, 17
Touche, Ross and Co., 15, 49–50, 56
turnkey contracting, 58, 62, 71–72, 76–77, 206
Turnkey Proposals, Inc., 67

Uniform Crime Report, 151

vendor influence in innovation adoption, 10, 167, 211
videocassettes, 20, 107, 114–117; and copyright laws, 110, 115; use in Salt Lake City, 116
videotape recorder (VTR), 17, 20–21, 104; case studies, 106–118; and copyright laws, 117–118, 207; model for adoption by secondary schools, 105–106; random adoption pattern discussed, 117–119

Walker, Jack L., 9, 40, 200, 205
Wallace, George, presidential vote, 7, 27
Whisler, Thomas L., 4, 10, 199
Williams, Oliver P., 7, 9, 211
Wilson, James Q., 11
Wisconsin Research and Development Center for Cognitive Learning, 18, 93
Wrinkle, Robert D., 8

Zaltman, Duncan, 11

About the Authors

Richard D. Bingham is an Assistant Professor of Political Science at the University of Wisconsin - Milwaukee. He received the BS in BA from Boston University and MAPA and Ph.D. degrees from the University of Oklahoma. He was Assistant Professor of Political Science at Marquette University from 1973-1976 and is author of *Public Housing and Urban Renewal: An Analysis of Federal-Local Relations* and has contributed to the *Urban Affairs Quarterly* and the *Social Service Review.*

Thomas P. McNaught received the BA and MA from Marquette University. He was Research Associate for the Office of Urban Research of Marquette University from 1974-1975.

About the Authors

Richard D. Bingham is an Assistant Professor of Political Science at the University of Wisconsin - Milwaukee. He received the BS in BA from Boston University and MAPA and Ph.D. degrees from the University of Oklahoma. He was Assistant Professor of Political Science at Marquette University from 1973-1976 and is author of *Public Housing and Urban Renewal: An Analysis of Federal-Local Relations* and has contributed to the *Urban Affairs Quarterly* and the *Social Service Review*.

Thomas P. McNaught received the BA and MA from Marquette University. He was Research Associate for the Office of Urban Research of Marquette University from 1974-1975.